A Very British Conspiracy

A Very British Conspiracy

*The Shrewsbury 24 and
the Campaign for Justice*

Eileen Turnbull

VERSO
London • New York

First published by Verso 2022
© Eileen Turnbull 2022
Foreword © Laurie Flynn 2022

1 3 5 7 9 10 8 6 4 2

Verso
UK: 6 Meard Street, London W1F 0EG
US: 388 Atlantic Avenue, Brooklyn, NY 11217
versobooks.com

Verso is the imprint of New Left Books

ISBN-13: 978-1-80429-014-9
ISBN-13: 978-1-80429-015-6 (UK EBK)
ISBN-13: 978-1-80429-016-3 (US EBK)

British Library Cataloguing in Publication Data
A catalogue record for this book is available from the British Library

Library of Congress Cataloging-in-Publication Data
A catalog record for this book is available from the Library of Congress

Typeset in Sabon by MJ & N Gavan, Truro, Cornwall
Printed and bound by CPI Group (UK) Ltd, Croydon, CRO 4YY

For Mark and all our family

If the past has nothing to say to the present, history may go on sleeping undisturbed in the closet where the system keeps its old disguises.

—Eduardo Galeano

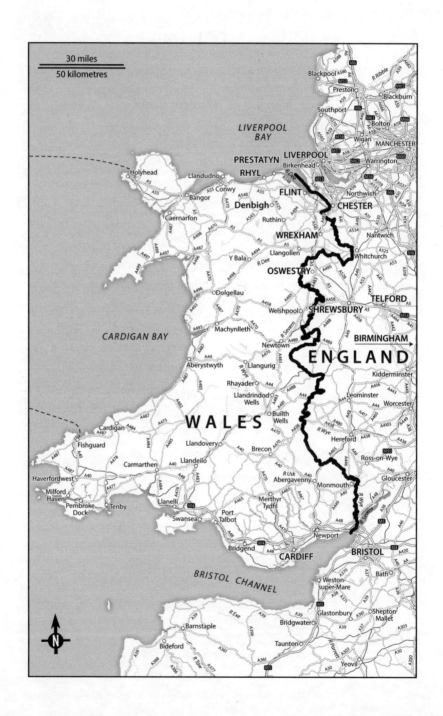

Contents

Foreword

Solidarity and an unwavering determination are the values Eileen Turnbull and her companions in the Shrewsbury 24 Campaign exemplified in their long march for justice – justice for twenty-four profoundly wronged union activists in North Wales and their families who are at the centre of this remarkable book. These men were framed by powerful elements in the construction industry and their allies in right-wing politics in the wake of the 1972 building workers' strike, and it took decades of tireless and intelligent campaigning to clear their names. That it took half a century is a telling commentary on enduring gross inequality before the law in Britain.

In the weeks and months running up to the outbreak of the strike fifty years ago, I had only just finished serving my time as a trainee reporter on a weekly paper called *Construction News*. This apprenticeship had come to a sudden and unexpected end, which, looking back, illustrated very well the improper leverage important people and powerful corporations are allowed to exercise illegitimately behind the scenes.

Sydney Lenssen, the paper's gifted editor, had been forced out of his post because of his campaigning instincts and his refusal to sack a member of staff he had encouraged to probe the shady side of British construction. The industry's appalling safety record, its poor conditions, and its practices of widespread corruption and 'the lump' (an early version of the gig economy, which prompted workers to avoid paying tax and joining unions) meant there was no shortage of important stories for the paper. Lenssen had a particular interest in the business practices of the twin companies Sir Alfred and Sir Robert McAlpine, and

it is abundantly clear that they intervened to bring his reform-
ing regime to an end. In the wake of the 1972 strike, as Eileen
Turnbull so clearly shows in her distinguished and revelatory
book, they would soon move to do the same to building union
activists in North Wales, an area deliberately targeted and one
where the McAlpine's industrial power was matched by extensive local political influence.

The book is an inspiring story on a number of fronts. Through
her persistent pursuit of lost and hidden documentation, endless
visits to obscure repositories and the National Archives at Kew,
Eileen Turnbull found irrefutable evidence which wholly dis-
credited the prosecution and which demonstrated, precisely and
devastatingly, how the fix and frame-up was put in. I salute her
skill in unfolding this tale and rescuing the reputation of hon-
ourable trade union activity as a key part of the age-old struggle
for justice and human rights and for a planet rescued from the
ravages of turbo-capitalism, unregulated and unreformed.

Laurie Flynn

Preface

A *Simple Twist of Fate*

I have been asked many times over the past fifteen years, 'Why did you become involved with the Shrewsbury pickets' case'? This would be followed with, 'How, more than four decades after the trials at Shrewsbury Crown Court, did you manage to obtain the documents that were relied upon by the pickets' lawyers to secure an historic successful outcome in the Court of Appeal?'

I have never really answered either of these questions, preferring instead to ensure that any interest in the case was focused on the pickets and the miscarriage of justice they faced in 1973–4.

I am a private person. To answer the question about my motivation to seek out the truth in this case I would have had to discuss my own personal association with the building industry and the case of the Shrewsbury pickets. Now, for the purposes of this book, I feel this is the time to explain why I have been so passionate about searching out the evidence that I hoped would clear the names of the convicted building workers. Their only crime was to strike against miserable wages and inhumane conditions of work. There have been many obstacles and some desperate disappointments over the past fifteen years but I have never given up. Hopefully, when you have read this book, you will understand why.

The 1970s: The Past Is Another Country

My connection to the building industry and the dispute was through my late husband, Tommy. He worked as a labourer for five years in the late 1960s and early 1970s on building sites in and around the North West.

I remember clearly the awful conditions he worked in on those sites. At the time, we lived in a two-bedroom terraced house in south Liverpool. When he arrived home from work each evening, Tommy would be covered from head to toe in mud, mostly dried in and set hard on his clothes and skin. He would routinely walk up the entry to our back door, take off his jeans, T-shirt and jumper and put them in a bucket of water in the yard to soak off the mud. Then, freezing cold, he would make a mad dash through the back kitchen and up the stairs to have a hot bath to try and remove the ingrained dirt that had stuck to him during the day.

The filth on the sites came second only to the dangerous working conditions: no laid-out roads or walkways, gaping holes in the ground filled with mud, water and all sorts of debris. The scaffolding had no toe boards or handrails; ladders were unsecured; no hard hats, protective boots or wellies. No safety equipment at all. Building debris was spread all over the landscape of the sites. It hid common dangers such as rusty nails sticking up from pieces of wood, broken glass and shattered pipes, strewn over the uneven ground.

These hazards were the bane of Tommy's life. He would often come home cursing that he had stepped on a nail or had another splinter or had building debris fall on him. There was an upside to the job. He liked the camaraderie of his workmates, the solidarity of the other labourers, and their sense of humour. But the work was hard and the wages for labourers were abysmal.

He always complained bitterly about the lack of trade union organisation. He was a member of the Transport and General Workers Union (T&GWU) and would bemoan the fact that the skilled tradesmen always benefited from higher wages and often had better hut or cabin facilities than labourers. They were members of separate 'craft unions' which often proved an obstacle to any form of united action on a site. When workers raised the matter of wages or conditions with the employer, they were more liable to be sacked, thrown off the site and blacklisted.

An Accident Which Was to Change Our Lives

In 1969 Tommy and his mate Jim were working on Fiddlers Ferry Power Station in Cheshire. The site was a shambles. When walking on site one morning they were run over by a car which was carrying workers to another part of the site. I remember the police coming to the house to tell me that he had been injured and that I should go to Whiston Hospital immediately. I was out of my mind with worry, terrified they were going to tell me he was dead. We lived miles away from the hospital and I had a young toddler and no transport. I left our daughter with my mother, who had just finished her shift in the Metal Box in Speke, and managed to get to the hospital. When I arrived, a nurse calmed me down and took me to the ward. They were both badly cut and bruised: Tommy had a broken arm and a badly twisted ankle; Jim had a broken leg and broken wrist. The nurse said that although they were battered and in shock, they were lucky to be alive.

This devastating episode proved to be the parting of the ways for Tommy and the building industry, where workers' lives were cheap. It had frightened the life out of us both and he decided there and then in that hospital bed to leave and look for work elsewhere. I remember walking away from the hospital so grateful he was still alive but angry because I knew nothing would change on the sites to ensure it would never happen to anyone else. The T&GWU's solicitors tried to claim compensation for Tommy and Jim but failed as the accident occurred on private land.

From Building Power Stations to Building Cars

Tommy got a job in Standard Triumph in 1971, where he became a member of the Amalgamated Engineering Union and was elected shop steward. We still had many friends who worked in the building industry and we took a keen interest in and supported the 1972 national building workers' strike. Tommy would talk to his workmates in Standards about his experiences on the sites. We had nothing but admiration for the union members in the building industry who had decided enough was enough and were taking strike action. The fact that the union demands included the eradication of 'the lump' and an overhaul of safety provisions on sites demonstrated that the building workers were serious and wanted to change the balance of power in the industry. If there were no lumpers, the workforce could be unionised and sites made safer. But what was indeed revolutionary about the dispute was that it brought tradesmen and labourers together for the first time in the history of the building trade. A joint pay claim for all building workers had been tabled with the employers; skilled and unskilled were fighting together. It was heartwarming for us to witness this solidarity.

We knew that the unions had a fight on their hands. The huge construction firms – the McAlpines, Laings, Wimpeys and others – had enjoyed such a tight grip on the industry for generations. They seemed all-powerful; it was truly a David-against-Goliath battle. In September 1972 we were absolutely jubilant to hear that the strike was settled and building workers had won the biggest pay increase in their history. We did not know the details but it was enough for us to know that, against all the odds, the building workers had succeeded.

The Calm Before the Storm

Then, out of the blue, on 14 February 1973, we heard the news that building worker pickets from north Wales had been picked up by the police and charged under the Conspiracy and Protection of Property Act 1875. We thought there must have been some mistake as north Wales had never been known throughout the labour movement as being a stronghold of trade union activity. But what really confused everyone was that the police had waited five months to charge them.

The police were not known to be slow when it came to dealing with picket lines of workers, as we witnessed in the other disputes in 1972 – the dockers, the coal miners and the engineers. It was widely believed among trade unionists that the north Wales pickets were being fitted up; none of the charges against them made sense. The West Mercia police had been with the men throughout the picketing in Shrewsbury on 6 September 1972, when most of the alleged offences were supposed to have occurred. Yet there were no arrests that day, no 'argy-bargy' with the police, no pushing or shoving, and no picket line!

We Go to Shrewsbury

Information about the plight of the pickets was thin on the ground. Tommy was able to pick up news about them from Liverpool Trades Council, which he attended as a delegate from his AEU branch. Simon Fraser, the Trades Council secretary, put out a call in September 1973 to all trade unionists on Merseyside to go to Shrewsbury for the opening day of the first trial, 3 October. Nationwide, support for the pickets was very strong; hundreds of Liverpool trade unionists travelled to Shrewsbury that day to show their solidarity.

Like many people in Liverpool, we had never been to Shrewsbury before. Indeed, we rarely travelled outside the boundaries of Merseyside. But we went to Shrewsbury in our small, dark green Austin 35 van with our toddler son, Stuart, and our friends Jimmy and Ethel and their son, Anthony. Tommy drove and Jimmy sat next to him, with myself, Ethel and the kids sat in the back of the van on wooden seats. There were no windows in the back so it was a bit claustrophobic. But we managed not to be stopped by the police, who had set up roadblocks on the roads surrounding Shrewsbury and were turning around cars and coaches. They must have seen us but thought it was two men going to work in their van.

Shrewsbury was a lovely town. I had never seen anything like it. Small windy streets, like something you see on Christmas cards. Very olde worlde, with individual little shops selling

LIVERPOOL TRADES COUNCIL
Shrewsbury 24 Committee

The RIGHT to STRIKE
The RIGHT to PICKET

NATIONAL CONFERENCE
calls for
DAY OF INDUSTRIAL ACTION
WEDNESDAY, 3rd OCTOBER

Mass Demonstration
at SHREWSBURY
WEDNESDAY, 3rd OCTOBER

PUBLIC MEETING
SHIRE HALL, SHREWSBURY - 12 noon
PROCESSION 2·00 p.m.

Published by Liverpool Trades Council
Printed by David Rume Ltd., Gildart Street, Liverpool, L3 8AG.

Appeal from Liverpool Trades Union Council to attend mass demonstration in Shrewsbury on the opening day of the first trial.

expensive wine and cigars, exclusive gentleman's outfitters, luxury food emporiums and fur coat shops for ladies. This was the poshest place I had ever been to in my life. But what really had me transfixed was a large, double-fronted shop. It had huge rounded windows on either side of the entrance. In one window it had a life-size model of a horse with rider all kitted out; in the opposite window there were saddles, an array of hunting knives, horse whips, spurs, riding boots and all sorts of other livery. But I could not take my eyes off the model of the horse and rider. The sight was truly amazing. I stood there for quite a few minutes in absolute wonderment. I have never forgotten it, a horse shop! This place was another world.

The March to Shrewsbury Crown Court

Although autumn, it was a crisp, beautiful, sunny day. We met quite a few people we knew from Liverpool and cheery greetings and humorous remarks were exchanged. There were trade unionists from all over the country with their union banners held high. The organisers formed us up to start our march through this sleepy Shropshire town to the Crown court, where the trial of the first six pickets was to begin that day. Spirits were high among the demonstrators. There is nothing like a trade union march to bring out feelings of mutual support and solidarity and this day was no exception.

Although we expected a substantial police presence, nothing could have prepared us for the hundreds of police who marshalled themselves either side of the march. Their helmets were almost touching each other, front to back, ensuring that we could not get through their lines to reach the pavement. Even so, there was a lot of friendly banter from the crowd towards the police lines, with shouts of 'Attention! Left-right-left-right-left-right-march'. It brought lots of laughter and then there was a loud cheer from the delegations as the march set off for the court to show our solidarity with the building workers on trial.

Our group walked with the Liverpool delegation of mainly building workers and dockers. We formed up in a line across the width of the street, starting with our son Stuart, with me holding his hand, Tommy next to me, followed by Ethel and Anthony, and by his side walked Jimmy. As we were slowly marching along, chatting about this and that, I don't know why, but I looked down over my son's head and was absolutely astounded to see the policeman next to Stuart was holding his hand. I froze. I did not know what to do. This was clearly a friendly gesture by the policeman and little Stuart was very happy being helped along. But this man was on the side of those who were prosecuting innocent trade unionists! I thought for a moment and then took action. I bent down and offered Stuart a lollipop. Predictably, he immediately released his hand from the policeman and put the lollipop in his mouth. I was so relieved, although I did acknowledge the show of kindness from the policeman and gave him a smile of thanks for helping my son along and he in return gave me a nod.

The Judge Takes Flight

When we reached the Crown court, the delegations folded up their banners and we all lined up outside. The court was a modern, long stretch of grey flat concrete with a pavement leading up to the entrance. It was a strange feeling standing outside the court, quite eerie. Although there were hundreds of demonstrators it was relatively quiet. Then, like something surreal, a shiny black limousine with a royal crest on the door drove up slowly and stopped outside the entrance. A very smart gentleman came out of the building and opened the door of the car. To everyone's surprise, out stepped the judge dressed in full red robe, white fluffy ermine around his neck and a white wig. There was a hush among the crowd and then the judge, who was a tall man, started to walk slowly towards the door of the court. As he did so, three trumpeters dressed in classic eighteenth-century court clothes began to herald the judge's entrance. The atmosphere suddenly changed. Loud boos, terms of abuse and curses rang out from the crowd. The sight of this centuries-old court ceremony of the great and the good hit a nerve and brought home to us all the seriousness of the situation. It was at this point that the judge bent down, lifted up his long red gown and ran the rest of the way into the court building. The sight of the judge taking flight into the court broke the tense atmosphere. The crowd roared with laughter and gave out loud cheers.

Pickets on Trial

As we started home our mood changed. It had been an optimistic and inspiring day but we left Shrewsbury with foreboding. It was as if we knew what was to come. As it turned out, our feelings proved to be prophetic. After a twelve-week trial three of the pickets were given prison sentences and the other three were given suspended sentences. The two trials that followed in the new year saw a further three pickets jailed and thirteen more given suspended prison sentences. Only one picket was found not guilty and another was found to have no case to answer and did not face a trial.

The prosecutions of the building workers have remained an open sore for trade unionists who were around at the time. A veil of secrecy has surrounded what happened to the pickets who travelled to Shrewsbury during the strike on that fateful day, 6 September 1972. I have never forgotten it. When the leading picket, Des Warren, died prematurely in 2004 it inspired the setting up of a justice campaign two years later. It aimed to overturn this miscarriage of justice and to uncover the truth about what really happened to the north Wales pickets.

This book tells the story of what really happened to the north Wales pickets, which led to many of their lives being destroyed. It sets out not only how I found the crucial evidence but also the story of how the government, the police and the employers set up the north Wales building workers, whose only crime was to stand up against the criminal conditions in which they were being forced to work. The fresh evidence I discovered was relied upon to persuade the Court of Appeal to quash all the convictions of the Shrewsbury pickets, which it did on 23 March 2021. It has been a long hard road, but the campaign succeeded in clearing the pickets' names.

Introduction

The 1970s – Days of Hope

The year 1972 was a momentous one for the British trade union movement. It was the high point of class confrontation in the second half of the twentieth century, with significant victories for working people. Many accounts have been written about the coal miners and their mass picket of a coking depot in Saltley, Birmingham. Likewise, the strike that led to the release of imprisoned London dock shop stewards, the Pentonville 5. But far less is known about another successful dispute that year, a twelve-week national strike by building workers, which won them the biggest pay rise in their history.

With the exception of Darlington and Lyddon's *Glorious Summer*, many of the books covering the 1970s make little, if any, mention of this lengthy dispute, the first and only national strike in the construction industry.[1] Compared with other strikes in that momentous year, coverage of it did not make daily television or radio news bulletins. No nationally recognisable trade unionists were involved, no household names such as Arthur Scargill, Jack Jones or Hughie Scanlon. What stands out about it, and should make it better known, was the subsequent extraordinary prosecution of thirty-two north Wales building workers for alleged picketing offences and the jailing of six of them at Shrewsbury Crown Court long after the strike had ended.

North Wales building workers, arguably, would have been the last to come to mind when it came to taking part in an industrial dispute, let alone being involved with picketing. Trade union membership was historically very low, on building sites that were spread out over a predominantly rural area. That pickets could lose their liberty through their involvement in an official national strike remains one of the most scandalous episodes in the history of trade unionism in this country. It puts fear in the hearts of rank-and-file trade unionists even today.

The whole saga of what happened to those pickets, twenty-four of whom were prosecuted in three trials at Shrewsbury Crown Court, has been the subject of speculation for many years. The only significant contemporaneous account was a book by Jim Arnison, *The Shrewsbury Three* (London,1974), which was based upon his daily reporting of the first trial for the *Morning Star* in 1973. Two pamphlets were written at the time by Laurie Flynn, *Pickets on Trial* in 1973 and *Workers against The Law: The Truth about the Shrewsbury Trials* the following year. Des Warren wrote a crucial account in 1982, *The Key to My Cell*, drawing upon his involvement in the strike, his trial and his imprisonment.[2]

Over the following years, many myths about the pickets were created and recycled. The research that I carried out to overturn the pickets' convictions, including recently obtained prosecution documents and police reports, allows these myths to be corrected. This book sets out the pickets' remarkable story and traces the steps that were taken by the British state to prosecute trade unionists.

Against massive odds the building workers won a significant improvement in pay and the twelve-week dispute was deemed a great success. Many of the activists thought that more could have been won from the employers. They campaigned for the continuation of the local action committees that had been set up during the strike. They were looking ahead to the 1973 pay round to build on the gains they had won. They remained determined to get rid of 'the lump' (described in Chapter 1) and to make building sites safer places to work.

The strike had increased trade union membership, strengthening their bargaining position with the employers. It also created a new generation of rank-and-file activists who developed skills and confidence in organising picketing, addressing mass meetings to explain issues, negotiating with site management and inspiring fellow workers. There was an air of optimism flowing through their ranks. What they could not have envisaged at the time was that all of their enthusiasm and hope for the future of the industry was to be dashed following the prosecution of north Wales building workers.

The main focus of the three Shrewsbury trials was a single day's picketing on Wednesday, 6 September 1972. A decision had been made the previous week, at one of the regular meetings of the Chester and North Wales Area Strike Action Committee, to picket sites in Shrewsbury. Several representatives from the Oswestry strike committee attended the meeting on 31 August to appeal for support. They were out on a limb in every respect. Geographically, this English market town by the Welsh border was miles from any significant working-class centre. The nearest, Chester, was thirty miles north and Liverpool forty-five miles away. The plan was not to picket in Oswestry, where support for the strike was relatively strong, but to go to Shrewsbury, where many sites were non-unionised and had continued to work during the strike. The chairperson of the Oswestry strike committee, John Llywarch, worked on the Wrexham bypass site, which brought their area into the orbit of north Wales building workers.

On 6 September five coaches of pickets travelled from north Wales to rendezvous at the Labour Club in Oswestry, where they met local strikers, whose own coach would lead them to working sites in Shrewsbury. Some of the pickets had come from three sites in north Wales that had been called out on strike from the beginning of the dispute on 26 June. Most of the men, however, had only been on strike for three to four weeks, after an all-out strike was called from 15 August. When the pickets boarded coaches that morning in Mostyn, Denbigh, Chester, Colwyn Bay and Wrexham, none of them could have imagined the train of events that they were to be caught up in and the devastating effects it would have on many of them and their families for the rest of their lives.

As was usual practice, they did not form a picket line at the building sites they visited, in contrast to picketing of workplaces by engineers, dock workers and coal miners. Unlike today, there were no gates or similar entrances to building sites in the 1970s. Generally, there were no fences around the perimeter; anyone could just walk on. They visited five sites in Shrewsbury. At the first site, Kingswood, the pickets were threatened with a shotgun by the son of a contractor. Shortly afterwards the police turned up and remained with the pickets for the rest of the day. Apart from that incident, many of the pickets described 6 September 1972 as just another day's picketing. At lunchtime they had intended to return home but decided instead to travel to sites in a new town that was being developed fifteen miles to the east, Telford. One of the developments was a major housing estate, Brookside, that was being constructed by Sir Alfred McAlpine & Son Ltd. At this point, additional West Mercia police were mobilised, and followed the pickets from site to site.

Photographs taken at the time on the Brookside site showed the pickets holding a mass meeting to address the workers about the aims of the strike while the police stood in twos and threes at the back, arms folded or hands in pockets. A report produced by West Mercia police to answer complaints that it received from employers noted the high-ranking police presence on the Brookside site: 'a Chief Superintendent, a Superintendent, three Chief Inspectors and three inspectors', as well as dozens of police constables.[3] Throughout the day there was no fighting, no arguments with the police and not a single picket was arrested or cautioned. This was remarkable given the subsequent claims of violence and intimidation that were presented in court.

At the end of the day the police escorted the coaches out of Shropshire and left them to return to north Wales. Just before the convoy headed north, a senior police officer, Chief Superintendent Meredith, boarded a coach and shook hands with the leading picket, Des Warren, and commended him for the behaviour of the pickets. This assessment was reinforced by the police communications that were reproduced in one of the subsequent reports prepared by West Mercia police.

But before the pickets even arrived home that evening a meeting was under way at the Oswestry home of one of the contractors whose Shrewsbury site had been picketed that day. He had summoned the local police to attend, to explain to him and several other contractors that he had invited, why the police had failed to stop the pickets. In the following days members and representatives of the National Federation of Building Trades Employers (NFBTE) contacted the police, the Home Office and MPs to demand action. Almost immediately, this behind-the-scenes pressure led to the establishment of a wide-ranging investigation by West Mercia police.

The building workers knew absolutely nothing about these events following their return to work on 18 September 1972. Many were surprised when a number of pickets were questioned by the police in November 1972. Six who refused to attend police stations voluntarily were arrested and, after questioning, were bailed. They were released from police bail in December 1972 and the pickets and their families assumed that this had brought the matter to a close. How wrong they were.

In early February, Gwynedd police served summonses on a number of men, charging them with offences on north Wales sites. But the main event was on 14 February 1973, five months after the strike had ended, when West Mercia police went into action. Of the approximately 250 building workers who went to picket in Shropshire, twenty-four were singled out. Six were arrested that evening and the rest were handed a summons to attend court on 15 March to answer charges. This came completely out of the blue. A total of 243 charges were laid against the twenty-four for offences that were alleged to have occurred on building sites in Shropshire and north Wales between 1 August and 28 October 1972. Many of the charges were for alleged offences at McAlpine's Brookside site on 6 September.

The thirty-two men were mostly ordinary rank-and-file workers. Many had never been on strike or picketed before. They were all born and raised in Wales apart from a handful who had moved there as adults. Some of them were time-served craftsmen but many were general labourers who had worked in a variety of jobs. Few of them were active trade unionists of the type you would find in industrial cities such as Liverpool, Manchester, Birmingham or London. Many of the labourers had been in and out of membership depending upon the degree of trade union organisation on building sites.

It is hard to imagine today the confusion and desperation of these building workers. The strike had been over for five months and many of them were just 'getting back on their feet' after twelve weeks of not earning any money. Now they found themselves facing criminal charges. Unfortunately, their plight was to get worse when they found out that there was no official support from their respective trade unions on the basis that the pickets were being charged with criminal offences. The craft union UCATT (Union of Construction, Allied Trades and Technicians) requested a legal opinion from its lawyer, who advised that the nature of the charges meant that the pickets' behaviour was inconsistent with proper trade union activity and therefore was ineligible for legal assistance under any trade union's scheme. UCATT's general secretary wrote to the North West regional secretary summarising the advice and directed him to inform the pickets that union legal aid would not be granted. Copies of the letter were sent to the three other unions on the National Joint Council for the Building Industry. Although, of the twenty-four men tried at Shrewsbury, only six were members of UCATT and eighteen were members of the T&GWU, George Smith took the lead as he was also secretary of the union side of the national negotiating body, the NJC.

The pickets' only lifeline was state Legal Aid, which turned out to be a two-edged sword. It was a vital benefit because it would cover the fees of the lawyers the pickets could instruct to act for them, but it was also, in some ways, a curse. In court each picket was represented by a separate QC and junior barrister. These lawyers were only interested in representing their particular client, indirectly undermining any collective defence by the pickets. Whereas the prosecution, conducted by the Director of Public Prosecutions, used just three barristers (a QC and two junior counsel) for all the trials and pre-trial hearings, the accused pickets had more than thirty barristers between them, instructed by four separate firms of solicitors.

The men were prosecuted at eight Crown court trials. Fourteen were tried in five trials at Mold, mainly in June and July

1973. Twenty-four, which included seven men who had already been tried at Mold, were prosecuted in three trials at Shrewsbury between October 1973 and March 1974. In addition, one picket had his case dealt with at Mold Magistrates' Court. In the event, the prosecution failed to get any significant convictions at Mold. A few pickets were found guilty of minor offences, principally criminal damage. They received small fines of between fifteen pounds for a guilty plea and fifty pounds for a guilty verdict by the jury. Many of the pickets who were due to stand trial at Shrewsbury were encouraged by these results, but this turned out to be a false dawn.

The prosecution was disappointed with the outcome but learned valuable lessons from the Mold trials and made a number of significant changes to its preparation for the trials at Shrewsbury three months later. This would produce the results that the employers and the government wanted. At Shrewsbury the prosecution split up the twenty-four and proceeded first with a trial of six whom they portrayed as the ringleaders. The six faced the most serious charges: conspiracy to intimidate, affray and unlawful assembly. After a twelve-week trial, three of them were convicted of all three offences and, six days before Christmas, were jailed for between nine months and three years. After the second trial of nine pickets, three more were sent to prison, each for six months for affray and four months for unlawful assembly. In total, six pickets were imprisoned, sixteen received suspended prison sentences, one was found not guilty by the jury and the final picket was found not guilty by order of the court.

After the Shrewsbury trials had been completed the pickets and their families, understandably, were in a state of shock. They had always maintained that they were innocent of all charges. They were stunned by the savagery of the sentences and bewildered as to why prosecutions had been brought against them. The leading picket, Des Warren, received the longest sentence: three years' imprisonment on all three charges, to run concurrently. During his incarceration he was administered with drugs by the prison authorities, which he subsequently blamed for causing him to develop Parkinson's disease.[4] He was released in 1976 but due to blacklisting and the increasingly debilitating effects of the illness he was unable to work again and died prematurely in 2004, aged sixty-six.[5] His death spurred trade unionists in the North West and north Wales to establish a campaign in 2006 to have the convictions of all the pickets overturned. The Shrewsbury 24 Campaign was born.[6]

In 2009, I volunteered to be the (unpaid) researcher for the campaign. I embarked upon a quest to locate the 'fresh evidence' that was necessary to persuade the Criminal Cases Review Commission (CCRC) to refer the pickets' convictions back to the Court of Appeal. This would prove to be a monumental task. The information that I managed to obtain over the following ten years not only uncovered that fresh evidence but also goes some way to answer the pickets' question: Why were we prosecuted?

I discovered a large number of crucial government files that had been released to The National Archives, Kew, in 2005 under the Public Records Act 1958.[7] These contained thousands of pages relating to the discussions and decisions by the Conservative government in 1972–3 to curb picketing. I also discovered Director of Public Prosecutions (DPP) files revealing how they prosecuted the north Wales pickets.[8] I have drawn primarily from these and other contemporaneous documents located in libraries and archives throughout the UK and from the papers of participants in the strike and the trials.

The files at Kew showed that there are many other government documents relating to the trials that have not been released. I made several requests to successive governments under the Freedom of Information Act 2000 to see them but was told each time that they were being retained under Section 23, relating to national security. The campaign launched a petition to demand their release; after all, what were the issues of national security involved in a building workers' strike over forty years ago? Despite a debate in Parliament in 2014 organised by Labour backbenchers, when MPs voted 103 to 3 for the release of all documents, the government continues to withhold them.

This book identifies the process and the decisions that were made to prosecute the north Wales pickets, the conduct of the trials, and the sentences that were passed. It shows why and how it was decided these men were selected to be prosecuted for picketing, rather than building workers from industrial centres in other parts of the UK. The outcome of the trials was the result of concerted action by building trades employers, Conservative politicians and the state to halt the emerging and successful trade union tactic of flying pickets and the growing strength of trade unionism in the building industry.[9]

Many in the trade union movement regarded the prosecutions as having been politically driven show trials, where trade union activity was in the dock. The overturning of the pickets' convictions would remain unfinished business for the labour movement in the years that followed. It has taken fifteen years to unravel this story and achieve justice for the Shrewsbury 24.

This book tells the story of the Shrewsbury 24 Campaign and our fight for justice. It describes the highs and lows of the legal battle to get the CCRC to refer the pickets' case to the appeal court. The search for truth took me on a long and winding road of discovery to find the crucial evidence which was to finally overturn this miscarriage of justice. The book also describes the campaign's work over fifteen years to spread knowledge of and gain support for the pickets throughout the trade union and labour movements. The solidarity we received encouraged the pickets and the campaign. Despite all the setbacks, we never gave up.

These prosecutions should never have taken place. The fact that they did is a salutary lesson for all trade unionists today.

PART I

1972: The Year of Strikes and Solidarity

1

A Strike Whose Time Had Come

Setting the Scene

The building workers' strike, the prosecution of pickets and the draconian prison sentences only make sense when seen in the context of the political and economic situation at the time. The strike began two years into the Conservative government of Edward Heath. That government, like the Labour one before it, was confronting the challenges of a British economy in long-term decline. It had been masked by the period of major reconstruction and economic expansion after the Second World War. But by the end of the 1960s the economy was showing the signs of weakness, relative to the other main capitalist economies, that had been developing since the end of the nineteenth century.

The economic conditions that created full employment in the 1950s and 1960s increased trade union membership and gave workers greater bargaining power, particularly in engineering. There was a willingness to take action to defend pay and conditions, including overtime bans, work to rule, go-slows and strikes. Although trade unions could negotiate industry-wide agreements at national level it was left to the representatives at the workplace level, the elected shop stewards, to negotiate productivity deals and enforce demarcation lines between trades. Local demands were made for improvements in pay and conditions that exceeded the basic terms in a collective national agreement between the unions and an employers' federation.

Table 1: Strikes in the UK, 1968–76

Year	Aggregate number of working days in stoppages in progress (thousands)
1967	2,787
1968	4,690
1969	6,846
1970	10,980
1971	13,551
1972	23,909
1973	7,197
1974	14,750
1975	6,012
1976	3,284

Source: *Department of Employment Gazette*, January 1979. See Robert Taylor, *The Fifth Estate: Britain's Unions in the Modern World*, London, 1980, p. 41

Table 1 shows that the number of working days lost as a result of strikes rose significantly from the end of the 1960s. Between 1950 and 1959 the annual average number of days lost was 3.25 million, and in the following decade, 1960–9, it had increased by just 10 per cent to 3.55 million days.[1] The picture changed sharply after 1967.

The Labour government established a Royal Commission on Trade Unions in April 1965.[2] Part of its remit was to address unofficial strike action (so-called 'wildcat' strikes) and shop steward power, which was blamed for wage drift and demarcation disputes. The result of the inquiry was the 'Donovan report', published in 1968. It was welcomed by the government and also by the Conservative's employment spokesperson, Robert Carr MP, who compared it favourably with their own policy document, *Fair Deal at Work*.[3] Donovan recommended restoring union power from the shop floor to full-time officials so that national agreements would be honoured and any local deals would be based on improvements in productivity.[4]

In 1969 Barbara Castle, the Labour secretary of state for employment, presented Donovan's main proposals in a White Paper, *In Place of Strife*.[5] It highlighted that 95 per cent of all strikes between 1964 and 1967 were unofficial, i.e. not sanctioned or ratified by the trade unions involved. Labour recommended secret ballots for strike action, legal penalties for trade unions that failed to comply and a twenty-eight-day conciliation ('cooling-off') period to allow negotiations with a management to continue, during which trade unions were prevented from taking strike action. Unions would be fined if they flouted this. There was significant opposition to these proposals from Labour-affiliated trade unions and from many union-sponsored Labour MPs. It contributed to Labour's defeat at the general election in June 1970 and the election of a Conservative government after six years in opposition.

The Industrial Relations Act

The Conservatives brought in the Industrial Relations Act 1971. It was based upon *Fair Deal at Work* and many proposals from the Donovan report. During the months when the new law was going through Parliament huge demonstrations were organised to 'Kill the Bill'. Although it became law, a mood of defiance throughout the trade union movement had been built up, not least through the campaigning of the Communist Party-led Liaison Committee for the Defence of Trade Unions (LCDTU).

Trade unions were required under the Act to register with a registration officer who would supervise a union's rules and have the legal power to examine workplace agreements. A union that did not register lost immunities from legal action if it was sued for damages arising from strike action. A new National Industrial Relations Court (NIRC) was set up to hear a variety of 'industrial' cases. These included complaints against trade unions for alleged breaches of company agreements or procedures and for flouting the 'cooling-off' period prior to strike action, and complaints from union members against their own union for alleged breach of rules and from non-union members who were affected by a union's conduct. This would enable disaffected workers, with encouragement from employers, the Tories and the Conservative media, to drag unions through the courts with spurious claims.

Table 2: States of Emergency called by the Heath Government 1970–4

Date of proclamation	Date state of emergency ended	Nature of dispute
16 July 1970	4 August 1970	Dock strike
12 December 1970	17 December 1970	Electricity workers' strike
9 February 1972	8 March 1972	Coal miners' strike
3 August 1972	2 September 1972	Dock strike
13 November 1973	11 March 1974	Coal miners' and electricity power workers' disputes

Source: figures taken from Keith Jeffery and Peter Hennessy, *States of Emergency*, London, 1983, pp. 274–5

The TUC adopted a policy of non-registration and non-compliance with the Act. During 1972 several trade unions were involved in significant disputes that challenged it. These included national strikes of engineers and dock workers over pay and working conditions. Some of these disputes brought the Amalgamated Union of Engineering Workers (AUEW) and T&GWU before the NIRC but both unions upheld TUC policy and refused to appear in court. Their defiance led to significant fines for 'unfair industrial practices' and for contempt of court, and to orders for the sequestration of union funds when they refused to pay.[6]

An indication of the level and seriousness of strike action during the Conservative government was the unprecedented number of states of emergency that it invoked (Table 2).

A state of emergency was an exceptional measure, contained in the Emergency Powers Act 1920. It could be called in the name of the monarch if it was believed that there was a threat to the supply of food, fuel, transport, water, light or any other necessities of life (Section 1(1)). Once called, the Privy Council could make regulations to ensure that those services were maintained, subject to subsequent parliamentary approval. No government, before or since, has invoked as many as Heath's Tory administration.

The NUM versus the Government

The successful coal miners' strike at the start of 1972 was an inspiration for industrial action by other groups of workers that year. The miners had not been involved in sustained national strike action since the defeat of the ten-day General Strike in 1926. The miners had continued their strike alone for a further six months but were forced back to work through starvation, accepting pay cuts and a longer working day. This crushing defeat was symbolic within the trade union movement and stifled any further significant opposition to wage cuts and unemployment for the next two decades. In 1947 the coal industry was nationalised and the miners were now public-sector workers with just one employer, the National Coal Board (NCB), instead of many separate private companies.

The National Union of Mineworkers (NUM) submitted a pay claim for 1972 ranging between 17 and 47 per cent, well in excess of the government's target. A detailed account of the strike is given by Darlington and Lyddon.[7] They cite an assessment of the forthcoming strike by a former Labour MP, Woodrow Wyatt:

> The coming coal strike billed for Sunday is the saddest cock-up since the War. Rarely have strikers advanced to the barricades with less enthusiasm or hope of success ... Even if the strike lasts two and a half months, it would have little effect on electricity supplies ... Alas it is as if some mystery siren is luring (the miners) zombie like to destruction. They have more stacked against them than the Light Brigade in their famous charge.[8]

Wyatt's prediction proved to be misjudged and indicated how unaware he was of the changes at work in the NUM, which led the union to adopt the pay claim and to win the strike so successfully.[9]

The turning point of the strike was the picketing of a coke depot in the Saltley district of Birmingham. The aim was to stop lorries from driving out with deliveries of coke for industry and power stations. After days of confrontation with the police at the depot gates the NUM appealed to local trade unions for support. On Thursday 10 February 1972 thousands of engineers and other workers stopped work and marched on Saltley Gates to join the miners' picket. The police decided to close the depot.[10] On 19 February the NUM leadership negotiated an improved offer which was accepted by the members in a pithead ballot, and they returned to work on 28 February. The union had secured a pay rise of 27 per cent from the NCB.

The significance of this victory was not simply that it destroyed the government's pay policy, or that it was achieved by coal miners. It was the tactics used that were unprecedented. The NUM organised thousands of its members to be involved in UK-wide picketing and to gain support from other groups of workers. Thousands of pickets were available to travel to other workplaces. Through mass picketing they were able to reduce electricity production and maximise the pressure on the government. The tactic of the *flying picket* was born.[11]

The Pentonville 5

Following the success of the miners came the dock workers' dispute. The employers were attempting to introduce a new technology, containers, without the agreement of the unions. It would mean that far fewer dock workers would be needed to load and unload cargo from ships. To protect jobs the dockers demanded that the loading and unloading of containers within a five-mile radius of a registered port should be reserved to them. The employers were also attempting to have cargo landed at 'unregistered' ports and wharves that were not part of the National Dock Labour Scheme. Both developments were a threat to thousands of registered dock workers' jobs.

A picket was organised by dockers at a container depot at Chobham Farm, east London, to demand that the employer hire registered dock workers to do the work. An application was made to the High Court on 4 July for an injunction to prohibit the dockers' leaders from continuing the picket. When the injunction was ignored, five dockers' shop stewards were arrested for contempt of court on 21 July and sent to Pentonville prison. Over the following days a huge outpouring of support for the 'Pentonville 5' developed. Workers from engineering factories, printing works and elsewhere joined dock workers in a national strike. The TUC General Council then took the unprecedented step of calling a one-day general strike. The issue quickly returned to court when the little-known Official Solicitor made an application to quash the jailing of the dockers on the basis that the national union was legally responsible for the picketing, not lay representatives.[12] The judges agreed and the five shop stewards were released. Yet again, mass strike action and trade union solidarity proved a success.

Building Workers' Trades Unions

When the building workers began their action on 26 June 1972 it was the first national strike that they had ever undertaken. They were encouraged by the success of the earlier disputes and the general anti-Tory atmosphere among the organised working class. This spurred the building workers on through three months of action, uniting skilled and unskilled in a common goal, to win a joint wages and conditions claim. The employers were used to seeing off the threat of industrial action and strikes but this time building workers were far more unified and determined.

In 1971 three craft trade unions amalgamated to form a major union for skilled building workers. The Amalgamated Society of Woodworkers and decorators, the Association of Building Technicians and the Amalgamated Union of Building Trade Workers became UCATT. The first national conference of the new union took place in Blackpool on 16 June 1972, ten days before the strike began. The amalgamation occurred more out of necessity than out of any feelings of solidarity. By the start of the 1970s, the three individual unions were in a weak position due to the growth of 'lump' labour in the building industry. Their decline was halted by the merger. For many members of the new union this was an historic event; for the first time there was a united building workers' union. Hopes were high among the rank and file. There was much excitement and optimism that at last they were to have the opportunity to fight together for long-overdue improvements in the industry.

The many individual craft trade unions had worked together for years. In 1918 they established the National Federation of Building Trades Operatives (NFBTO) to negotiate collectively with the employers. Each union had relied upon its control of entry into its trade through long apprenticeships of five to seven years to secure improved pay and to maintain wage differentials over labourers. The latter were often treated like second-class citizens by time-served tradesmen, although numerically they were a large and essential body in the building industry.[13]

On its formation, UCATT had a top-heavy structure: an executive council (EC) of thirteen full-time officials and a general council (GC) of fifteen lay representatives. The latter comprised nine woodworkers, three painters and three builders; ten of them were members of the Communist Party.[14] Writing of the merger, John Elliot, Labour editor of the *Financial Times*, observed,

> The trouble is that merging the three main partners of UCATT merely compounded their individual financial and organisational problems. With about 200,000 of its 268,000 members in construction, UCATT has approaching 200 regional officials plus another 25 national officials, including a 13-man national executive council which mysteriously finds business to occupy it in full council sessions for two days every week.[15]

Two of the general trade unions had sections for members in the construction industry, including the largest, the T&GWU. It was the main union for labourers. The General and Municipal Workers Union (GMWU) had labourer members, including in a number of construction-related manufacturing companies. The fourth union involved in the strike was the Furniture, Timber and Allied Trades Union (FTAT), which was also the product of a recent merger of two NFBTO affiliates.[16]

The Building Workers' Charter

A crucial influence within the various unions and the strike was a rank-and-file grouping, the Building Workers' Charter. The Communist Party was the leading force but, unlike similar groupings in other unions, it was more open and inclusive, involving members of the Labour Party, other left-wing groups and unaffiliated building workers. It was formed at a conference in the Downing Street Co-op Hall, Manchester, on 25 April 1970. The 288 delegates at the conference agreed a charter of demands for all trades:

- a basic rate of pay of £1 per hour;
- a reduction in the basic working week to thirty-five hours;
- four weeks' paid holiday;
- de-casualisation of the industry, including the registration of all building trade operatives;
- the abolition of 'the lump';
- a comprehensive pension scheme;
- greater union democracy, including election of all full-time officials every three years and branch officials every year;
- the formation of one democratic union for the building industry;
- establishing 100 per cent compulsory trade union membership;
- full recognition of elected shop stewards and regular area meetings of stewards;
- full protection of shop stewards;
- adequate safety and welfare regulations to be introduced and rigidly enforced;
- full nationalisation and public ownership of the building industry.[17]

These demands proved to be popular among building workers, and as a result a second charter conference was held on 24 April 1971 and a third the following year, on 29 April 1972, in Birmingham. The latter attracted 900 delegates and was opened by UCATT's Midlands regional secretary, Ken Barlow. It produced a regular newspaper, the *Building Workers' Charter*, which was read widely on sites.[18] Supporters were influential in persuading the unions to adopt parts of the charter, though the national pay claim that the unions submitted to the employers in June 1971 fell short of many of the charter's demands. The official claim called for a thirty-five-hour week, a basic wage of thirty pounds per week and an improvement in the number of paid holidays.[19] Modest though this was, charter supporters had little confidence that union officials would fight for it, given the history of previous wage claims.[20]

The Employers and the Conservative Party

The employers were represented by several bodies. The NFBTE, covering small and medium-sized contractors, had been founded in the nineteenth century.[21] The Federation of Master Builders (FMB) was formed in 1941 and by the 1970s it had 20,000 firms in membership compared with the NFBTE's 14,000.[22] The companies that dealt with the larger civil construction projects – roads, bridges, pipelines and other infrastructure – were united in the Federation of Civil Engineering Contractors (FCEC), founded in 1919.[23]

The Conservative Party had long-standing links with the construction industry. Sir Keith Joseph, the Cabinet minister responsible for health and social security, was connected with Bovis.[24] Nicholas Ridley MP, a junior minister in the Department for Trade and Industry, was a construction company director and engineer.[25] The home secretary, Reginald Maudling, had resigned in July 1972 following a scandal related to his connections with property companies.[26] Sir Ernest Marples was a Conservative MP from 1945 to 1974 and a government minister between 1957 and 1964. He had owned 80 per cent of the shares in Marples Ridgway before it was taken over by the Bath and Portland Group. As minister for transport, he championed polices that slashed Britain's railway network (the Beeching cuts) and promoted extensive road building, from which his company benefited enormously.[27] The minister of employment,

Robin Chichester-Clark, became a consultant to the NFBTE when he stood down from Parliament in 1974.[28]

Conservative councillors had regular contact with small and medium-sized firms that routinely bid for council contracts. Many builders were members of their local Conservative association. A leading example was Idris Owen, who had been a Conservative councillor in Stockport since 1946, chairing its housing committee for a period, and served as the town's MP during Heath's government, from 1970 to 1974. He was a former vice president of the NFBTE.[29]

Political donations were made to the Conservative Party by major construction companies, including W&C French, Sir Robert McAlpine & Co., John Mowlem & Co., Tarmac, Taylor Woodrow and Wood Hall Trust. Several building materials companies also donated: BPB Industries, Hanson Trust, International Timber Corporation and Kelsey Industries.[30] In 1974 the

---

'Anyone who can hold a private party and make it virtually impossible to get a cabinet quorum cannot be without influence or friends. In what other industry can any person boast of such a wide and diverse circle of acquaintances? None.' Construction News 17 December 1970

The Occasion: the McAlpine's Christmas beano December 1970
The Venue: The McAlpine's own hotel, the Dorchester, Park Lane, London
The Menu: La Friande de Perdreau, whatever that may be, washed down with Chateau Rancan Gassies and rounded off with a copy of a biography of Ted Heath as a presentation for every guest.
The guest list: Unbelievable, 700 of the wealthiest, most powerful people in Britain. The following were on the top table.

Edward Heath yachtsman

Lord Chandos of Panmure Gordon stockbrokers

Sir Gerald Templer ex boss of the British Army and chairman of the British Metal Corporation

Harold MacMillan ExTory Prime Minister

Sir Joseph Lockwood boss of EMI director of Smith's Industries, Beechams and Hawker Siddeley

Lord Thomson owner of Thomson Newspapers

Lord Inchape boss of P&O, director of Burmah Oil and BP

Lord Renwick of W Greenwell, stockbrokers

Selwyn Lloyd former Tory chancellor and Foreign Secretary

Sir Charles Forte boss of Trust House Fortes

Sir Desmond Plummer former boss of the Greater London Council

Lord Perth boss of Tate & Lyle

Lord Amory former Tory chancellor of the Exchequer, ex director of Lloyds, ICI and John Heathcoats

Ray Gunter former Labour Minister of Labour and director

of Securicor

Gordon Brunton boss of Thomson Newspapers.

Lord Citrine former Electricians Union official, former Genral Secretary of the TUC, former Chairman of the Electricity Board

Charles Clore boss of the British Shoe Corporation, director of Scottish Motor Traction, Selfridges etc,

Dr Finniston boss of the British Steel Corporation

Sir Ronald Leach of Peat Marwick company doctors

Lord Hall former head of the Post Office

Lord Stow Hill formerly Frank Soskice, Labour Home Secretary

Sir David Brown owns David Brown Tractors

J A Boyd Carpenter ex Tory Minister and chairman of the Civil Aviation Authority

Lord Mancroft Ex Tory minister, Cunard and Great Universal Stores director

Sir Louis Gluckstein head of Great Universal Stores

Sir Alec Douglas Home smallholder

Sir Halford Reddish free enterprise fanatic, boss of Rugby Portland Cement and director of Granada.

Reginald Maulding director of dubious companies

Lord Showcross former chairman of BSA, and former Labour Attorney General

Sir Arnold Weinstock boss of GEC

Duncan Sandys former Tory Minister director of Llonrho

Lord Hill former boss head of the BBC and the ITA

Sir Max Rayne head of London Merchant Securities, the property empire

Lord Aldington friend of Jack Jones, director of English China Clays and GEC

Sir Harold Samuel property king and boss of Land Securities

John Peyton Tory Minister of Transport

Sir Miles Thomas director of the Thomson Organisation and of a dubious gambling club, 'The Pair of Shoes'

Sir Paul Chambers formerly of ICI now insurance magnate and director of National Westminster

The political influence of the McAlpine dynasty.

Conservatives received donations totalling £67,703 from companies in the building and civil engineering sector and £30,299 from companies in the building materials sector.[31] The highest-ranking donor to the Conservatives was the McAlpine-owned Newarthill, giving £43,540.[32]

The NFBTE was the best-organised grouping of the small and medium-sized employers and led the negotiations for them on the National Joint Council for the Building Industry (NJC). The NJC had been established in 1926 as the body to organise national collective bargaining between building trade employers and workers. The NJC adopted a Working Rule Agreement (WRA) covering rates of pay, hours, overtime rates, allowances, holidays and apprenticeships. Over the years, following regular negotiations on the NJC, the WRA had expanded to over 160 pages in length.[33] Despite the detail, it only applied if the employer on a particular construction site adopted it. That, in turn, depended upon the strength of trade union membership and organisation on the site. The growth of 'lump' labour in the 1960s and the employers' thirst for higher profits increased the likelihood that national agreements would be ignored.

The nationally agreed pay rates, though low, were important because they formed the starting point for wages on any job. On well-unionised sites, shop stewards would negotiate bonus, overtime and other payments based upon the national rates, so that most workers could end up earning more than the basic rate. But it was a constant fight, when one site finished and a new one started. By the start of the 1970s, construction industry wage rates were in the bottom half of the table for UK manual workers.

The position was acknowledged by the NFBTE's national president when he reflected upon the aftermath of the 1972 strike:

Now in June, when our troubles really started, our national rates *were* relatively low. Our 1969 wage negotiations had perhaps been *too* successful. Pay anomalies existed right across our industry from one trade to another, from one town to another, from one firm to another. The weather has always undermined our

Table 3: Average gross weekly wages – male adults – as of April 1971

	£ per week
1. Vehicles	34.0
2. Petroleum and Coal Products	33.4
3. Paper Printing and Publishing	33.2
4. Shipbuilding	32.1
5. Transport	30.8
6. Chemicals	30.5
7. Bricks, Pottery, Glass and Cement	30.4
8. All Manufacturing	30.2
9. Mechanical	29.8
10. Food, Drink and Tobacco	29.6
11. Electrical	29.1
12. Gas, Electricity, Water	29.1
13. All Industries and Services	28.8
14. Mining and Quarrying	28.2
15. Instrument Engineering	28.1
16. Building and Construction	27.8
17. Textiles	26.5
18. Clothing and Footwear	25.6
19. Miscellaneous Services	23.6

Source: New Earning Survey, Department of the Employment Gazette, December 1971

men's confidence in what their wage packet will contain. We had, in fact, allowed a pay jungle to develop in our industry – fertile ground for militants to step in, pressure the unions and the men to go for a mammoth pay increase, and show them how to bend employers into submission.[34]

Building workers had few work-related benefits, particularly compared with manual workers in engineering, vehicle manufacture and council direct works departments. Access to an occupational pension scheme, sick pay or paid holidays was rare. A holiday stamp scheme had been set up in 1942 by the building and civil engineering employers and trade unions. Each week a 'B&CE' stamp could be purchased by the worker to put on a holiday card. When the employee moved to a different employer, they took the card with them for new stamps to be added. The card could be cashed in, usually in the summer, when the employee stopped work and needed 'holiday' pay. Many employers did not take part in the scheme though.

A Bloody Industry

Conditions on building sites were appalling. In 1972 alone 190 building workers were killed and tens of thousands were injured through accidents at work.[35] UCATT's monthly journal, *Viewpoint*, had regular reports of accidents. One was the prosecution of an unnamed employer manufacturing bricks. It had failed to prop up a damaged kiln that needed repair. It collapsed onto an adjacent kiln, which should also have been propped up, killing three men who were working inside. The company was fined just £100 plus £4.50 costs.[36] Another three deaths occurred in 1972 on the Loddon Bridge site of Marples Ridgway,[37] which resulted in a £300 fine.

Life was cheap. The maximum penalty that an employer could face at that time for allowing death or injury in a workplace was just £300.[38] There was no pressure on them to improve site safety, no reputational damage to worry about. Newspapers reported workplace deaths either as a footnote story or in a sensationalist manner, depending upon the location or the manner of death. The reader was left to conclude that accidents were the fault of careless workers, not criminally negligent employers.

At his trial, Des Warren highlighted that, during the period of the strike, July to September 1972, when he was trying to get employers to sign up to a national agreement, forty-nine building workers were killed in accidents on sites that were still working.[39] Despite lurid press reports, not one single building worker was killed or suffered serious injury due to picketing by trade unionists.

The Notorious Lump

Trade union members were determined to halt the growth of 'lump labour'. This was a system where the main site contractor would not employ workers directly but instead would pay the worker a *lump sum* for doing a job and leave that worker with the responsibility of paying income tax and National Insurance contributions. Often, a sub-contractor would agree to do a job for a fixed lump sum and then hire one or more men to work for him, cash in hand. This practice was known as 'working on the lump' and the men who worked this way were known as 'lumpers'. Its main features were summed up succinctly by *Socialist Worker*:

> The short-term advantage to the lump worker is that he avoids his obligation to pay National Insurance contributions and income tax, often by living and working under an assumed name. Since he is on the move from contract to contract, it is difficult for the income tax men to catch up with him. He therefore seems to earn more than anything the union can negotiate ...
>
> They work all the time even in the rain since they are on lump sum payments. They do not quibble about safety and as soon as the job is finished, they vanish into thin air ... The employer gets out of his obligation to pay National Health and Insurance contributions and holiday stamps. He gets out of his obligations to provide a safe working environment with proper amenities.[40]

The lump was a means by which the employers could save money and undermine trade union organisation. Abolition of the lump was an important demand of striking building workers in 1972, and they took up the chant 'Kill, kill, kill the lump' on demonstrations and when picketing sites.[41] Des Warren's barrister highlighted the practice as part of the defence at his trial:

> The Lump is a fraud on the Revenue and on Social Security and on all those who contribute to them ... It is also accompanied by a steady increase in the proportion of accidents and a steep decline in the number of apprenticeships and of the men in the building trade unions.[42]

The adoption of lump labour by the employers was helped by the very nature of the construction industry. The process of construction involves building, adapting, repairing or demolishing a structure. This can range from an individual house to entire housing estates, from a section of road to a motorway, to bridges, hospitals, shops and factories. The various jobs that need to be done can be divided and sub-contracted out to individual firms to complete specific parts, e.g. brickwork, electrical work, steel fixing, scaffolding, plumbing, joinery and so on. On a construction site there could be half a dozen or more firms, each with their own workmen, doing a particular task towards the overall construction project.[43]

Building Sites: Reploughing the Same Field

Demand for labour on a building site varies during the course of the contract. Different trades come and go. When a construction project is completed all the workers involved have long since moved on to new projects. This prevents a trade union presence from being maintained in the workplace; the workplace for a building worker moves around.

Conflict between employer and worker is endemic due to the economics of construction. The profit made by a contractor on any project is the difference between the contract price agreed with the client and the money paid out in wages and materials during the contract. This simple economic equation was and remains the nexus for conflict between building worker and building contractor. Workers would start a new contract of employment each time and this put terms and conditions up for negotiation, beginning with pay rates for overtime, attendance, inclement weather and so on.[44] This system gave plenty of opportunities for an employer to make more profit than they had originally planned by reducing the wages bill and by avoiding the cost of equipment that makes working conditions safer and more humane.[45] An employer that did not provide basic tables and chairs for a canteen, lockers, toilets and washing facilities saved money, even though they had a legal duty to provide many such facilities.[46] Warren described one workmen's hut in Shrewsbury as being such an unhealthy hovel that was fit only to have a match put to it. Subsequently, he was accused of threatening to commit arson and criminal damage.[47]

The Blacklist: Trade Unionists Out of a Job

A major consequence of the temporary nature of a building site was and remains the power that it gives to employers to deny further employment to a worker. Each time a new building site was opened the trade unions would often have to start the process of recruiting members, electing shop stewards and negotiating recognition with the employer. Anyone who was known to be a trade union activist had their name kept on a centralised list which employers could check when deciding whether to offer work to someone.[48] Des Warren had to use aliases to get work on sites and would even have to change his appearance to avoid being recognised by some employers.[49]

The blacklist was dehumanising and soul-destroying for any trade unionist who argued for better wages and conditions and who highlighted health and safety issues. Many were denied the opportunity to work in their trade and provide for their families. It deterred workers from joining a union and 'putting their head above the parapet' by becoming a shop steward. Often a worker would be sacked on the spot for raising a complaint about pay or conditions of work.

The 1972 Wage Claim

Although the unions had submitted their claim to the NJC in June 1971, a year before the existing three-year agreement was due to end, the employers did not reply until November. They rejected it and refused to negotiate until the reconstitution of the NJC, which was necessary following the mergers on the union side. At the NJC meeting in February 1972 the employers finally responded with a 7.5 per cent increase in pay, which the unions immediately turned down. The employers' offer maintained the differential between skilled and unskilled workers: it would increase the hourly rate for craftsmen by £1.40 to £21.40 per week and by £1.20 to £18.20 per week for labourers. The employers made further minor increased offers of settlement on 16 March and 17 May 1972, which were also rejected. The latter was a nineteen-month deal with an immediate pay rise from the start of June of £2.40 for craftsmen and £2.00 for labourers; rates would increase again in February 1973.

While the national negotiations progressed there was a growing willingness and confidence to take action, which was demonstrated in local disputes that broke out in spring 1972. One such strike involved Peter Carter, a bricklayer and well-known Communist Party member among Birmingham building workers who was to play a leading role in the national strike later in the year. He had been the trade union convenor at one of the large Bryants' sites in the city, where he and another shop steward, Phil Beyer, had been sacked. They led a successful strike that not only gained their reinstatement but also secured a 50 per cent increase in basic rates of pay.[50]

Despite the trade unions' prompt rejection of the offers the employers did not expect any serious consequences. They believed that the unions would continue negotiating until a deal was agreed, as had happened on every previous occasion in the past fifty years. The assistant general secretary of UCATT recalled that

> in May and June 1972 strike action commenced against certain selected firms. The employers for their part found it difficult to believe that building workers were serious in their intentions. National strikes were a rarity in the building industry and as on previous occasions when industry-wide strikes had been threatened but failed to materialize, the employers decided again to call what they thought was the union's bluff.[51]

This time, building workers were emboldened by being part of the new union, UCATT, and were in no mood to give up without a fight. The common pay claim of thirty pounds for a thirty-five-hour week had a unifying effect upon the rank and file. For the first time, skilled and unskilled would take action together, leading Warren to declare that this was a revolution in the industry.[53] Building workers were also influenced by the major industrial disputes which workers in other sectors had won and sensed that history was with them. If they took strike action, they too had a chance of success.

Building workers knew that they faced a fierce battle with their employers, who were well connected with the Conservative Party. They were up against thousands of different firms throughout the UK, which created many geographical and organisational challenges for the unions. There were few permanently established workplaces. It was going to be a baptism of fire for many workers in the industry who had never before been involved in a national dispute. When the strike began on 26 June 1972, the odds appeared to be stacked against them.

2

The Strike Begins

All in It Together?

The negotiations between the trade unions and the employers on the National Joint Council for the Building Industry (NJC) finally broke down on 25 May 1972. It had been three years since the previous national agreement had been signed and the union leaders were now in the unexpected and uncomfortable position of having to make plans for industrial action. They formed an ad hoc National Action Committee (NAC) of eight members: four from UCATT, two from the T&GWU and one each from the GMWU and FTAT. These were the same full-time officials that formed the operatives' (trade union) side of the NJC.

The NAC held its first meeting on 30 May and it adopted two tactics to force an improved offer from the employers. First, strikes would be called at selected sites. The NAC asked regional action committees (RACs) to identify those companies that had 'vulnerable contracts', e.g. ones that had time penalties built into the contract. These would be the ones at which members would be called out on strike. Second, the unions would offer to sign individual agreements with the large national and regional firms. This, they hoped, would create divisions among the employers. The sites of those firms that signed up '... would avoid strike action being taken against them'.[1]

Two weeks later, UCATT held its inaugural conference, on 16–17 June, and heard a statement from its general secretary, George Smith. He informed delegates of the NAC's plans for action but remained hopeful of an agreement with the employers. The main resolution on the dispute, supported by the north-western, Yorkshire and northern regions, endorsed the proposed tactics. It called upon UCATT's executive council to 'organise a national campaign, through the medium of the regional Councils, on the question of our wages demand and further to organise *selective* action against individual firms'.[2]

In moving the resolution, Tony McClelland, a Liverpool painter, emphasised the importance of imposing a levy of a pound per week on members who weren't called out on strike. He was confident that the union could raise millions of pounds from them and from solidarity collections within the wider trade union movement, which could sustain striking building workers for a long period if necessary.[3] The members brought out on strike at selected sites in each region would be given strike pay (known as 'trade privileges') from union funds.

Another Liverpool delegate, Bill Jones, urged the conference to be bolder and begin the campaign with a one-day stoppage of all building workers. This would inspire them and show the employers that they meant business. He also called for lay representatives to be appointed to the national and regional negotiating bodies to prevent a sell-out, as had occurred in previous years.[4]

Selected Sites Only

When the action started on 26 June, thousands of building workers throughout the country stopped work at lunchtime to take part in demonstrations.[5] In Liverpool, 10,000 marched in support of the claim. UCATT issued a leaflet to members who were not called out on strike, headed, 'Back the wage claim'. Halfway down it stated in capital letters, 'Your site is asked not to stop work but to support this industrial conflict with financial contributions to the strike fund'. It suggested that working sites should 'adopt' a site that had been called out on strike and guarantee it a fixed sum of money each week. They were also asked to ban overtime. Harry Chadwick, a Wigan joiner who became chairperson of the Shrewsbury 24 Campaign, was active throughout the strike. He recalled,

At the beginning, there was hesitancy in calling for an indefinite all-out strike, even amongst charter supporters. We were not certain that it would be supported by all union members. But this changed very quickly when pickets visited working sites to talk about the dispute. Many workers joined a union and willingly paid the levy. They were keen to join the strike.[6]

Peter Carter was also initially hesitant: 'Some people say we should have had an all-out strike from June 26. I don't believe we had the forces available to make the call realistic.'[7] But he, like many Charter supporters, was to change his mind when he saw the level of support for a total stoppage.

On some larger, city-based sites, where trade union membership was strong, employers conceded the claim and signed an agreement with the unions, stating that they would pay the new higher basic rates. Signs would be posted on such sites boldly proclaiming, 'This site is working because our claim has been met.'[8] The unions agreed that members on those sites could return to work.[9] This policy of selective strikes and local deals with employers was criticised later for being divisive. John McKinsie Jones, who was prosecuted at the first Shrewsbury trial, told me, 'It caused animosity as those on strike were sacrificing the most while others were still earning. It was a divisive policy. Everyone should have been out.'

Regional Action Committees

The day-to-day organisation of strike action was devolved from the NAC to the regional committees composed of full-time trade union officials, members of each of the four unions' regional committees, site convenors, leading shop stewards, and branch officers. The NAC held regular meetings with regional representatives during the dispute. As it progressed, the regional bodies encouraged the formation of local action committees in towns and cities throughout the country. These local committees were open to all building workers, irrespective of unions, and met regularly, often in the open air, to discuss the campaign. They would also organise the picketing of working sites in their area.

This level of organisation was remarkable, given the historic divisions between different crafts and between them and unskilled labourers. They quickly learned that unity was the only way that they could win. There were many newspaper reports of meetings of hundreds of striking building workers organised to maintain morale and to arrange picketing. The North West RAC, which included north Wales, had forty-four such local action committees at the height of the strike.

Many striking members were eager to picket working sites in their area. At this early stage the purpose of picketing was not to get other sites to stop work but to hold a mass meeting of those at work to explain the aims of the strike. They would encourage workers to join a union if they were not members, elect shop stewards and contribute to the levy to replenish the strike funds.

In the first week of the strike, seventy sites struck nationwide, fifty-seven more from 3 July, and a further forty-five from 10 July. This involved approximately 8,000 union members. In a speech on 12 July, UCATT's George Smith announced, 'Regional secretaries are now reporting that they are being approached by firms and the union has now circulated a draft agreement to provide the basis of negotiations with companies.'[10] Any agreement had to be ratified by the NAC. Agreements with regional companies and employers' federations were to be agreed at a regional level.

Deadlock – Employers Dig In

The formal position of the NJC was that national talks had broken down; the employers had no further proposals to make following the unions' rejection of their most recent offer on 25 May. During the following two months, behind-the-scenes channels of communication were set up by the two sides involving an ad hoc group of negotiators. On each occasion they failed to reach an agreement that could be put to the full NJC.

After three weeks of selective strike action the NFBTE was intransigent. At a special meeting of UCATT's executive council on 19 July it was 'decided that the whole strategy of the existing dispute would have to be reviewed'.[11] They still did not consider an all-out national strike, as many members were now demanding. Instead, the union proposed to advise members on strike at selected sites to return to work and the RACs would organise lightning strikes over a wider area to maximise the disruption to the employers. The executive also suggested that striking members seek employment at working sites:

> Where sites were withdrawn over any period at all attempts should be made to have our members take up other employment with other Employers because this factor in itself would cause division among Employers because of their contractual difficulties arising out of the supply of labour.[12]

The NAC met the next day and decided to escalate the selective strike action. The Yorkshire RAC was given permission to call out all members in Irwins, Mowlems and Humber Joinery in the county and to organise half- and full-day lightning strikes throughout the region at its own discretion. Other regions made plans to identify further sites to bring out, including eight in the South West, three in London and six in the North West. Other regions reported that they were meeting to select additional sites for strike action.[13] Following the NAC meeting, a press release was issued on 20 July expressing the unions' frustration at the employers' cynical repackaging of an earlier offer that had been rejected. It announced the escalation of the campaign of selective strikes throughout the country.[14]

As the strike progressed, reports from the regions showed that members wanted to go beyond selective action. At the NAC meeting on 27 July one regional secretary 'reported that support for the campaign was snow-balling in Yorkshire and the main difficulty involved was keeping men in ... they were under continual pressure for the escalation into a National Stoppage'. The north-western region 'reported that there was increasing popular pressure for increased action and the overtime ban had now been made effective'. In the Midlands, the 'feeling of the membership was that selectivity had meant the effective strikes being spread too thinly, which was involving too much sacrifice by too few people. They proposed an escalation of strike action involving the suspension of Trade Privileges'.[15] The eastern region reported that the strike was solid and shop stewards on sites that had been recommended to return to work to finance other strikers rejected this proposal. Only the southern and south Wales regions reported any weaknesses in support. It was also noted that the FTAT was not backing the strike campaign and its members were crossing picket lines.

The Employers' New Offer – They Think It's All Over

Building workers in many areas were voting with their feet, stopping work even though their site had not been selected to come out on strike. The overtime ban was widespread. This moved the employers to make a further improved offer at a meeting of the ad hoc negotiating group on 28 July. They would increase pay rates, the bonus level and additional holidays, in four stages over an eighteen-month period.[16] The union representatives said that the overall structure of the offer was acceptable except for the immediate increase in pay. The employers pushed for immediate acceptance but the unions replied that they were not in a position to accept the package on the spot. It was agreed that the offer would be discussed at a full meeting of the NJC on 2 August.

At that later meeting the employers made some minor improvements to pay rates and changes to the start dates of the various stages. From 7 August 1972 the basic minimum rate for skilled workers would increase to £25 per week and to £21.40 for labourers; from May 1973 the rates would increase to £29 and £24.80 respectively. An extra day's winter holiday would be given for 1972–3 and a further day's holiday from 1973–4. UCATT, the FTAT and the GMWU agreed to the offer but the T&GWU, though supportive of the proposals, wanted time to consult its members.

Despite the T&GWU's insistence on consulting its members, the other three unions proceeded as if the strike was over. UCATT's executive met regional representatives on Thursday 3 August and, although it heard reports that the deal would not be acceptable to members, decided to sign up to it, as did the FTAT and the GMWU. The three unions had nine votes on the Operatives side of the NJC to the three of the T&GWU. Preparations were made for the publication of the settlement and amendments to the Working Rule Agreement. George Smith wrote to UCATT regional secretaries on 4 August enclosing the terms of settlement, including sufficient quantities for distribution to shop stewards.[17] He informed them that confirmation of ratification of the deal would shortly be sent by telegram following the next NJC meeting.

The T&GWU's decision to consult its members created a vacuum. Over the following days rank-and-file UCATT members discovered that their own union executive had accepted the offer without referring it to them for approval. Charter supporters mobilised. There were strikes and demonstrations by building workers throughout the country to demand that the offer be rejected and that the strike be extended to all building workers.[18] UCATT's North West Regional Council meeting on 7 August was lobbied by hundreds of angry building workers. It heard a report from Albert Williams, the executive council member for the region. At the end of the meeting a resolution was carried, nineteen votes to two, to reject the offer and to move to 'all out tactics in areas where possible, without trade privileges'.[19] Resolutions rejecting the agreement and calling for an escalation of the strike were also passed by UCATT's Southern, Yorkshire, Eastern, and Midlands Councils. On the same day, 7 August, the T&GWU executive rejected the offer.

The NJC meeting scheduled for 8 August to rubber-stamp the agreement with the employers was cancelled. Instead, the UCATT executive council met that day and 'it was agreed that as a result of the pressure through the Regions by our members against this proposed agreement, it should not be ratified.'[20] *The Times* clearly saw the influence of the charter: 'The militants have first captured key sites, then regional officials, and finally forced the moderate union leadership into an unprecedentedly tough bargaining position.'[21] The UCATT executive was now in retreat, following the humiliating reversal of its earlier decision. It called a meeting with regional representatives for 11 August

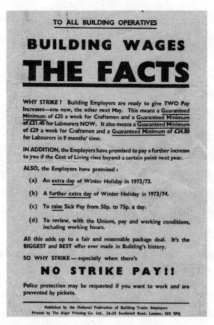

Employers' strike-breaking leaflet urging building workers to accept the August 1972 offer and return to work.

at the Birmingham regional office to discuss how to develop the campaign.[22]

The Escalation of Selective Strikes

On 15 August, the trade unions, under mounting pressure from their members, issued a joint statement to escalate the strike:

> That the regions be advised that the most rapid intensification possible should now take place. The Operatives' Side took into account that it was essential that middle-range firms which up to now had not been affected to a great extent, should be the type of construction firms upon which the Regional Action Committees should concentrate.[23]

The statement highlighted that the main obstacle to a settlement was the smaller building contractors, which were the backbone of the NFBTE:

One particular feature of the strategy of the present escalation is to ensure that there is a complete stoppage of work of small and medium-sized firms, i.e. firms from 30 men to 200 men. It is most important that this is done with utmost speed and should be completed by the end of the week. It is therefore anticipated that a full stop of these firms will bring companies to the negotiating table regionally for company agreements.[24]

As the dispute entered its seventh week, the numbers now involved meant that there would be no strike pay ('trade privileges') because the unions did not have enough money to pay hundreds of thousands of striking members. The T&GWU issued a telex message to its regional secretaries: 'Jointly with other Unions and at the request of large sections of our members it has been agreed to escalate the stoppage to complete national action but without payment of dispute benefit.'[25] This would cause hardship, especially for single men who could not claim social security benefits. Despite this, the escalation of the strike created a greater sense of unity and solidarity among building workers. Although the statements of the T&GWU and UCATT called for a complete stoppage, some regions still selected sites to go on strike rather than declare that all building work should stop.[26] Most other areas just got on with it and organised picketing to get everyone out. For the first time since the strike began they could all act together.

This turning point was noted by Lee Wilson, writing eight weeks into the strike in the London *Evening News*:[27]

The only untypical thing about the strike of Britain's building workers, is that until now few people have been affected. At least visibly, immediately affected. Incredibly the dispute has been going since June 26.

Rampaging pickets have not tossed bricks at the police. No one has been asked to tighten his belt. We haven't been warned that we are losing the flavour of Greatness, and so far the Government has not declared a State of Emergency.

After the miners and the dockers, the building workers seem to be as menacing as a walk-out by a church choir.[28]

He ended his article by warning, 'But now things might change.' Press interest in the strike increased as building workers took up the flying picket tactic.

Local Action Committees

The planning of the escalation of the strike was left to regional and local officials. In turn, they encouraged the development of more local action committees in every town and city in their region. The South Wales RAC met on 17 August and decided to organise flying pickets and agreed to put this to a rally in Swansea two days later to encourage members to use their cars to transport pickets around. At a meeting between regional secretaries and the NAC on 17 August, the chairman of the North Western RAC

> reported that there had been a very good escalation within the North Western Region and that all parts of North Wales were now closed and in addition Liverpool, Wigan, Oswestry, Skelmersdale and Southport had been closed down and that union unity had been absolutely first class.[29]

The meeting also heard reports that over 100,000 building trade workers at more than 5,000 sites had come out on strike. As well as Liverpool, construction work had stopped in Bristol, Stoke, Birmingham, Norwich, Ipswich, Glasgow, Aberdeen, Leeds and Sheffield. By 22 August the unions reported that 200,000 workers on more than 7,000 sites were on strike. The South Western RAC proudly reported to the NAC two days later, 'In sum total and I can only approximate, I consider that there are about 15,000 building trade workers on strike in this region which is about twice the total of membership of all of the four unions in the building industry before this dispute started.'[30]

Jim Arnison, who covered the strike for the *Morning Star*, commented,

Stopping the big sites proved no difficult obstacle for it was there that one could guarantee some form of trade union membership and organisation. The problem lay with many of the smaller sites and on the new Motorway and road construction jobs. Then the real issue facing the strikers was revealed.[31]

The 'real issue' was the lumpers, many of whom refused to join a union as they were only interested in the lump sum they were paid for the current job that they were doing. They would only be persuaded to back the strike if they saw the tremendous support that it had from their fellow building workers. A group of fifty or more pickets was more inspiring and persuasive than a handful. In addition, mass picketing kept striking building workers involved in the dispute. Arnison wrote that it threw up new young leaders of the unions, 'eager and willing to join the struggle and to win victory. Many of these were raw and inexperienced in the formalities of trade unionism. They were often impatient – they were having a go, some of them for the first time in their lives'.[32] The experiences that these men did share were of the harsh working conditions, low pay and bullying site management that were endemic in the industry.

The NFBTE recognised that the dispute had reached a turning point. A paper for its council meeting on 17 August reported that, following the rejection of the employers' latest offer, strikes had spread beyond the selective strikes that the unions had called initially:

The pattern changed again in the week beginning 7th August, when militants began spreading the action without reference to the unions' official policy. Groups of men went from site to site, often using intimidation and threats to get work stopped. This was particularly marked in Yorkshire, where pickets approached operatives even at bus stations and company's pick-up points and warned them not to go to work. Within two or three days, nearly every major site in the Yorkshire Region was at a standstill. There had been instances of unofficial action of this kind earlier in the dispute in several regions, including London and the

South West, but it was only at this stage that the unions seemed to lose control of the industrial action.[33]

The language used by the employers to rally their members mirrored that used by trade unions – the need for *unity*, *solidarity* and a *levy*. An NFBTE emergency newsletter advised members on the latest stage of negotiations and declared, 'Unity is important. Stand firm.' It concluded by expressing gratitude 'for the solidarity shown by Regions'. It had a defence fund that would make loans to member firms provided that they

1 have acted in accordance with any decisions, recommendations and advice which have been, or may be issued by or on behalf of the Council of the Federation.
2 That the member must be suffering severe financial hardship as a result of strike action ...[34]

The NFBTE president recognised that the prolongation of the strike would place huge demands on the fund and appealed for member firms to contribute to a levy:

> As a guide, the Council suggested that the amount should be up to £1.00 per direct employee but, in the interests of general fairness, you will no doubt take into account the use made of labour-only sub-contractors and, for this purpose, regard them as direct employees.[35]

Despite the decision to escalate the strike the unions were still keen to sign agreements with employers locally where the latter were prepared to accept the unions' main wage demand. In a telex message on 18 August from the T&GWU national secretaries to the union's eleven regions, they wrote, 'there was now no reason why there should not be company regional agreements covering national contractors.' At the beginning of September George Smith announced that ninety-one firms had signed up to the claim. Agreements with forty-six Scottish firms included four extra days' holiday by 1973–4 and plans to reduce hours to thirty-five 'over a period'.[36] The union leaders still thought that by picking off firms, the employers' united front would be broken, forcing them to improve their collective offer.

One Out, All Out

Not all regions supported local deals. Ken Barlow, UCATT's Midlands regional secretary, issued a rousing appeal letter to all members, using capital letters in part to promote support and solidarity:

A few Company Agreements have been signed in other Regions NO SUCH AGREEMENTS HAVE BEEN SIGNED IN THIS REGION

ALL BUILDING AND CIVIL ENGINEERING WORK IN THIS REGION MUST NOW BE BROUGHT TO A COMPLETE STANDSTILL. IT IS NOT NECESSARY FOR AN OFFICIAL TO VISIT YOUR SITE (IT WOULD BE PHYSICALLY IMPOS-SIBLE FOR THIS TO HAPPEN ANYWAY!)

IF YOU ARE STILL WORKING ON ANY SITE YOU SHOULD STOP WORK IMMEDIATELY, ORGANISE A PICKET LINE. AFTER THIS IS DONE, AND PROVISION MADE FOR A ROTA OF MEN TO COVER THE SITE DURING ALL WORKING HOURS [sic]. WHEN THIS IS DONE, ANY SPARE MEN SHOULD REPORT DAILY TO THE UNION OFFICE AT 8.00 a.m.

If you are already on strike and reporting to your picket line or this office daily you are playing your part ...

AS LONG AS YOU STAY AT HOME WE SHALL NOT WIN OUR BATTLE.[37]

Pickets Get Organised

As the strike spread from mid-August onwards the challenges of picketing came to the fore. Many construction sites were not fenced off, unlike today. Workers, pickets and the public could walk onto and through many building sites from any number of directions.[38] The workplaces of miners, dockers, engineers and others were permanent, physical presences. The National Union of Mineworkers knew where every pit was and the name of every local union representative. The building workers' unions did not. Building sites were temporary and one of the pickets' first tasks was to find them. They had to rely upon local knowledge, word of mouth and reconnaissance trips. This was painstaking work in the days before mobile phones and the Internet, text messaging and emails.

Often the only means of communication was public telephone boxes, which were not widely available in semi-rural areas like north Wales. Not everyone had a car and pick-up points had to be planned over a large area. When a site had been successfully picketed, there was always a risk that some men would drift back to work in the following days if there weren't sufficient union-minded workers among them who would inspire their colleagues to join the union and continue to support the action. Consequently, pickets would return to sites that they had visited previously to check that work remained at a standstill.

Despite these challenges, striking building workers would work tirelessly each day, travelling throughout their area to ensure that all sites stopped work. In addition, just as striking coal miners in 1972 had picketed power stations and coke depots, so striking building workers in the bigger cities also picketed workplaces that were connected with their industry: supply companies such as cement works, timber yards and brick manufacturers.

After 15 August the ranks of striking building workers grew as more of them stopped work. Pickets from local action committees were no longer simply visiting sites to explain the issues and raise a levy on builders who continued to work. They were asking all building workers to join the strike, irrespective of trade. Over the following weeks the north Wales building workers, like their counterparts in many parts of Britain, were successful in spreading the strike to most sites in their area. Their confidence and determination to win the dispute were behind the decision of the North Wales and Chester Action Committee to take part in a flying picket to Shropshire on 6 September 1972. That day was to be a life-changing event for many of them. Little did they know that they would eventually become caught up in the counteroffensive against picketing that had already been launched by the Conservative government, the employers and the police.

3

The North Wales Pickets and the Fateful Day

North Wales in the 1970s, like today, did not have any significant urban centres apart from Wrexham. The towns and villages dotted across the coastline and inland were relatively small. The nearest English cities, Roman Chester and industrial Liverpool, were important focal points for shopping, entertainment and football. There were a handful of large employers: British Steel at Shotton, Courtaulds textiles, Hawker Siddeley aircraft and even a few surviving collieries in the north Wales coalfield. Apart from the public sector, most people worked for small local firms. This was not fertile soil in which the seeds of trade unionism flourished.

The Organisation of the Strike in North Wales

Three building sites in the north Wales area had been selected to come out on strike from 26 June: the Holst contract at Shotton Steelworks, John Laing's at Colwyn Bay police headquarters and the Taylor Woodrow site at Chester Telephone Exchange.[1] In the following weeks, pickets from these workplaces visited building sites across north Wales to explain the dispute and get support for the levy. A local district organiser at the T&GWU's Wrexham office, Ted Hughes, described their work:

The Committee Members and myself would approach the Site Agent, identify ourselves and ask for a Meeting with the Labour Force on site. At these Meetings other Members of the pickets were invited on to the site. Should this not be granted by the Management then a Meeting was arranged to take place outside the site boundaries.[2]

As the strike spread, local action committees were set up in Rhyl, Shotton, Denbigh, Flint, Wrexham, Bangor, Ellesmere Port and Chester. A hybrid local coordinating strike action committee for the north Wales and Chester area met weekly in Chester from August onwards. It consisted of representatives from each of the local action committees, full-time union officers and lay trade union branch officers. The role of the local action committees was to organise mass meetings of all striking building workers, sometimes daily, often in the open air, to update them on the progress of the strike and the places that needed to be picketed. The Flint strikers met daily outside the Raven pub. It was also a means to maintain morale and show to each other that large numbers were supporting the action. Occasionally, the mass meeting would end with a march through the local town.

Picketing in North Wales

One of the working sites visited in July 1972 by the strikers employed by contractors at the Shotton steelworks was McAlpine's Wrexham bypass road project, which employed over 200 people. Of the six pickets prosecuted in the first Shrewsbury trial, two came from this site, John Llywarch and Eric Tomlinson. Ironically, neither of them were trade union members when the strike began on 26 June. It was a predominantly non-union site and there were no experienced trade unionists working on it, like a Des Warren, who would instinctively try to recruit fellow workers. Llywarch was employed as a pipe-layer ganger and described how the visit of pickets in July encouraged him to join the T&GWU. He then obtained 180 forms from the local union office and persuaded many of his fellow workers to join.

He stated that Tomlinson, who worked as a labourer on the site, 'was against the strike at first and against joining the union. In fact, I recruited him, and then he was all for it, he seemed to enjoy it'.[3] The newly unionised members on this McAlpine site were not asked to strike at this stage but to contribute to the levy. The site eventually stopped work when a national all-out strike was declared from mid-August 1972.[4]

The following list shows some of the significant places in north Wales that were picketed by members of a local action committee during the strike and that featured at the pickets' trials.[5] These sites were not situated in any significant towns or cities. Apart from Shropshire on 6 September, the number of pickets that visited any of these sites varied from a few car-loads to a coach. The north Wales pickets were a diverse group, organised in separate local action committees. In general, the pickets from Denbigh did not visit the same sites as pickets from Chester; those from Flint did not picket with those from Wrexham. The one and only time that they picketed together was on 6 September.

August 1972

1 Padeswood sewerage construction site, near Mold
7 Padeswood
8 Penrhyn Bay, site of Eldon R. Gorst & Son Ltd
14 Cefn Parc, Penycae, Wrexham
14 Padeswood
18 Penrhyn Bay, Eldon R. Gorst & Son Ltd
18 Penrhyn Beach, Llandudno
18 Brynford (Narrow Lane), site of Rawson and Roberts of Holywell (a contractor pulled a shotgun on the pickets)
23 Brennig Reservoir

September 1972

6 Shrewsbury and Telford
7 Penycae, Wrexham, Caergwrle Investment Ltd
8 Cambrian Road works, Llansannan
11 Brennig Reservoir
11 Crewe Lane, Farndon, near Wrexham

13 Penrhyn Beach, Llandudno
14 Crewe Lane, Farndon

October 1972
24, 26, 28 Greenfield sewerage construction site, Flintshire[6]

As can be seen, there were several sites that pickets had to return to repeatedly, such as Penrhyn Beach and Brennig Reservoir. This was also the experience of striking building workers throughout Britain. Such sites were where large numbers of lump labour worked. There were insufficient trade unionists working on them who could maintain a token picket to ensure that work remained at a standstill.

The tireless efforts of striking building workers in July and August ensured that most building work in north Wales eventually stopped. The *Morning Star* reported on 14 August, 'In North Wales, there was a meeting of 1,500 in a hall at Connah's Quay, with nearly 1,000 outside, at which there was a vote for a total stoppage with no strike pay as soon as possible.' Three weeks later, a local T&GWU district secretary, Eric Roberts, wrote that support for the strike was solid:

> I attended a meeting at Wrexham Miners Institute yesterday 4th September 1972, there were approximately 900 to 1,000 members present and they reaffirmed their decision ... they were prepared to carry on and not give in until the National claim had been made and that there should be no surrender.[7]

Oswestry Local Action Committee

The success of strikers in north Wales led them to agree to a request to picket further afield, in the English county of Shropshire, on 6 September. It was a centre for lump labour where, the *Shropshire Star* reported, 'They say they have little to gain from any pay award because they negotiate their own price for a job.'[8] The police also noted that the county had become a magnet for building workers opposed to the strike: 'There is reason to believe, as the strikers did believe, that some of these had drafted themselves into the Shropshire area when their original sites were closed by the strike.'[9]

The West Mercia police summarised an earlier attempt to picket sites in Shrewsbury:

> Oswestry strikers picketed Shrewsbury sites during August but with little success. There was a short-lived Strike Action Committee in being for Shrewsbury, but its members did not visit Chester and it was in fact reduced to a mere two men after only a few days. Building sites in Telford were not visited by pickets until 6th September – the date of the events leading to this report.[10]

The initial picketing had persuaded several Shrewsbury sites to stop work on that visit, including a Laing's site at the Square, Fletchers, Boots the Chemist site, the Tarmac site at the Weir over the river Severn, Watkin Starbuck & Jones, and the new police station site in Monkmoor Road. Several of the pickets recalled that police were present throughout their time in the town.[11]

Union membership in Shrewsbury was low and members were not experienced or numerous enough to maintain support for the strike. There were also many workers who had refused to join the stoppage. Men gradually drifted back to work in the days following the Oswestry pickets' visit on 18 August, despite the strike spreading throughout Britain. This was reported back to the Oswestry Action Committee by two workers from the Laing's site. Both towns were in England and trade unions within the county usually came under the Midlands region of individual unions. The Midlands Regional Action Committee was very active during the strike and was the obvious body to contact to seek support for a further picket of sites in Shrewsbury and in Telford.[12] Llywarch lived and picketed in Oswestry and was chairman of the local action committee. He was also the secretary of the T&GWU branch covering the Wrexham bypass site, where he worked. Most of his members on the bypass picketed with the Wrexham Action Committee and his link with them caused Llywarch to attend the weekly meetings of the North Wales Area Action Committee in the Bull and Stirrup pub in Chester, rather than the nearer Midlands Regional Action Committee.

The Bull and Stirrup Meeting

On Thursday 31 August, the area action committee held its weekly meeting in an upstairs room of the Bull and Stirrup public house in Chester, chaired by Alan Abrahams, a member of UCATT's North West Regional Committee. He estimated that around seventy people were present.[13] They included several full-time officials and regional council members, including, from UCATT, Albert Prest, Lou Armour and Charlie Jones, and from the T&GWU, Eric Roberts and Jim Morris.[14] Four representatives from the Oswestry Local Action Committee had travelled the thirty miles northwards to attend the meeting: John Llywarch, John Batterbee (treasurer), Gary Davies and Geoff Davies. The meeting heard reports from full-time officials about the progress of the strike and from representatives of each of the local action committees.

A copy of the *Shropshire Star* of 21 August 1972 was circulated, with an article headlined, 'Freelance builders to defy pickets'.[15] It stated, 'An anti-picket force has been formed by Shrewsbury building workers to defend themselves against pickets who have threatened to swoop on sites in the town.' One sub-contractor from the Severn Meadows site in the town centre, John Price, told the paper that he hoped to have enough men to ward off the pickets and persuade them to leave. At the end of the article, he warned that any confrontation with pickets would not come to violence, but that his force 'will fight the pickets if necessary'.[16]

Abrahams gave evidence at the first Shrewsbury trial, which included his recollection of the meeting:

It was moved from the floor that there should be a picket sent out to assist the Action Committee in Oswestry which was seconded. I asked how many of the action committees could supply pickets, and they all indicated that they could supply pickets and transport. We had done an estimate of how many pickets would be raised, agreed it was in the proximity of 300 and then voted to send those pickets to assist the Oswestry Committee. The vote was unanimous.[17]

Warren's statement to his solicitor gave the same account:

It was still being suggested in Shrewsbury on various sites that the strike was not official and because they were so poorly organised and inexperienced they could never get a large number of pickets out on the site. They suggested that if we had a large number of pickets attend it would impress the workmen and convince them that it was an official dispute. As it was the employers were able to say it was only a handful of cranks and extremists ...

I said ... that I could bring about 40 men from the Prestatyn area ... We arranged to meet Llywarch at Oswestry Labour Club, each district arranging its own transport. We expected about five coaches and we had no idea which particular sites we were going to. We did not expect any trouble nor did we want any. We had not given much thought to the anti-pickets force talk as I thought this was just newspaper talk.[18]

Commitments were given by representatives from Flint, Denbigh, Rhyl, Wrexham and Chester action committees to each organise coaches from their respective areas. This was the one and only time during the strike that building workers from all over north Wales came together to picket.

The Fateful Day

Wednesday 6 September was a warm sunny day when five coachloads of pickets, totalling around 200 men, made the trip from north Wales and Chester. Photographs taken on the day show that the pickets wore everyday, casual clothes. Many of them turned out in white open-neck shirts, smart trousers and casual shoes. Several of them, including John Carpenter and Kevin Butcher, wore suits.

The coaches arrived over a thirty-minute period at Oswestry Labour Club, where Llywarch spoke briefly at an impromptu meeting. When they all left just after 10.30 a.m., local Oswestry strikers boarded a sixth coach which would act as the lead for the journey down the A5 directly into Shrewsbury. The police later identified the six coaches and obtained statements from several of the drivers:[19]

> *Denbigh* coach, led by Des Warren and Ken O'Shea (Chairman of Denbigh Action Committee). It started from Prestatyn and then went to Lenton Pool, Denbigh, to pick up more. It included John Seaburg, Colin Kelly, Gwyn Roberts, Michael Pierce, Ken O'Shea, Des Warren, Ken Thomas, Derek Hughes and Lennie Williams.[20]
> *Flint*, two coaches. Met at the Raven Hotel. Barry Scragg booked them. He was in charge of one and John McKinsie Jones the other.
> *Oswestry*. Booked by John Llywarch from Crosville Motor Co.
> *Chester*. Picked up men at 9 a.m. outside the Odeon cinema, Chester.
> *Wrexham*. Booked by Eric Tomlinson and led by him and John Carpenter.

Alan Abrahams, chairman of the North West Regional Action Committee, was due to lead the pickets in Shropshire on 6 September. He had led many pickets in north Wales and Merseyside during the strike, including one of a motorway site near Liverpool involving 1,000 men. In the event he could not attend because he had been called to another meeting but was confident that other members of the North Wales Action Committee would take charge. One of them was Des Warren, a skilled steelfixer and secretary of UCATT's Rhyl branch, whom Abrahams had known since 1963.[21]

Warren wrote, 'Our pattern of activity during the day was to hold meetings on sites, urging workers not only to stop work but to join the pickets. Police were with us during the whole of that day.'[22] He had picketed north Wales sites in this way during the strike and had never been arrested or cautioned:

I had a copy of an agreement prepared by the National Action Committee for the employers to sign agreeing to the conditions which were sought for by the strike and which would apply to the site once the dispute was over. It was my intention to get the Manager to sign this agreement and that was what I did on every occasion.[23]

Apart from seeking to persuade the manager to sign the agreement, the pickets' leaders would go to the office of the site agent and request a meeting with the workers on the site. At the open-air meeting, members of the action committee would address the crowd and explain the dispute.[24]

West Mercia police prepared two reports about the picketing,[25] which included records of radio communications between various officers and the police control centre. The timeline of the picketing on 6 September is drawn from it, listing the name of the site and the main contractors involved, starting in Shrewsbury:

11:00 Kingswood – AH Woodhouse & Sons Ltd and J. Parry & Sons
11:25 Shelton roadworks – Wrekin Construction Ltd
11:45 The Mount – Maurice Graham Ltd
12:30 Severn Meadows – Watkin, Starbuck & Jones Ltd and Fletcher Estates Ltd
12:45 The Weir – Tarmac Construction Ltd

While having lunch the pickets took a decision to visit working sites in Telford, twenty miles away.

14:25 Brookside – Sir Alfred McAlpine & Son Ltd
15:35 Maxwell Homes, Stirchley Lane (near Brookside)
15:45 Woodside – Morris & Jacombs Ltd, Park Lane
16:25–16:40 coaches leave Telford
16:57 Police return to station

The six coaches of pickets arrived on the outskirts of Shrewsbury and parked outside the Oak Hotel on Shelton Road. When the coaches parked up the pickets got off and went across the road to the Kingswood site. Warren recalled,

We went onto the site and, as I always did, I headed straight for the site office to see the Manager or whoever was in charge. The men spread over the site to speak to the men and get them to come to a meeting. This was a standard procedure at all the sites we adopted. There was only a small number of men working on the site, about 25/30. The strike had been escalated about three weeks prior to that and all sites should have been stopped so the men were not in a particularly cheerful frame of mind. We had stressed, however, to the pickets that we were there to convince the men of our argument. There was only a third of the men in the Building Industry in a Trade Union and we wanted to persuade people to join a Trade Union and stay in a Trade Union and violence could not achieve the end we wanted. It would have the effect of losing support rather than gaining it.[26]

During the picketing of Kingswood an incident occurred involving a shotgun. This was the second time during the strike that the north Wales pickets were confronted by a contractor wielding such a weapon.[27] The owner of the shotgun was a contractor on the Kingswood site. He held it up to the pickets but was forced to put it back into the boot of his car. Shortly afterwards some pickets removed it and broke it in two to prevent the contractor from trying to wield it again. Half of it was handed to the police, who went on to list it among the property damaged by the pickets ('cost £20').[28]

Police on the Scene

The first recorded notification that the police received of the pickets' arrival was a 999 emergency call at 11.13 a.m. PC Philips reported that there were between fifty and 100 pickets and that he needed some assistance. Inspector Martin put out a call to any available car in the Shrewsbury area to go to Swiss Farm Road to assist. The police arrived ten minutes later, after the pickets had been to Kingswood and Shelton roadworks sites. On arrival, Chief Inspector Gradwell asked to speak with the strike leaders by their coaches and ten came forward. Seven were identified in the West Mercia Constabulary report from police photographs: John Carpenter, John McKinsie Jones, John Llywarch, Ken O'Shea, Barry Scragg, Eric Tomlinson and Des Warren.

By 11:30 a.m., fourteen police were present and for the rest of the day there were always police present at the sites that were picketed. Further police arrived on Shelton Road but senior officers took the decision that they were not needed:

> After some discussion the pickets were allowed to make their way to The Mount building site a short distance away. Meanwhile, a Sergeant and Constable had been directed to the site from Bayston Hill, the dog handler was in attendance and Detective Chief Inspector LEWIS, with one of his Sergeants, arrived at The Mount having heard about the shotgun allegation. On arrival he learned that the shotgun affair had been partly resolved and, there being no apparent disorder, he instructed four Constables in one Police vehicle to leave the scene and return to Divisional Headquarters.
>
> During this time two Traffic Department vehicles with a total of three Constables were standing by in the area, but were not called upon to assist.[29]

Later, Chief Inspector Hodges admitted,

> the decision to dismiss four Constables from the scene, albeit with a view to not 'overplaying our hand', was premature and ill-advised to a degree. It would have been logical – and in keeping with intentions at the time – to instruct them to leave the scene but to remain at a designated place nearby in case of need.[30]

The pickets visited three more sites in Shrewsbury in the morning: the Mount, Severn Meadows and the Weir. These were typical sites where workmen were dispersed over a wide area and needed to be told that a central meeting was going to be held to discuss the strike. Warren recalled,

> At the next site, The Mount, I met a representative of the Management. There was myself, John Carpenter, Scraggs, Murray,

Llywarch, O'Shea, John McKinsie Jones. I arrived last and there was an Inspector in the hut laying down the law. I asked him to leave the office because he was not part of the dispute. I told him to either leave the office or abide by the conditions which were agreed. I asked the Manager if he was prepared to sign the agreement ... He said that he was not in a position to sign any agreement, but said that we could have the meeting in the canteen. The canteen was a make-shift place, it was dark and the clothes were hung about. The seating comprised of planks on bricks and there was an open burner on which the men brewed their tea and, quite honestly, when I saw this place I just started laughing. This was where the men changed and where they had their lunch. We held the meeting and I addressed them and I talked about the aims of the dispute and I included reference to our hope that we could improve conditions and during that time I referred to their canteen and said that all it was fit for was setting a match to. This was subsequently interpreted as a threat, but this was never intended.[31]

The Decision to Go to Telford

During a break for lunch there was a discussion among the action committee representatives about further picketing. Most of the pickets were unfamiliar with Shrewsbury and had to rely upon Oswestry men to direct them. As far as they were all concerned it was a national dispute and all building work in Britain should stop. If they saw a site that was working, they would picket it. A decision was taken to travel to Telford, twenty miles to the east of Shrewsbury, as there were several large sites in the area that were still working. There had been no prior agreement to picket sites in Telford, either at the Chester meeting on 30 August or at the rendezvous at Oswestry Labour Club. One of the six coaches that had travelled to Shrewsbury had to return to Chester as it had only been booked out for half a day and needed to be back for a 'school run'. Most Chester pickets stayed and found seats on the remaining five coaches. A phone call had to be made to the owner of the Wrexham coach to ask for the hire to be extended by several hours as it was also due back by mid-afternoon. This was agreed, subject to the payment of an additional hire charge.[32]

The police summed up the position at that time:

> One of the coaches left the area to return to Chester but the remaining coaches stayed in the Severn Meadows locality for almost an hour, during which time the pickets purchased fish and chips from a shop nearby. These were consumed, some on the coaches and some as the pickets strolled about.[33]

Sir Alfred McAlpine's Brookside Site

The first site that the pickets visited in Telford was an extensive new housing estate named Brookside, which was being constructed for Telford New Town by Sir Alfred McAlpine & Son Limited.[34] It was vast and, according to Llywarch, had become a magnet for lumpers who could not get work on sites in other areas due to the strike.

When the pickets arrived, they had to split up because of its size. It had several site offices. Warren went to site office number 3 and other spokespersons searched for the other site agent

Michael Pierce walking with a group of pickets past their coaches at Brookside.

© David Bagnall, *Shropshire Star*

offices to request meetings with the workforce. The main body of pickets walked through the site to inform those working to come to a meeting. There were some heated exchanges and Thomas Brian Williams recalled workmen on scaffolding throwing bricks and mortar at the pickets as they walked through the site.[35] Not surprisingly, some pickets threw them back. Williams was subsequently charged with throwing a brick at Albert Blackham, causing actual bodily harm but was never tried for the offence.[36]

Warren described his role:

> Brookside was a very big site. I did not know where the offices were. It was a McAlpine housing estate, so the men all spread out. I walked through the site and went into the office on my own. I spoke to the agent who brought the contracts manager. I asked him about signing the company agreement, but he said it was not up to him to sign such an agreement. There were about 30/40 McAlpine men outside the office. There was just me and another picket. I addressed them for about 5 minutes and asked them to get all the men down and get all the fellow workmen.[37]

Chief Superintendent Hodges suggested that there were sufficient police present when the mass meeting at Brookside was under way: 'Officers who arrived on the civilian coach whilst

Des Warren, standing on a platform, centre, addressing workers and fellow pickets at Brookside, 6 September 1972.

© David Bagnall, Shropshire Star

© David Bagnall, Shropshire Star

Des Warren addressing workers and fellow pickets at Brookside 6 September 1972. To his left is John McKinsie Jones; to his right facing the crowd is Terry Renshaw and below him with the striped shirt, Ken O'Shea. Clifford Growcott is standing in the right-hand corner with the bobble hat, after he claimed to have been assaulted.

the meeting was going on were held in reserve on the coach and, in fact, were not required for any part of that operation.'[38] Chief Superintendent Meredith, Chief Inspector Gradwell and a constable arrived at 14:50, when the site meeting was in progress. Meredith recorded that he saw a group of 300 men, pickets and site workers, assembled outside the McAlpine office. 'Whilst I saw no incidents involving physical violence at this stage, the situation was generally rowdy and a great deal of verbal abuse was being exchanged between individuals and small groups.'[39]

Another senior police officer, Superintendent Landers, identified Warren and John McKinsie Jones as two of three pickets standing on a mound at Brookside addressing a large crowd of men, including workers from the site and pickets:

There was no shouting or acts of violence, but several of the workers obviously did not want to hear what was being said, because one or two were heard to say, 'We're getting more than that now, why can't they leave us alone?' I saw no damage whatsoever to property and I heard no mention of damage or violence at that stage, and no one made any complaint to me at all.[40]

The large size of the senior police presence, as noted by Hodges, was remarkable: '[at] the height of the Brookside incident there were a Chief Superintendent, a Superintendent, three Chief Inspectors and three inspectors on the site.'[41] Overall, he noted, 'Indeed, it must be said that the Police responded quite quickly during this incident and a total of 82 Officers were actually involved throughout the day with several others readily available if required.'[42]

Despite these numbers, none of them witnessed any damage or considered that any action should be taken, though Hodges later claimed that 'this meeting was held after the damage and violence had been committed.'[43] He wrote that Gradwell, Inspector Powell and two constables attended, but 'it must be said that the purpose of their visit was not so much to render numerical support but to provide continuity of identification of pickets.'[44] He was critical of the evidence-gathering:

> It was clear to the police that damage had been committed by the pickets but no specific complaint was received and, in the absence of any person in authority to describe the damage to them or any other person to identify offenders, it appears that the decision was taken not to make an immediate investigation but to hold one subsequently. Yet the police at the scene made no real attempt to identify the pickets at this stage.[45]

After Brookside, the pickets went by coach to the Maxwell Homes site, Stirchley Lane, Telford. Most of them stayed on their coaches while a small delegation entered the site. They returned quickly to report that the site was closing down and there was no need to hold a mass meeting. They drove off to the final site, Woodside. This was a smaller version of Brookside, a housing development where the main contractor employed large numbers of non-union lump labour. The pickets followed the same practice, spreading across the site to call everyone to a mass meeting while Warren and others went to the office to speak with the site agent.

When we got to this site we were met by someone who claimed he had been nominated as spokesman for the men. And we went to a meeting which was held in their canteen. It was the usual meeting and I discussed the conditions as set out in the agreement which I normally ask the employers to sign. They nominated the spokesman as a shop steward and they agreed to contact the local action committee. They then voted to withdraw the labour.[46]

Despite the presence of a large number of police officers and the later claims of damage and intimidation, not one picket was arrested or cautioned on 6 September in Shropshire. The north Wales building workers wanted to visit as many sites as possible to explain the reasons for the strike and to inspire those who were working to join a union and join the strike for the benefit of them all. Warren recalled,

It is not widely known that all the police officers who accompanied the pickets round the sites made written statements in which not one of them could claim they had seen us commit any violence. That is why there were no arrests (or even mention of charges) that day in the Shrewsbury area.[47]

This led Warren to conclude, 'we had completed a normal day's picketing.'

On the biggest site, McAlpine's at Brookside, which we reached toward the end of the day, Chief Superintendent Meredith shook my hand and congratulated me on the conduct of the meeting we held. He made no complaint about the activity of the pickets.[48]

Police Assessment

The police radio communications on the day confirm that they did not consider that anything serious was taking place. At 13:47 one control room officer, PC Nash, without disguising his contempt for the pickets, informed a colleague,

Yes, now then, you've got to remain in the Wellington area to watch for 5 bus loads of pickets coming from Shrewsbury, the tow rags [*sic*] – they've been floating around Shrewsbury, not causing bother much ... in the Castle Fields, Shrewsbury ... heading in your direction and its anticipated that they will go to Wellington ... to do some picketing, God knows why ... be available if required.[49]

PC Amies contacted the control room at 14:31 to ask, 'We can do with a little bit of assistance at Brookside here, they're tending to get out of hand. We could also do with a loud hailer, we've got one in the traffic office at Wellington.'[50] Twenty minutes later he reported, 'I'm now resuming from Brookside, Telford. We've got about 20 odd beat men here. They're keeping these pickets in line so I'm resuming back to Shrewsbury over.'[51]

Amies's assessment was confirmed in an exchange between two police inspectors at 15:39:

RADFORD: I've just heard a lot of squitter on the radio, what's going on up at Dawley, can you tell me?
WILLIAMS: Yes, there's some pickets come down from Liverpool picketing building sites.[52] They were at Telford but they've moved on and they can't find them at the moment. That's all it is, there's no trouble.
RADFORD: 'There's no trouble?
WILLIAMS: Its just picketing and the A.C.C. informed all Divisions that this was going on you see. But as at the moment they don't know where they are and there's no trouble reported at the moment.

Radford finished by mentioning that some of his dogs' vehicles had been contacted about the picketing but Williams confirmed that they were not needed.[53] When the five coaches left the Woodside site in Telford, the final report to the police control room at 5 p.m. stated, 'for your information the coaches intend to rendezvous at Prees Heath for tea, understood over.'[54]

Just Another Day's Picketing

These contemporaneous radio communications between police officers did not indicate that an affray was taking place or that the pickets were an unlawful assembly. The police did not receive any complaints from workmen or interview any of them on the site. It was understandable that there would be arguments between the pickets and those working on the site, especially lumpers. The pickets had been warned of an anti-strike force in Shropshire and when the pickets arrived on the Brookside site they were met with a shower of bricks and other missiles until the lumpers realised that there were dozens of pickets, who would not be intimidated. The objective of Warren and the other action committee members was not to drive the workers off the site. They wanted to explain the aims of the strike and appeal to their fellow workers to join a union and support the national stoppage.

As far as the pickets were concerned, 6 September was just another day's picketing. In the following days the local action committees in north Wales held their usual meetings and continued to organise pickets at sites in their areas. Fellow building workers throughout the country were doing the same in the belief that this would lead the employers to meet the unions' claim.

By early September, the all-out strike appeared to be working. Hundreds of thousands of building workers had now stopped work. Local action committees were leading the campaign on the ground, maintaining the picketing of all building sites. The Glasgow Action Committee sent a report to the Scottish RAC on 6 September:

> Overall the situation is very satisfactory, as near to a 100% strike situation as anyone could hope to get to. The incidence of men going back to work is minimal, though we are reaching a critical period in the view of the Committee.
>
> The weekly meeting of the Shop Stewards continues on Sunday mornings, and the Committee meets daily. We are now considering the idea of a weekly mass meeting, to keep the spirits up, as hardship is now becoming severe for some lads.

The other point I should make concerns our plans for another massive march through the city. Would you ask George Smith and L. Kemp for a date of September, 19th or 20th?[55]

The extended action had its effect. The employers decided to improve their offer. At a meeting of the NJC on Thursday 14 September, the employers offered a two-year deal up to 11 November 1974. It provided for an immediate increase in basic rates of weekly pay to £26 for craftsmen and £22.20 for labourers, with further rises on 25 June 1973 and 10 June 1974. A threshold clause would also operate to increase wages from 1 October 1973 if the Retail Prices Index increased by more than 5.5 per cent between August 1972 and August 1973. An extra day's holiday was given and sick pay was increased from fifty to seventy-five pence per day.

The Strike Ends

The NJC took a vote on the new offer. UCATT, the GMWU and the FTAT voted to accept. Only the T&GWU opposed acceptance, but it recognised it was in a minority and went along with the majority decision. The employers were told there and then that they had a deal. George Smith sent a letter to all UCATT branch secretaries and regional secretaries the following day:

> At a meeting yesterday of the National Joint Council for the Building Industry, agreement was reached to provide for an increase in wages, improved holidays and sickness or injury payments. As a consequence, members are advised that there will be a normal return to work with effect from Monday, 18th September 1972.[56]

The deal was still well short of the unions' claim of thirty pounds per week basic for a thirty-five-hour week. It also prevented any further negotiations for two years at a time when price inflation was rising sharply. Crucially, the demands that building workers had made about the use of 'lump' labour on construction sites and improvements in health and safety were not addressed at all.

The offer was not put to a vote of members; they were simply told that it had been accepted and everyone was to return to work. The UCATT national executive argued that acceptance was necessary for several reasons: first, that they were coming under pressure from other trade unions whose members were being affected adversely by the strike; second, that the Federation of Master Builders had approached the CBI and TUC to have the dispute settled through their arbitration procedure; third, that they feared that the government was going to introduce a statutory wage freeze.[57] None of these seemed compelling arguments when set against the growing support for the strike.

The T&GWU did not agree with the deal. Its two national secretaries for the building trade, G. P. Henderson and L. C. Kemp, issued a statement on 15 September setting out the terms of the employers' new offer and began by stating, 'What has not been reported however is the fact that the T&GWU representatives voted against the proposed terms of settlement.' They objected to the terms for bonus payments, to no reduction in basic working hours, to the widening of the differential between trades and labourers and to the duration of the agreement.[58] Despite this they acknowledged that the majority of the union side accepted the employers' offer and the strike would end.

In the following days mass meetings of strikers were held regionally and locally. While many rejected the deal they voted to return to work. There was considerable opposition to the settlement, particularly from supporters of the charter. UCATT's North West Regional Committee rejected it and demanded a recall of the National Action Committee to discuss the issue before any return to work. In Liverpool, building workers did not accept it and remained on strike for a further week. The Midlands Regional Council of UCATT passed a resolution on 16 September, deploring 'the action of the Executive Council in respect of the Settlement of the Construction Industry Dispute', noting that the national union had acted

3 ... without real consideration of the position of strength from which they were negotiating –

a) an increase in membership

b) a preparedness by the operatives who had been out the longest to sustain their efforts for an even longer period for a more just settlement ...

5. It further requests and urges all members to keep intact the organisation of site stewards that has been built up over the recent months.[59]

A resolution equally hostile to the settlement was approved in Scotland at a 2,000-strong meeting in Aberdeen:

> THAT this meeting of Building Workers, disgusted with the cavalier treatment at National level when agreement was signed without reference to the members, calls for their immediate resignation.
>
> Democracy has been trampled and the perpetrators should not be allowed to remain in office. We pledge our future energies to the removal of our present negotiators and work for their replacement by representatives who better reflect the asperations [sic] and hopes of the members.
>
> It is with the utmost reluctance we have to accept the situation since we are faced with a 'fait accompli'. We urge an orderly return to work accepting that whilst we have not had the success we deserve in this battle, we have not lost the war.
>
> The fight for improved working conditions goes on and must be fought at site level. The unity we forged in this dispute must not be wasted. A Shop Steward on every site must be our slogan.
>
> A strong Shop Stewards movement must be our weapon.
>
> Lets waste no time in recriminations. Lets get organised.
>
> Kingsway Hall – September, 17th 1972[60]

Maintain the Local Action Committees

Although Warren advised fellow members to accept the offer at a mass meeting on 18 September, he also saw the strike as the start of a new era of rank-and-file action:

We had plans for extending the scope of the committees after the dispute. We aimed to win 100 per cent trade union membership, improve wages and conditions, smash the lump and the blacklist with 'recruitment of labour' agreements under which unions would supply the labour.[61]

In contrast, one of the UCATT officers for the north Wales area, Albert Prest, typified the attitude of a number of full-time officials. He considered the strike to have been a backward step, never to be repeated:

Let us hope that Improvements can be achieved without resort ever again to a National Dispute, which at the time achieved its aim, but not without a very high price in individual misery and hardship, and left reflections which cannot be said to be of any credit ... may it be another fifty years before the Construction Industry is again subject to such an upheaval.[62]

Prest's unpublished memoir revealed his strong dislike of industrial action, preferring instead the cultivating of 'good relations' with employers. He believed that improvements in members' pay and condition would be achieved through his superior negotiating skills. This outlook led Prest to oppose those active rank-and-file members who believed that the only way to get decent pay and basic dignity at work was through strong union organisation on every site and a willingness to stop work to secure it. At the end of the strike Prest described a demonstration and mass meeting that was planned for 19 September at the Roodee racecourse in Chester to discuss acceptance of the settlement: 'Up to that time I had never taken part in a demonstration.'[63] He had been a full-time union official since 1956!

Three Good Wallops

At the end of 1972, anyone reflecting on the events of that year would have recognised it as one of militant trade union activity that defied government attempts to limit wages. More working days were lost than in any year since the General Strike of 1926. The Conservative government declared two states of emergency – in February (miners) and August (dock workers) – but to no effect. The government's industrial relations law, designed to reduce the number of strikes by placing power back into the hands of full-time trade union officials, was being ignored. Dock workers defied court injunctions and when their shop stewards were imprisoned for contempt of court an escalating national strike won their release. The significance of this year was summed up acutely by Darlington and Lyddon:

> What distinguishes 1972 from many other peaks of working-class struggle in Britain is not just the spirit of rebellion shown by workers involved, or the militant tactics adopted and pursued by them, but their relative success: 'The miners made their ... strike effective by large-scale picketing of power stations, sending mobile groups of pickets to areas remote from the coal fields. The dockers and building workers copied this tactic. Sit-ins and factory occupations occurred in engineering disputes.'[64]

Although the settlement in September did not meet the building workers' full demands, many members believed that they had won a considerable victory. It was the biggest pay rise in the history of the building industry and it had been won through concerted strike action. It had started to overcome the divisions between different crafts and between unions that had existed for decades. There were new groups of workers with skills that were not represented by the old craft unions of bricklayers, carpenters and plumbers. They included steel fixers, like Warren, concrete layers and scaffolders, whose work was in demand due to new construction methods. Instead of each craft negotiating on its own they were now acting together, presenting a unified claim for all construction workers.

The coordinated picketing, mass meetings and demonstrations organised by the local action committees, particularly from mid-August onwards when the all-out strike had been called, was a historic experience for building trade unionism. It forced the employers to make improvements in their offer of settlement which they had vowed not to do. The strike involved all trades and began to develop a common, united identity among them. This would be the foundation for the future struggles that were anticipated by Midlands UCATT.

Arnison wrote that the Conservatives were not going to let this success pass: 'Tory MPs were screaming for the blood of pickets.'[65] One of the Pentonville 5 dock workers, Bernie Steer, warned that trade unionists should prepare for a counterattack from the Conservative government and the employers:

> These people are not finished ... they are vicious people and, in my view, they will be like a wounded animal now. They will retreat in a corner; they have had three good wallops and now they are going to start slashing out.[66]

Building workers were not one of the leading battalions of the trade union movement in 1972, despite the enormous achievements that they had made in mobilising during the strike and in picketing sites. No one expected, least of all them, that they would be the ones against whom the 'vicious people' would slash out at first, confirming Steer's prophesy.

PART II

The Employers Take Action

4

The Employers Mobilise

The success of trade unions in 1972 in using strike action and picketing to defend living standards and resist job losses was met with a hysterical response from employers, Conservative Party members and the main newspapers. Each was determined that steps should be taken by the government to prevent a repeat. The building industry employers were part of that chorus, keen to prevent the spread of trade unionism on sites. They considered the outcome of the strike to be a defeat. Derek Fowler of the Federation of Civil Engineering Contractors summed it up in a letter on 18 September 1972, four days after the trade unions had accepted a revised offer:

> The outcome ... is a settlement both in building and civil engineering *higher than would have been necessary* to meet the aspirations of the bulk of our labour force, of which it is estimated that only about 30% are union members.[1]

Fowler attributed the 'unnecessarily high' pay increase to '"strong arm tactics" and extremely large groups of mobile pickets which are organised locally and which the unions make no attempt to control'.

The NFBTE tried to find some crumbs of comfort by emphasising that the only immediate changes 'are simply an increase in the standard wage rate and in sick pay'. It also pointed out, 'You will, I am certain, consider the initial wage increase high. But on the other hand our negotiators have secured a period of 26 months during which there will be only comparatively modest wage adjustments.'[2] It followed this up by giving a more detailed account of the final negotiations:

> Some members will consider that the initial wage increase is high. However, in the light of all the things at stake, there is no doubt whatsoever in my mind that our negotiators secured the most favourable terms they possibly could ...
>
> We fought – and fought hard – to gain more acceptable terms. In the end we had to accept the fact that what the Operatives' leaders said were minimum acceptable proposals were, in fact, just that. They pointed out that they had got only grudging support for their acceptance, anyway, and for them to suggest anything less to their own side would bring negotiations to an end. We sensed that they meant what they said. So we had to agree to the big initial increase. For what were the alternatives? They [sic] could only be another breakdown and the strikes continuing indefinitely. We also had to face, in these circumstances, the high probability of individual settlements on a big scale, which would have demolished our negotiating position in no time.[3]

Before the strike ended, the NFBTE were taking steps to identify leading pickets. It had sent out letters to its 15,000 members, 'urging them to prepare dossiers on intimidation by squads of so-called "flying-pickets"'.[4] The NFBTE Newsletter of 8 September 1972 argued that 'if it were not for the militant action being taken by a relatively small number of activists this strike would never have got off the ground on anything like the scale it has.'[5] It informed members that it was compiling an 'intimidation dossier' and it appealed for examples so that it could be sent to the government, 'with a view to trying to stop similar kinds of pressure being exerted in the future'.

The FCEC shared the NFBTE's concern about the activities of flying pickets. Two days before the strike ended the FCEC wrote to the minister for housing and construction, Julian Amery MP, highlighting the mass picketing in the Shrewsbury area on 6 September. The letter concluded by asking the government to pursue this matter strongly in the appropriate quarters, with a view to action being taken, e.g.:

1. by the improvement of police organisation and co-operation; and

2. amendment of the law governing picketing, including trade union responsibility.[6]

The NFBTE asked its regional secretaries for evidence that would assist with its submissions to the government and to an interdepartmental committee that was reviewing the law on picketing. But their letter repeated the earlier request for intelligence: 'Especially valuable would be signed statements from eye-witnesses ... photographs of at least some of the more notorious occurrences (from local newspaper photographers) and tape recordings and personal photographs.'[7] The planned dossier was therefore not just a propaganda tool to persuade the government to toughen the laws against picketing. It would also add names to the blacklist that the industry-backed Economic League had operated for decades.

It has to be emphasised that, contrary to many later reports, the activities of north Wales pickets on 6 September did not trigger the compilation of a dossier. It had been under way for several weeks and the NFBTE often cited events in Yorkshire as the reason for compiling it. The unions were well aware of the employers' propaganda campaign during the strike, of supposed picket violence. On 22 August George Smith wrote to the national secretaries of the T&GWU, G&MWU and FTAT, and to UCATT regional secretaries. He warned that, of the complaints made by employers about picketing, the majority

emanated from the Yorkshire Region of the N.F.B.T.E., whose Director, Colin Hogan, appears to have been particularly irresponsible in his comments. The Operatives' Side Secretary for the Yorkshire Region confirmed that flying pickets in Yorkshire are accompanied by the police and that the police had had no complaint to make whatsoever about the peaceful picketing union members were engaged in.[8]

There were countless reports during the strike of pickets being threatened and of contractors driving cars at picket lines. Smith noted,

> A thorough investigation was held into all accusations of violence and intimidation which had been made by certain officials of the employers' organisation. These were found to be completely without foundation as far as union pickets were concerned. The only instances of violence reported were of attacks on pickets by labour only sub-contractors whom certain firms in the industry were employing.[9]

The NFBTE Dossier

The dossier was presented to the home secretary, Robert Carr, at the end of October 1972.[10] It was titled 'Violence and intimidation: a dossier of examples of personal violence, injury, arson and damage during the building strike 1972'.[11] It contained 10 pages of alleged incidents, drawn from two sources of information: newspaper reports that had been sent to the NFBTE and private reports that were unattributed but appear to have come from member firms. There was no indication of the number that replied to the multiple appeals for information. The source of many of the allegations against pickets was described as 'Private'. Overall, the dossier gives the impression of a scrapbook compiled by someone using scissors to cut and paste any newspaper article available, without questioning the truthfulness of the reports.

The dossier drew three conclusions. First, that the most militant picketing took place in five regions – Yorkshire, the Midlands, the North East, the North West and Scotland. There were very few reports from Greater London, southern England and south Wales. Second, that the use of flying pickets increased towards the end of the strike, 'culminating in the events of notorious "Black Wednesday" – September 6 – when building sites over much of the West Midlands were subjected to deliberate and well-directed attack'. Third, that the picketing was 'the work of comparatively small, but co-ordinated groups of people who were well organised, well directed and well financed.'

It broke down the reported incidents of picketing into two phases to support its argument that mass picketing intensified during the final weeks of the dispute. This would not be surprising as the unions escalated the strike from mid-August onwards. The dossier reported incidents in the following areas:

Phase 1: 7–31 August
East Midlands: 8 incidents (including Derbyshire, Gainsborough, Brigg 2, Kings Lynn, Scunthorpe 3).
West Midlands: 13 (Birmingham 4, Cheadle, Coventry 6, Leek, Oswestry).
North East: 3 (Hartlepool 2, Newcastle).
North West: 4 (Blackpool, Bolton, Southport, Wigan).
Scotland: 4 (Edinburgh, Glasgow 3).
South East: 7 (London 3, Milton Keynes, Northampton, Sittingbourne, Southsea).
Wales: 4 (Buckley, Colwyn Bay, Denbigh, Penrhyn Bay).
Yorkshire: 23 (Barnsley, Darfield, Elland, Halifax 2, Hoyland, Huddersfield 2, Leeds 5, Ossett, Rotherham 3, Selby, Sheffield 3, Sowerby Bridge, Wakefield).
Unknown: 2.

Phase 2: 1–8 September
East Midlands: 1 (Leicester).
West Midlands: 6 (Birmingham 2, Coventry, Shrewsbury, Stoke, Walsall)
North West: 5 – (Blackpool, Sale 3, Skelmersdale).
South East: 4 (Basildon, London, Lowestoft, Southampton).
Wales: 1 (Flintshire).
Yorkshire: 9 (Barnsley, Bradford 2, Keighley, Leeds 2, Sheffield 2, York).

The main geographical concentration of alleged incidents was in Yorkshire and the West Midlands. Of these, it was in Yorkshire that most occurred, indicating higher levels of picketing throughout that county. The incidents in the Midlands happened mainly in Birmingham and Coventry, though it also included the north Wales pickets' visit to Shrewsbury and Telford on 6 September, referred to as 'Black Wednesday' in the introduction to the dossier. Almost a whole page of the dossier is devoted to accounts of that day, taken from the *Birmingham Post*, the *Shropshire Star* and 'several private reports'. It also quoted a *Daily Mail* article of 11 September 1972 featuring Clifford Growcott, whom the article alleged had been attacked at McAlpine's Brookside site in Telford.[12]

The dossier was one part of a concerted attempt by the NFBTE to get the home secretary and police to act against picketing. It fitted the theme that the employers and the Conservative Party wanted to promote: that a minority of militant trade unionists were using unlawful intimidatory picketing to impose their way on moderate co-workers and on employers. The *News of the World* prepared the ground with a two-page spread on 22 October alleging communist-led violent picketing during the strike. Following this 'exposé' the dossier received extensive press coverage between 29 and 30 October. The *Sunday Times* commented that Robert Adley, Conservative MP for Bristol North East, would be asking the home secretary and the employment secretary to hold an inquiry into the allegations in the dossier.[13] The *Financial Times* noted,

Fresh pressure on the Government to take action against mass picketing in labour disputes is likely to build up as a result of a report sent to the Home Secretary alleging 'virtual mobster tactics' by 'well organised, well directed and well financed' groups of pickets during the country-wide building strikes two months ago.[14]

Not all journalists were convinced by the dossier's exaggerated claims, though. Joe Rogaly, political editor of the *Financial Times*, wrote,

This document is itself flawed, since in its introduction it suggests the existence of a sinister plot without being able to substantiate the allegation. Many of the incidents that have been listed seem to be little more than the ordinary, spontaneous angry behaviour that might be expected on a building site at any time (and especially during an industrial dispute): the net effect of the list provided is that the publication reads more like a politically-motivated [*sic*] pamphlet than a serious study.[15]

Rogaly's criticisms were borne out by the results of several police investigations, discussed in Chapter 6.

Magistrates' Court Hearings

It would be wrong to conclude from the dossier that the police were not present or did not intervene on picket lines. Pickets were arrested during all the main national strikes of 1972 and, if charged, were usually tried promptly at the local magistrates' court. For example, Jim Burnham, the leader of a picket outside a building site at the London Stock Exchange in August, was fined twenty pounds plus twenty pounds costs for obstructing a police inspector who was trying to clear a path for non-striking electricians to go into work.[16]

In another case the *Financial Times* reported, 'Three building pickets were fined £50 each at Gloucester for assaulting a workmate who had refused to join the recent national building strike.'[17] According to the *Guardian*, the three were part of a group of twenty to thirty pickets outside the site of Gloucester's new hospital. It claimed that their colleague was cycling off the site, pulled to the ground, kicked and punched. The three were charged with assault occasioning actual bodily harm.[18]

Pickets arrested in 1972 were generally charged with obstruction, breach of the peace or criminal damage. The arrests took place immediately on the picket lines, not days or weeks later. Not a single north Wales picket was cautioned or arrested in Shrewsbury or Telford on 6 September 1972, despite the presence of police during most of the day and despite newspaper claims of intimidation and damage to property. Likewise, none of the pickets prosecuted at Mold Crown Court in June or July 1973 for alleged offences on sites in north Wales had been arrested at those sites.

The mass picketing in Shrewsbury and Telford was not qualitatively different from picketing that occurred elsewhere. An example was the report of a trial in Yorkshire which illustrates the difference between the routine treatment of arrested pickets in Britain and the careful management of the prosecution of the north Wales pickets that was to come:

> About 150 pickets from Leeds and Wakefield 'frightened and intimidated' 12 workers at a small clinker block making firm at Heck, near Goole, during the builders' strike, Selby magistrates were told … Three Leeds scaffolders who were among the pickets denied obstructing the police and using turbulent and belligerent behaviour likely to cause a breach of the peace. They were each fined £15 and bound over in the sum of £100 for a year … two police constables were trying to handle between 100 and 150 pickets, who were milling round the office block of the company shouting abuse. When a lorry loaded with ash arrived at the yard the pickets started to threaten the driver.[19]

The small number of police compared with the number of pickets present did not prevent arrests from being made.

Confederation of British Industry

The publication of the NFBTE dossier was part of a determined effort by employers to persuade the government and the police to prohibit mass picketing. The NFBTE raised its concerns at a CBI Working Party on Industrial Relations, on 9 November 1972:

> The Chairman reminded the meeting that when the EPC had considered the question of picketing in March it had expressed the view that the existing law was in general adequate and that the real problem was one of enforcement. Since then, however, picketing, particularly in the Building Industry strike, had reached new heights of violence and intimidation and it had been decided to reconsider the matter.[20]

The meeting could not agree on the steps that needed to be taken:

> It was generally felt that in view of the organised violence of flying pickets in the Building Industry strike, the previously held view that the existing law was adequate was no longer tenable. There was, however, some difference of opinion as to whether it would be politically practicable to tighten up the law at the present time.

It was noted that 'the activities of flying pickets in the Building Industry strike suggested that there might need to be some restrictions on the number of pickets and on the persons who might be allowed to picket.'[21] The meeting concluded that the CBI would seek a meeting with the Home Office, 'to try to establish what practical difficulties existed in the proper enforcement of the law.'

The CBI ratcheted up the pressure. Its director general, Campbell Adamson, wrote to the home secretary, Robert Carr, on 30 November, urging him to 'tighten up the enforcement of the present law and to consider the introduction of certain changes in the law'.[22] Adamson referred to a recent meeting that he and the CBI's president had had with the prime minister, at which they raised the issue. Adamson copied in Heath and the employment secretary, Maurice Macmillan, to the letter. Both Carr and Macmillan had addressed the issue at the previous month's Conservative Party conference and stated that the law was adequate; the problem was a failure of the police to enforce it.[23] Macmillan repeated this line in the House of Commons the following month, in answer to questions from several backbench Conservative MPs: 'It is already illegal to do many things. The problem is one of enforcement against those carrying out illegal practices.'[24]

The government's message to employers was that it was for the police to make the decisions on policing picket lines and for charging those who were arrested. This may have deflected some of the pressure, but a head of steam was building within the Conservative Party for the government to take action that was more difficult to ignore.

5

The Conservative
Party Reacts

The Conservative Party was alarmed at the many successful national strikes and mass picketing in 1972. Discussions took place at all levels, from local constituency associations and Members of Parliament to the hidden world of advisers and ministers in government. Like the employers, various Conservatives put forward suggestions to strengthen the law, and demanded that the police act more firmly in future disputes. For Heath's government these options had to be weighed up in the context of the next steps in its counter-inflationary economic strategy and the need to avoid a further confrontation with trade unions over wage restraint.

Discussions took place at unminuted, informal meetings, although references to such conversations appear in documents. In a mass political party like the Conservatives, there were open discussions in which groups of members tried to influence party policy. The Central Fife Conservative Association sent a letter to all local party associations as early as March 1972 expressing grave concern about picketing during the recent miners' strike. It sought support from fellow Conservatives for its motion on picketing that it had submitted for debate at the annual party conference that year. It encouraged members to support a letter-writing campaign to the government to urge it to act on picketing. The Fife Tories also wrote to Chichester-Clark at the Department of Employment.[1]

The South Norfolk Conservative Association backed the initiative and wrote to Maurice Macmillan on 17 July 1972: 'On 14 July this Association considered a Central Fife appeal for support, both for their letter to you and for a conference motion. It was unanimously agreed to give full support.'[2] The Fife Conservatives also wrote to Macmillan and his Cabinet colleague, John Davies, secretary of state for trade and industry, criticising 'the use of coercion, intimidation and violence in recent disputes ... We are convinced that more serious threats are posed by unions using their monopoly power and would urge upon you the need for the Government to take suitable action.'[3]

At a more senior level, Lord Hugh Molson, a former MP and junior minister, wrote to Lord Hailsham, the Conservative lord chancellor, on 20 September 1972,

> Mr dear Quintin, The Government must do something about forcible picketing ... You said that a picket of three has been held not to be 'peaceful'... I want a simple test of what the police can prevent or stop without complicated proof. One hundred men with menacing expressions is not really peaceful, even if they neither say or do anything.[4]

Hailsham replied five days later and was 'very glad to have your suggestion and will keep it in mind'.[5] Hailsham wrote to Macmillan shortly afterwards to advise that he favoured only limited legislative changes (to the Emergency Powers Act 1920) because 'if understood and obeyed the present law is adequate.'[6] Hailsham recognised that any change was 'basically a political decision' rather than a legal one, but thought that regulations 'ought to prohibit picketing in excessive numbers and by parties extraneous to the dispute'.

The Conservative Party Conference 1972

The government knew that picketing would be debated at the Conservative Party conference in Blackpool in October 1972. It was an annual forum for the grass-roots party members to argue for 'their' government to take even more right-wing and reactionary steps. In the 1970s the annual conferences of the main political parties were broadcast live on the BBC during the daytime. Extracts from the key speeches and debates were featured in the evening news bulletins on BBC and ITV.[7] This national platform gave the government an opportunity to stage-manage the presentation of strong messages to its supporters; in this case, that firm action would be taken against picketing.

The government set out its position in a number of pre-conference speeches, starting with an address by the attorney general, Sir Peter Rawlinson, in his Wimbledon constituency on 21 September.[8] It was reported prominently in the following day's Times, Financial Times and Daily Telegraph.[9] It was noted that his speech 'coincides with the publication of motions for the Conservative party conference calling for action against violence in industrial disputes'.[10]

Rawlinson accepted that trade unionists had a right to picket, but it had to be peaceful and only for communicating information:

> If pickets, by sheer numbers, seek to stop people from going to work or from delivering goods, they are not protected by the law since their purpose is to obstruct rather than to persuade … it is likely to be intimidating even if no violence is involved.[11]

For Rawlinson, as for Molson, picketing in large numbers was intimidatory even if the pickets did nothing but stand quietly. He reassured his audience that the existing law dealt adequately with preventing the type of mass picketing that was used during the miners' strike and other industrial disputes that year. Pickets had no right to stop people or vehicles; their actions were limited to peaceful persuasion, for which purpose only a small number of pickets was needed. The Daily Telegraph repeated the government's position, that the problem lay with the lack of action by the police: 'A clear indication that the Government expects the police to enforce the law against unlawful picketing more vigorously than in recent strikes was given last night by Sir Peter Rawlinson, Attorney-General.'

In a speech to the Magistrates' Association on 5 October, Carr also focussed on picketing. It too was reported widely. One account began, 'A strong warning about the increasing growth of violence, particularly in industry and in recent strike picketing, was given last night by Mr. Robert Carr, the Home Secretary.' He identified picketing as part of a general problem of law and order in society, a favourite subject for debate at each year's Conservative Party conference. Carr noted, 'And there is industrial violence in the form of violent picketing which seems frequently to be inspired by people not directly involved in the dispute.' He urged his audience of magistrates to impose harsher sentences, including imprisonment, for picketing offences: 'I think it is right some treatment is severe. Indeed, I should not be ashamed to use the word punishment when referring to the treatment given to serious offenders, particularly those who commit violent crimes.'[12]

At the same meeting a crossbench peer and former Labour attorney general, Hartley Shawcross, also spoke on the issue.[13] He criticised the previous Tory home secretary, Reginald Maudling, for suggesting that most picketing had been peaceful, and 'that it was only occasionally that there were breaches of the law'. Shawcross declared,

> The whole thing was an unlawful conspiracy. Whenever three or more people gather together to carry out any common purpose in such a manner as to cause people of ordinary courage and firmness to be in fear, that very quickly becomes a riot.[14]

On the day that the Conservative Party conference opened in Blackpool, 9 October, the *Glasgow Herald* published an article headlined 'How the Communists plan to take over Britain'.[15] It referred to picketing of building sites in Birmingham led by Peter Carter, a building worker and prominent member of the Communist Party in the city. It would reinforce the arguments put forward by speakers at the conference during the week.

Carr replied to the conference debate on law and order. The *Daily Telegraph* reported, 'Mr Carr's main message to the conference was that the law as it now stands is adequate to deal with the danger of obstruction and intimidation without special legislation.'[16] The existing law 'makes it absolutely clear that the right to picket is not a license to intimidate, and that sheer numbers of pickets can of itself constitute intimidation'. The next day the *Guardian* added that Carr 'was expected to urge chief constables from police forces all over the country to consider setting up special police "flying squads" to cope with groups of "flying pickets" such as those which have operated during recent industrial disputes'.[17]

The speeches of senior Conservatives before and during the Conservative Party conference tried to claim that the spread of mass picketing in 1972 was not the fault of the government. Although laws relating to picketing did not specify a maximum number that could be present, the government argued that existing laws prohibited large numbers as they were, by definition, intimidatory and often obstructed the highway. Some minor changes could be made to the law, but the problem lay with the police and the courts. The Conservatives were giving both bodies a clear message: that they should take tougher action.

Pressure Mounts to Change the Law

The pressure on the government continued in the weeks following the conference. The chief whip, Francis Pym, wrote to Carr on 29 November setting out the opinion of many backbench MPs following a meeting of the Conservative Party Home Affairs Committee at which Rawlinson had opened the discussion. Pym urged Carr to take action, whether simply a restatement of the law on picketing or a change to limit the number and type of people who could picket.[18]

The government's special adviser, Michael Wolff, had argued for both: 'I do not think that it is enough to concentrate on enforcement: for the law cannot be enforced unless it is amended.'[19] He commended a recently published pamphlet from the Bow Group that took the same line, including the suggestion that there should be a statutory limit on the number of pickets at a workplace.[20] Wolff also advocated an increase in the penalties for intimidation under Section 7 of the Conspiracy and Protection of Property Act 1875:

> This would be largely window-dressing, *because of course charges could in many cases be brought under laws which carry higher penalties*; but it might have a good effect on police and on magistrates, as well as on the general public and the responsible trade union leaders.[21]

Wolff's comments were a reminder that there were a wide range of public order offences that could be used against picketing. But the more serious ones had rarely been used by the police.[22] It was precisely these types of common law charges that were to be brought against the six pickets arrested on 14 February 1973 and tried at the first Shrewsbury trial, in October 1973. A conviction for the common law offences of conspiracy, affray or unlawful assembly could result in a much higher sentence, just as Wolff suggested.

At the Conservative Party conference, Carr had praised the Lincolnshire police operation during the dock workers' strike in July and August 1972 and announced that he would be highlighting the lessons to all police forces, including the need for good intelligence on the movement of flying pickets so that they could be intercepted. He also commended cooperation between local police forces.[23] Shortly after the conference, Carr met fifteen chief police constables 'to discuss violent picketing during industrial disputes. A Home Office official said later: "This is the first of a series of meetings with chief constables to discover whether the law needs strengthening in view of recent violent picketing."'[24] The importance of cooperation and coordination of police resources was also noted at a meeting of a government Inter-departmental Committee on picketing. It was suggested that the government must make further efforts 'to improve enforcement of the existing law by strengthening, as necessary, the arrangements for mutual aid between police forces'.[25]

The Parliamentary Platform

In addition to the party conference, Conservative MPs used Parliament as a platform. Several of them initiated or spoke during debates on picketing in the House of Commons in autumn 1972. These were reported enthusiastically by the press to amplify the demand for urgent government action. The *Financial Times* reported a speech by the Conservative MP for Bolton West, Robert Redmond, during a debate on industrial relations.[26] Redmond observed,

> What we saw in the building strike and some other strikes recently is tending, I believe, to go far beyond what one can regard as industrial relations ... The 'Rent-a-Picket' style of operation, it seems to me, has something in common with the Provisional IRA in Belfast. [Laughter] ... We are seeing something now which is threatening the security of the State, and what I suggest ... is that there is a Mafia at work forcing men to strike against their will ... It seems to me that the reports one read in the News of the World on Sunday were probably far from exaggerated ...
>
> A friend of mine on Merseyside – this is hearsay evidence, I know, but I am asking for an investigation to test the truth of these things – told me of how he had approached a picket, or so-called picket, to ask what he was doing, and the picket replied 'We are doing this because we wish to destroy the constitution of this country'.
>
> However much hon. Members opposite may laugh at this desperately serious situation, I urge the Government to take the reports one hears seriously and to recognise the danger which exists.[27]

This alarmist theme, which provoked hysterical laughter from many Labour MPs, continued during the final weeks of the year. On Friday 8 December another Conservative MP, Kenneth Lewis, opened a debate on industrial relations and argued that the building workers' strike was the work of extremist groups:

> Their declared main aim is revolution. They move in on strike situations simply to further the revolution. During the building

strike the agitation was led by the Building Workers Charter Group, a breakaway from the Communist Party and based at the headquarters of the International Socialists.

In April there was a national conference of building workers. The speakers included a former Young Communist organiser, Peter Carter, and a Liverpool Communist, Alan Abrahams. These men and these organisations had been holding meetings stimulating the building strike.

I have here a book. It is a considerable document. I shall not read extracts from it, but it has been compiled by the National Federation of Building Trades Employers. It is not just what that federation says, because it contains pieces from the Press, comments, letters and the like. There are over 100 examples of violence and intimidation during the building workers' strike.[28]

A lengthier debate, on the role of trade unions in industry, took place in the Commons later in December, introduced by another backbench Tory, Sir Edward Brown.[29] Chichester-Clark replied for the government. He pointed out that any violence that occurred during picketing could be dealt with under Section 7 of the Conspiracy and Protection of Property Act 1875 or under other statutes, including the Public Order Act 1936 and the Police Act 1964. He also reported that there had been many arrests on picket lines in 1972 – 350 during the miners' and dockers' strikes – and fines were imposed averaging forty pounds, which he considered to be a severe punishment.[30] He then went on to claim,

As the House knows – this has been made plain over and over again in the country – the Government do not direct the police. However, it is true that my right hon. Friend the Home Secretary has recently met the chief officers of police to discuss the whole range of problems involved in picketing, including manpower reinforcements between police forces and other forms of co-operation, and he has stressed the importance which the Government attach to the preservation of the right to work. He has assured the police that they will have the fullest support of the Government in enforcing the law.[31]

Chichester-Clark's claim that the government did not direct the police was misleading. The senior government law officer, the attorney general, had directed the DPP to order police investigations into allegations of criminal activity by pickets that were reported in the *News of the World* and *East–West Digest*. As will be shown in Chapter 7, the F4 Division of the Home Office was behind the inquiry set up by West Mercia police into the activities of the north Wales pickets in Shropshire.

Controls on Picketing: Code of Conduct or Change the Law?

The picketing during the miners' strike in January and February 1972 led the government to establish an Inter-departmental Working Party on Picketing, but nothing came of it until the autumn, when pressure on the government caused it to be resurrected:

> It issued a report in May, which Ministers reportedly failed to consider properly, and now had before it a request from the Prime Minister to urgently update this report in the light of developments which had taken place (eg the events of the dock strike).[32]

Despite Heath's intervention, there was no rush to make dramatic changes to the law even though the government was constantly urged to act. A Department of Employment memo observed, 'Pressure from Government back benchers, and from the CBI, still remains for some Government action on the law on picketing, which is known to be under review.'[33] It suggested the reintroduction of Section 3(1) of the Trades Disputes Act 1927, which would make it 'a specific arrestable offence to picket in a way (eg in excessively large numbers) which led to intimidation, or obstruction or a breach of the peace'.[34] It was also suggested that regulations could be issued under the Emergency Powers Act 1920, 'to make it a criminal offence to picket essential installations (such as power stations)', unless it was a dispute between power station workers and their employers, the CEGB.

The memo concluded, 'It must be admitted that it is doubtful whether either alternative would in fact make significant differences to the balance of industrial power.' What they were clearly searching for was a means to weaken the ability of trade unions to take action to defend members' living standards and jobs.

Throughout autumn 1972, the employers and Conservative Party members clamoured for changes to the law and to police action that would affect *future* industrial disputes and picketing: restrictions on the number of pickets at the entrance to a workplace and on the category of person that could picket premises during a strike. They wanted the police to be more willing to arrest any picket who acted unlawfully in the future. One thing was certain: as the British economy remained in deep crisis, it was inevitable there would be more strikes and other industrial actions, which the employers would be determined to defeat.

6

The Propaganda War against Mass Picketing

The national press played a significant part in promoting the Conservative government's agenda during and after the strikes of 1972. Newspaper circulation at the time was extensive, both national and regional, compared with today. Although building workers were engaged in a national strike it did not receive, at least initially, the same level of reporting as the other major industrial disputes that year. The relatively sparse coverage of the strike reflected its lack of direct impact. It did not affect the general public dramatically, unlike the earlier miners' strike (power cuts) or dock workers' strike (shortage of imported food and of materials for industry). That all changed after August when the building workers were the only remaining group involved in a national strike going into the autumn. It coincided with the escalation of the strike from limited to all-out action.

It was remarkable to discover in The National Archives at Kew that a number of police forces had been ordered to carry out inquiries into newspaper allegations of picket line violence that had been reported in August and September 1972. The police reports discussed below show that many newspaper accounts were false but were part of a carefully orchestrated propaganda campaign to encourage the police and the courts to take tougher action. It also reveals that the subsequent treatment of the north

Wales building workers by the state was in marked contrast to that of striking miners, dock workers and other building workers in 1972.

The Long Reach of East–West Digest

Several newspaper reports of picketing were featured in *East–West Digest*, a fringe journal edited by Geoffrey Stewart-Smith, an obsessive right-wing Conservative MP who spent his career promoting anti-communist causes through his Foreign Affairs Publishing Company. He sent the *Digest* to every Member of Parliament as well as to senior civil servants.[1]

The September 1972 edition of *East–West Digest* contained an article headed, 'The menace of violent picketing', which led to several police inquiries.[2] Tony Hetherington, a senior civil servant in the attorney general's office, was prompted to write to Ryland Thomas, deputy director of public prosecutions, enclosing a copy of the September editorial from *East–West Digest*. Hetherington asked the DPP to

> consider whether there is any material in this article which would justify police investigations of criminal offences. In particular, he would like to have some information about the incidents described on pages 644–5 concerning the picketing at Scunthorpe, at page 645 concerning Halifax and at page 646 concerning Sheffield. He would be grateful if you could ask the appropriate police forces for some information about these matters.[3]

The decision of the attorney general to order police inquiries was a response to wide concerns within the Conservative Party about picketing, which Stewart Smith's article highlighted. Just before the party conference Wolff had noted, 'Every Minister who has visited the provinces in the last few weeks has testified to the depth of feeling that violent picketing, especially in the recent building strike, has aroused.'[4]

The DPP took the request seriously and obediently wrote to the chief constables of West Yorkshire, Lincolnshire and Sheffield and Rotherham asking each one to investigate the alleged incidents in their area and prepare a report.[5]

Neap House Wharf, Lincolnshire – dockers

The first report in *East–West Digest* involved the dock workers' strike:

> A statement issued by Lincolnshire Constabulary … at the height of the clashes said 'it is very disturbing that after so-called peaceful picketing we have five police officers detained in hospital. Two of these officers have back injuries and cannot move and two others were brought in unconscious.' The situation arising from the violent clashes outside the Neap House Wharf resulted in sizeable police reinforcements having to be called in.[6]

The chief constable of Lincolnshire replied to the DPP two weeks later. He enclosed two reports on the policing of picketing during the dock workers' strike in August.[7] The main report had been completed on 13 September and covered the police operation to deal with mass picketing at the ports on the rivers Trent and Humber, including Neap House Wharf. It described the deployment of hundreds of police to keep the ports open. The summary noted that sixty dockers were arrested during the four weeks of picketing and thirty-one were dealt with at court. Of the rest, twenty-eight were bailed to appear at the Scunthorpe Magistrate's Court on 14 September and one had been committed for trial at the Crown court.

When the DPP passed on the report to the attorney general it included a note of the outcome of the prosecution of pickets:

> All but about 14 now dealt with. The vast majority charged with Sec. 5 Public Order Act and each fined £40 and bound over for 12 months in a sum of £100.
>
> One man charged with Sec. 5 Public Order Act and also two offences under Section 51 Police Act, 1951 (assault on police). Fined total of £190 and six months imprisonment suspended for 2 years.

One man charged with possession of offensive weapon and Sec.5 Public Order Act. Fined £25 and £40.

One man charged with Sec. 47, ass.a.b.h. and fined £60.[8]

Most serious charge was one of wounding (Sec.20) and has been committed to Crown Court – should be dealt with on 19.11.72.[9]

The police report included several photographs that showed pickets appearing to pull down wire fencing. In addition, there were photographs of items confiscated from dockers' cars, including dockers' hooks, wheel braces, shovels, a cricket bat and a bag of golf clubs.[10] The implication was that the dockers brought these to attack strike-breakers. After all, what docker ever played cricket or golf? Those were the sports of the professional middle class!

As far as the Lincolnshire police were concerned, they had dealt with any unlawful behaviour on the day. They did arrest pickets if they thought offences were being committed. The report shows that pickets were charged with public order offences for which they received fines if found guilty. The most frequent charges were obstruction (of the police or the highway) and breach of Section 5 of the Public Order Act 1936:

> Any person who in any public place or at any public meeting uses threatening, abusive or insulting words or behaviour with intent to provoke a breach of the peace or whereby a breach of the peace is likely to be occasioned, shall be guilty of an offence.

The events at Neap House Wharf and the subsequent prosecutions of dock worker pickets are in marked contrast to what happened on 6 September in Shrewsbury and Telford.

J & J Fee Ltd, Halifax – building workers

The next *East–West Digest* report alleged that '120 pickets had taken over a housing development in Halifax where 60 men were at work. Threats were uttered to bring in "the heavy gang from Leeds" unless work stopped at once.'[11] West Yorkshire police's report for the DPP stated that seventy pickets were present at a site of forty non-striking building workers.[12] A police inspector and sergeant attended, by which time the pickets had already addressed the non-strikers. The inspector explained the law on picketing to the pickets' leader, particularly commenting on the number of pickets present. The pickets' leader replied that they were going to disperse into small groups to picket the many building sites in Halifax that were still working.

The police then spoke with the non-strikers at the site. Comments were made about threats and intimidation but none of the builders would give a formal statement and they decided not to continue working for the rest of the day. The report concluded that it would now be difficult to trace the pickets but that if the DPP wanted the workers to be reinterviewed they would attempt to trace the picket leader and some of the other pickets.

Pressure for a further investigation came from the main contractor on the site, J & J Fee Ltd, which was building several hundred council houses for Halifax Corporation. Peter Fee sent a statement to his local Conservative MP, Wilfred Proudfoot, who in turn sent a copy to the home secretary, Carr, with the following comment: 'The agitation within my constituency is not only from dyed in the wool [sic] Tories but from those whose political affiliations I do not know but who are moderates but all insist that this evil must be stopped.'[13] Proudfoot's intervention led to further, half-hearted, police inquiries but neither the DPP nor the attorney general's office believed that they would lead anywhere.[14] The conclusion was that there was little prospect of arresting and prosecuting pickets, weeks after the alleged incidents had occurred.

Peter Fee's lobbying of his local MP, Proudfoot, was no different to the Shropshire building contractors who lobbied their local Conservative MPs about the events in Shrewsbury on 6 September. The difference, as will be seen in the next chapter, was that West Yorkshire police did not use Fee's complaint as the basis for a major investigation into the actions of the so-called 'Leeds heavy gang' or other Yorkshire pickets.

Motorway development at Sheffield – building workers

The *East–West Digest* reported, 'three huts and an excavator caught fire and a gas cylinder exploded at a motorway construction site in Sheffield after 90 workers had defied pickets by carrying on working.'[15] Rotherham CID sent a one-page report to the DPP on 5 October. It stated that fires were started using oil and paraffin stored on the site, destroying two wooden huts completely; a lorry used as a mess room was gutted and a grader machine was extensively damaged. The report noted, 'Extensive enquiries have been made, a number of pickets have been traced, interviewed, and eliminated, and the matter remains undetected.'[16]

The three police reports show the inconsistencies in the application of the law towards pickets in 1972 and the charges that were laid against them. None of these three police forces gave a fraction of the time and resources to their investigations that was given by their counterparts in West Mercia and Gwynedd, who had started, secretly, to investigate the north Wales pickets as soon as the strike ended, on 18 September. It supports Des Warren's claim that the decision to investigate and charge the north Wales pickets was a carefully calculated one. As will be shown later, it was guided by the Home Office from the very beginning.

The Lies and Distortions of the News of the World

A second set of police inquiries was instigated as a result of a two-page spread about the building workers' strike published in the *News of the World* on 22 October 1972.[17] The attorney general wrote to the DPP,

> The Law Officers have asked me to send to you the enclosed cutting from The News of the World relating to industrial sabotage. They ask whether you can 'take it on board in the course of your present and future enquiries' into this matter.
> The difficulty as I see it is that there is no hard evidence on which the police can act. It is one thing to write a newspaper

article but another to have sufficient evidence to found a police investigation.[18]

The feature was headed 'The strife makers exposed', and claimed that it was the result of a *News of the World* team spending months 'seeking the truth about The Strife Makers'. Significantly, it was published several days before the NFBTE sent its dossier to the government and the media. A second article, published a week later, suggested that the newspaper's earlier research was now supported by the contents of the dossier. The article was unattributed and concluded, 'Criminal charges are almost certain to be preferred against some picket leaders.'[19] This was the first report that any pickets were likely to be arrested and charged for incidents arising from the building workers' strike that had ended weeks earlier.

The following analysis of the *News of the World* reports suggests that, far from spending months investigating anything, and certainly not 'the truth', the team had simply been given an advance copy of the dossier, which its journalists then used as the basis for concocting stories.

Simon Regan

Henry Boot Site, Corby
The *News of the World* feature included a report about the Henry Boot site written by a staff journalist, Simon Regan. He claimed that he posed as a picket during six weeks of the strike:

> On August 30, at the height of the strike, I watched pickets in action at the Henry Boot site at Corby, Northants. Two workmen were injured with bricks. Another man, chased by pickets, was so scared he locked himself in his home. A site office was set on fire, three windows were broken and car tyres were slashed.[20]

Northampton and County Constabulary investigated Regan's claim and prepared a report for the DPP.[21] Police Inspector

Cooper was responsible for supervising the policing of the picketing of the two Henry Boot sites and said of Regan's article,

> I have read the account of this industrial dispute in the 'News of the World' Newspaper and the comments surrounding the alleged trouble at Henry Boot site have been brought to my notice. I have no evidence at all to support this claim and at no time did I see or received [*sic*] any notification of incidents as setting light to huts or car tyres being slashed. No subsequent complaint was made to my knowledge at this station that damage had been caused as a direct consequence of this industrial action. I remained in contact with both sides of this dispute locally and neither of these parties brought to my attention anything of this or a similar nature.

Cooper's evidence was supported by statements from three other police officers that attended the site and by the Henry Boot site manager, Norman Bawdon, who told police,

> I have been shown the article in the News of the World newspaper regarding events which are supposed to have taken place on these sites on the 30th August, 1972. I can quite definitely state that no workmen were injured by bricks being thrown at them, no-one was chased off the site, no site office was set on fire nor windows broken and no car tyres were slashed.[23]

Detective Sergeant Wright prepared a summary of the evidence and concluded, 'From the enquiries made the investigating officers are of the opinion that the alleged incidents on 30 August 1972 never took place.' He ended,

> 10. It is the contention of the investigating officers that the author of the article, Simon REGAN was either:
>
> 1. Never present at the Henry Boot and Sons (Midlands) Ltd. Site at Corby on 30th August 1972, or
> 2. if present, completely fabricated the incidents referred to in this article.

The result of the police inquiry was clear, that Regan's eyewitness report in the *News of the World* was fictitious. Nevertheless, Regan repeated his story to camera in a documentary produced by Woodrow Wyatt, *Red under the Bed*.[24] It was broadcast on 13 November 1973, halfway through the first Shrewsbury trial, on the evening when the prosecution concluded its case (see Chapter 10).

Blue Circle site, Birmingham

After Regan's claims about his activities in Corby he wrote a similarly fictitious account of events in Birmingham:

> On August 23 he [Peter Carter] led about 100 pickets, including me, on the Blue Circle Cement depot at Sparkbrook, Birmingham. One policeman was kicked in the mouth and lorry windows were smashed with bricks. The previous day at another cement depot, there was much spitting, swearing and scuffling and six men were arrested ... Twelve days earlier, Carter led a coachload of pickets, carrying pickaxe handles, who chased men off a site at Rotherham, Yorks.[25]

Regan claimed to have visited Yorkshire as well.

> One of the most notorious picket squads became known as 'The Leeds Mob' formed at a meeting of 4,000 strikers in Leeds on August 5. Repeatedly as I toured the North with the pickets I heard workers told: 'You'd better come out – you don't want the Leeds Mob here, do you?'[26]

There is no evidence that Peter Carter led picketing anywhere in Yorkshire. He lived in Birmingham and was active in the West Midlands region. It is unlikely that Yorkshire strikers would need support from coachloads of pickets from Birmingham, over ninety miles away, if there was a so-called 'Leeds mob' formed at a meeting of 4,000 strikers on 5 August.[27]

The Birmingham police sent a report to the DPP within three weeks of the request.[28] Once again a police force concluded that Regan had fabricated his story:

With regard to the 'News of the World' article of 22 October 1972, on that particular day Peter CARTER was not seen in Sampson Road North and at no time were there 100 pickets in attendance. The article describes the premises as the 'Blue Circle Cement Depot' and claims that on the day in question a policeman was kicked in the mouth, also that lorry windows were smashed. None of these incidents occurred ... and it would appear that the author is either mistaken in the location of the incident, or suffered at the time a figment of imagination.

The police did arrest some pickets at the Blue Circle cement depot. Its report noted that on 23 August 1972 there were scuffles between pickets and police when the former attempted to prevent a lorry from leaving the cement works. Six pickets were arrested. Later that afternoon two further pickets were arrested after they

> commenced to play a game of chess, placing the board for that purpose on the roadway immediately in front of the gateway of the depot, and sitting either side. They were warned about their action but paid no heed, so were also arrested and charged later with obstructing the highway.[29]

The following day four more pickets were arrested for trying to block a lorry from entering the depot. A report in the *Morning Star* the following month noted that six men appeared in court and denied charges of 'disorderly conduct'. They were remanded on bail. Another man 'admitted committing a disorderly act outside the depot on August 24 and was given a conditional discharge'.[30]

In the end, of the twelve pickets arrested at the Henry Boot site, six pleaded guilty at the magistrates' court on 19 October 1972 to charges of obstruction or disorderly conduct. Four of them were fined between five and ten pounds;[31] two were given a conditional discharge for obstruction. One was fined ten pounds for assaulting the police. The six pickets who pleaded not guilty appeared in court the following day, when they were all found guilty of disorderly conduct and fined between five and fifteen pounds.

Regan's Connections

An insight into Regan, his contacts and his motives for writing the *News of the World* article was revealed in a government file dealing with Wyatt's television programme.[32] It shows links between Regan and government propaganda agencies, starting with a memo of 21 November 1973 from a civil servant, T. C. Barker, of the Information Research Department (IRD), a secretive branch of the Foreign Office.[33] Barker noted that Woodrow Wyatt 'approached of his own accord another old and trusted contact of ours, Mr. McKeown of Industrial Research and Information Services Limited (IRIS)'. Barker considered the film to be 'a feather in the cap of the modest but well-informed, and effective, anti-Communist organisation IRIS'.[34] He continued,

> It is ... worth noting that the News of the World reporter [Regan] who figured prominently in the programme as a witness of violent picketing had been originally brought to Mr Wyatt's attention by IRIS and ourselves, and that the newspaper series to which he had contributed in 1972 had been completed with the active help of IRIS in the first place.[35]

Sunday People: 'The Wrecker'

Two other national newspapers published articles that were used against the pickets, principally Des Warren, at their trials in Shrewsbury. The *Sunday People* article of 10 September 1972 was headlined 'The wrecker' and was illustrated with a large picture of Warren. It was used as a prosecution exhibit at his trial in October 1973.[36] It was a witch-hunting, anti-communist profile of Warren and described him as 'the leader of pickets at housing sites at Shrewsbury last week'. Remarkably, it was based upon an interview by two of their journalists on the evening when he returned home after twelve hours' picketing on 6 September. Warren recalled, 'On arriving back home in Prestatyn later that same evening, I found two Sunday People reporters waiting for me. They had been there since 2 o'clock in the afternoon.'[37] The journalists were not named on the article.

It is not known why they had travelled all the way to rural north Wales to feature Warren in an article in a national newspaper about picketing during the strike. They could have profiled Communist Party building workers in large industrial cities who were more prominent during the strike. The *News of the World*'s two-page feature named and printed photographs of several men, including Alan Tattam, Peter Carter and Lou Lewis. It described them as leading communists and organisers of flying pickets throughout the strike.[38]

The newspaper articles in the left-wing press in July and August 1972 also referred to several senior Communist Party members who were active in the dispute. They were among dozens of active CP building workers throughout the country. The most prominent were Carter, Lewis and Alan Abrahams, who were leading the strikes in Birmingham, London and Merseyside respectively.[39] Their names appeared frequently in the *Morning Star*, whereas Warren was not mentioned at all. He was an unknown compared with them.

Nothing New in Fake News

Although the various police investigations into press allegations of picket line violence concluded that many were lies and distortions, the damage had been done. The newspaper reports were a deliberate propaganda offensive against strikes and picketing. Little coverage was given of an attack on the chairman of the Birmingham Strike Action Committee, Mike Shilvock, just after the strike ended, on 20 September. A remarkably full account was given by the former army major turned right-wing academic Richard Clutterbuck:

> The attack was presumably made by or on behalf of a Lump sub-contractor who was exasperated with the flying pickets. The men who carried it out were clearly well practised in the art of beating-up. They picked a night when his wife was out at a choir

practice, and knocked on Mr Shilvock's door. Being suspicious, he kept the chain on the door. Through the gap, a knife was flashed at him; he drew back to keep out of range, and the men tore the chain out of the wall with a shoulder charge on the door. They 'did him over' for two minutes in absolute silence, and then broke his arm at the elbow and left him.[40]

The government was aware of the importance of the press in portraying its message, including that of a 'red menace'. Shortly after the dock workers' strike ended in July a letter from the prime minister's office noted,

> It was also important to keep in front of the public the Communist affiliations of Mr Steer, the Secretary of the unofficial Shop Stewards Committee. The Press Office at 10 Downing Street in consultation with the press offices of the other Departments concerned would do what they could to put these points over to the media.[41]

The West Mercia Police report of December 1972 acknowledged the impact that press reporting had upon their inquiries. It claimed that potential witnesses among non-strikers and 'passive pickets' were initially 'frightened' to give evidence due to possible reprisals. Their mood changed because of the breadth of the police inquiry and the coverage given to the issue of mass picketing in articles in the *Observer* and the *News of the World* and exchanges on the subject in both Houses of Parliament.[42]

The national press was an important platform for employers and Conservative MPs to talk up the threat of strikes and violent mass picketing. This propaganda offensive was used to build support for tough action that would weaken grass-roots trade union organisation and any possible resistance to the Tories' plans to deal with Britain's economic crisis. The year 1972 had shown that mass picketing had been successful for large groups of workers. The question for the Tories was, what action could and should be taken to stop it?

The government itself relied upon the press to report ministerial speeches setting out its position: that the law was adequate but needed to be enforced by the police. It wanted to appease employers and Conservative Party members but needed to avoid a further direct confrontation with the trade unions as it was seeking TUC support for its policy of wage restraint. A carefully constructed message from the Conservatives made a distinction between lawful strikes and picketing (involving peaceful behaviour by a small number) on the one hand and the violence and intimidation inherent in mass picketing.

The message that the government put across in the final months of 1972 was that the problem lay with the police and the courts. The former had not been active enough in controlling pickets at workplaces and arresting those who were behaving unlawfully. The latter were not imposing sufficiently severe sentences when pickets were convicted of offences. The NFBTE dossier fuelled parliamentary speeches and press coverage thereby setting the scene for the compilation of two police reports about the activities of north Wales pickets. The reports were sent to the director of public prosecutions on 18 December 1972 and were the beginning of a process that would end with the imprisonment of pickets for conspiracy to intimidate a year and a day later.

PART III

The Police, the DPP and Maurice Drake QC

7

West Mercia and Gwynedd Police Investigate

West Mercia Constabulary covered three semi-rural counties: Shropshire, Herefordshire and Worcestershire. It included the towns of Shrewsbury and Telford that the North Wales pickets visited just once, on 6 September. During its inquiries West Mercia worked with Gwynedd Constabulary, which covered an equally semi-rural area. Despite being named Gwynedd, it was the police force for all of North Wales, including the counties of Caernarvonshire, Flintshire and Denbighshire.

As the pickets headed home from Telford to north Wales on 6 September, they were unaware that a meeting was being held that evening at the home of Walter Watkin. It is something that the pickets did not learn of until I uncovered the information forty-five years later. Watkin was a director of Watkin Starbuck & Jones, the main contractors at the Severn Meadows site in Shrewsbury that had been picketed that day. He was a Conservative alderman on the local council and a magistrate. The police were to describe him as 'a man of substantial local standing'.[1]

In attendance at the meeting were his co-directors, Peter Starbuck and Brian Jones; Maurice and Graham Galliers, directors of Maurice Graham Ltd; and the press relations officer of Sir Alfred McAlpine & Son Ltd, who had travelled over fifty miles from Hooton to attend.[2] Watkin's influence was reflected in the ranks of policemen that he could summon to his house at short notice, Superintendent Brookes and Chief Inspector Gradwell.

Both of them had been present shortly after the pickets coaches arrived in Shrewsbury that morning.

Watkin was incensed that the pickets had visited his site and wanted to complain about the police inactivity in containing the pickets. Brookes later reported that the 'meeting accomplished nothing', perhaps because, as far as he was aware, there were no incidents that day and certainly no arrests of any pickets.[3] But several of the attendees at Watkins house did follow it up with written complaints and meetings with Tory MPs. The first was his co-director, Starbuck, who met John Biffen, Conservative MP for Oswestry, on Saturday 9 September. Biffen had already denounced the pickets in a front-page article in the *Shropshire Star* on Thursday 7 September, headlined 'Biffen blasts sites terror'. He declared, 'These hoodlums and bullyboys from Liverpool are a disgrace', though he had no evidence to support such claims. But to the sleepy county of Shropshire the spectre of militant Scousers invading their town was more alarming and newsworthy than a group of workers from the small towns and villages of north Wales.

When Biffen met Starbuck he asked him to put in writing his complaints about the picketing at the Severn Meadows site. When he received the letter, which included a two-page report prepared by Starbuck's company,[4] he forwarded it to the home secretary, Carr. In Biffen's covering letter of 18 September he told Carr that he had recently had

> a personal meeting with a number of building employers ... On a personal note I would like to assure you that the activities of building strike pickets is causing immense anxiety in north Shropshire. It is an anxiety I share; and I believe that we now stand measurably nearer bloodshed in industrial disputes than six months ago. I have not reached this judgment casually.[5]

Further pressure from the employers came from the director of the Midlands region of the NFBTE, Peter Smith. He wrote to the West Mercia chief constable, John Willison, on 11 September, the day after the *Sunday People* article profiling Des Warren as 'The wrecker':

We understand that there was to be some form of Enquiry, and my officers hope that the results will be communicated to them and will give some reassurance that effective measures will be taken to protect persons and property from this kind of violence in the future.[6]

This letter led to Superintendent Patrick being sent to visit Smith at the NFBTE office in Birmingham two days later. Smith gave a three-page statement in which he emphasised that he did not want his letter to be recorded as a complaint against the police:

I am of course anxious that an investigation should take place, but this I hope will be with a view to tracing the culprits responsible for the outrages in Shropshire last week, and not with a view to getting any police officer into any kind of trouble.[7]

Although Sir Alfred McAlpine & Son Ltd did not make any complaint to West Mercia police, the company had powerful contacts at national level. Its managers at Brookside prepared a two-page report for the company's head office.[8] The police were later to note that 'they were not slow in sending a representative to the meeting at WATKIN's house and it is understood that they have taken action in other ways, for example, by privately petitioning members of Parliament with a view to changes in the law on picketing being instituted.'[9]

It was the combination of this sustained lobbying from the Midlands NFBTE, Watkins and his fellow Shropshire contractors, local Conservative MPs like Biffen, and sensationalist press reporting of picketing, which culminated in the setting up of an unprecedented clandestine police inquiry into the north Wales pickets.

Robert Carr, the Home Office and Assistant Chief Constable Rennie

The police officer at the centre of the investigations was West Mercia assistant chief constable Alex Rennie. The police inquiries into picketing elsewhere had been led by more junior ranks, typically a detective inspector and a chief superinten-dent.[10] It was unusual for such a high-ranking police officer to lead an investigation of this type. A later report on West Mercia by an HM inspector of constabulary noted that

> the area is normally law-abiding and police work is not difficult. The 'Shrewsbury pickets' case was very much an isolated inci-dent and the violent activity of the 'flying pickets' took the force by surprise. The vigorous follow-up action was due, to a large extent, to the energy and determination shown by Mr. Rennie who, although Assistant Chief Constable (Administration) at the time, took over personal supervision of the investigation and brought the case to a successful conclusion.[11]

An insight into Rennie's background was contained in his self-published autobiography, in which he wrote of his links with the security services during his wartime activity. While training in North America to become an RAF pilot he claimed that he was recruited to work for the British security services, and 'once you were involved in security affairs it was for life.'[12] He recalled that during this overseas training he was approached to spy on fellow cadets, his trainers and others. He also became a liaison officer with CIA agents while in the USA. Despite passing all the necessary pilot tests he was not awarded his 'wings' because they did not want his name recorded due to the clandestine work that he was undertaking overseas. In this capacity he met Churchill twice.[13]

Rennie sent an initial report to 'Miss Green' at the Home Office on 18 September 1972 and a further report, date unknown, to Mr E. D. Wright, assistant undersecretary of state at the F4 Division of the Home Office. The functions of the F4 Division included '[p]ublic order and subversive activities'.[14] It was responsible for monitoring the Communist Party and 'domestic subversion'. Rennie informed Green that on 18 Sep-tember, 'Chief Superintendent F. R. Hodges, with a team of 12 experienced officers under my cammand [sic], have been struck off normal duties to investigate all aspects of the complaint and to endeavor to investigate with a view to taking proceedings where appropriate.'[15] Green wrote back on 6 October asking for Rennie's comments on the letter that had been sent to Home Secretary Carr by John Biffen MP. In reply Rennie referred to a second report.[16]

Rennie later outlined his detailed involvement in the investigations of the pickets, 'I know more about this than anyone else in the county because I read all the reports on a day-to-day basis and co-ordinated every step in the inquiry.'[17] Rennie was not present at any of the building sites on 6 September but visited the Telford sites several days afterwards. He claimed that he spoke with several building workers, and 'felt strongly that the perpetrators of the crimes should be brought to justice'.[18]

It was the Home Office that ordered reports from Rennie about picketing in Shropshire, not the attorney general or DPP. It was the driving force for an investigation and knew that Rennie, given his background, was a safe pair of hands to do their bidding.

The Police Investigation

On Monday 18 September 1972, the day the strike ended, the hand-picked team of police officers led by Hodges began its work. One of the problems that he had was that the police on duty twelve days earlier had not witnessed anything and had not received any complaints on the day from the builders on any of the sites. The police had already conducted a number of interviews of Telford lumpers in the days following the meeting in Watkin's house. These statements proved to be of little value as the lumpers could not give an accurate description of any picket or eyewitness evidence of unlawful acts. Hodges then interviewed Watkin and Jones on 19 September, followed by the Galliers brothers.[19] Their position was that 'the complaint is not that the Police took no action, but that such action as was taken was ineffective'.[20]

A small front-page article in the *Shropshire Star* of 29 September 1972 was headlined, 'Pickets may be prosecuted.' It began, 'Police are hoping to prosecute members of the bands of roving building pickets which hit Shropshire nearly a month ago.' It reported that 'extensive inquiries were proceeding in conjunction with other forces in North Wales and the north-west. Several men are being interviewed.' These would have been lumpers and contractors.

At this early stage the West Mercia police were trying to identify the north Wales men who had visited Shropshire on 6 September. Hodges wrote that they sought assistance from Gwynedd and Cheshire police forces: 'it soon became apparent that similar problems existed in the Cheshire, North Wales and Staffordshire areas, and throughout this enquiry close liaison has been maintained with those forces.'[21] His colleague, Super-intendent Glover, later reported, 'Following a conference at Chester on 9th October 1972, a concurrent enquiry was under-taken by Gwynedd Constabulary into similar incidents in North Wales during the same building trade dispute.'[22] It became a joint inquiry between the two forces. West Mercia police set up a base at the Grand Hotel on the seafront in Prestatyn. From there they would attend local police stations in north Wales to question pickets, alongside Gwynedd police. What started as an investigation by West Mercia police into picketing in Shropshire on one day now became a general inquiry into the picketing of north Wales building workers throughout the full twelve weeks of the strike. Up to the end of September there was no indi-cation that Gwynedd police had any intention of investigating alleged incidents involving picketing in their area during the strike. They started only when prompted by the inquiries begun by West Mercia. The investigations by Gwynedd police took them back to the beginning of August.

The work of the two police forces was extensive. They produced draft witness statements between 8 September and 11 December 1972 for their reports to the DPP. At the end of the inquiry, the *Liverpool Daily Post* announced,

> Detectives have seen nearly 800 people in a mammoth inquiry into alleged incidents involving pickets during the building strike last summer ... Most of the inquiries have been in Shropshire

and North Wales and have lasted nearly three months. Claims made by employers in a dossier are among those that have been probed.[23]

A police report gave a breakdown of the extent of the investigation:

During the West Mercia enquiry the number of witnesses interviewed and statements obtained was:–

	Interviewed	Statements
On sites (workers)	466	158
Miscellaneous (householders, press, etc.)	38	27
'not involved' pickets	74	33
Police Officers on sites	73	73
	651	291

An unknown number of persons were interviewed by Gwynedd but the joint total is well in excess of 700 persons. The actual number of statements taken in North Wales was 43 – a joint total of 334. 24 officers were involved in interview evidence, either as conducting the interview, or as corroboration.[24]

The police acknowledged that many of the witnesses whom they interviewed in the beginning could not give a clear description of any picket, especially the people the police claimed were ringleaders. When they interviewed the pickets themselves, a number of them refused to speak to the investigators, 'no doubt, because they had something to hide and were quickly aware that *we had nothing to allege against them.*'[25]

Remarkably, although statements were prepared from seventy-three police officers in the autumn, none of them could say that they saw any picket doing anything unlawful. The police acknowledged at the end of its inquiries that the officers' statements 'are largely non-evidential as to specific offences but do fill in the background of the sites'.[26]

The police decided to obtain photographs taken by local newspaper and police photographers to use for identification purposes in interviews. First, they had to put names to the faces of the many pickets. Once they had identified a group, the police prepared marked copies of the photographs which had the names of individual pickets written on them, particularly Warren. These would then be used when witnesses were reinterviewed over the following months and fresh statements prepared.

Pickets Questioned

After the police forces had spoken with building contractors, lumpers and householders, they turned their attention to the pickets. Most were interviewed in November and were not given any notice. They were being asked questions about events that had taken place up to three months earlier, which was difficult to recall due to the passage of time.[27] Some were seen at home, some at work. Many of them were requested to attend the local police station. A number complained about the manner in which they were interviewed by the police, describing it as an interrogation rather than a voluntary interview. Even those who were not arrested felt intimidated and unable to leave the police station.[28] At the end of many of the interviews the police stated that they proposed to report the picket for alleged offences including assault, criminal damage and making an affray.

The police did not use a standard approach to interviews. Some pickets were cautioned straight away but others were not advised until midway through the interview. In some cases, an officer would take notes during the interview and then prepare a statement for the witness to sign at a later date (John Lly-warch).[29] In others, the officers would not take any notes but then write up a statement when the witness had left the station and then have it signed at a later date (Leonard Williams). Some pickets complained that a statement would be written up during the course of a lengthy and oppressive interview but it was not read back to them and they simply signed it to get out of the police station. Only later did they discover that it contained information that they did not agree with (John Seaburg, Gwyn Edward Roberts, Gwyfor Williams, Henry James).[30] Seaburg actually returned to the police station the next day to withdraw the whole of his statement. Only later did he discover that the police were still going to use it at his trial at Mold.[31]

Glover reported that six pickets were arrested during November and taken to police stations to be interviewed: Des Warren and Roy Warburton on the 14th; Arthur Murray, Beverley Skinner and John Bithell on the 15th; and John McKinsie Jones on the 16th. They all received bail letters except Skinner.[32] These six arrested pickets had good reason to believe that no action would be taken. After questioning, Warren was released and bailed to attend Rhyl Police Station four weeks later. He was later informed, on 5 December, that he did not need to attend and was released from bail.[33]

John McKinsie Jones, treasurer of the North Wales Strike Committee, received a letter from the committee's solicitors at the end of January 1973: 'Further to this matter we have now received your telephone message with regard to this case indicating that the matter has now been completed and accordingly following your instructions we are closing our file of papers.'[34]

The Police Reports Sent to the DPP

On 18 December 1972, West Mercia's chief constable, John Willison, sent two reports to the DPP.[35] His covering letter makes no mention of the origin of the request for the police inquiries that led to the two reports. This contrasts with the letters sent to the DPP in the autumn by Northampton, Birmingham, West Yorkshire and other police forces enclosing reports about picketing in their districts. Willison makes no such mention; his letter to the director appears to come out of the blue.[36] It begins simply, 'Two files are forwarded, one by Gwynedd and one by West Mercia Constabulary, concerning the actions of pickets on a number of dates and places in Gwynedd and on one day in Shrewsbury.'[37] This gives the impression that the DPP were expecting the reports, but there is no publicly available paper trail between the police and the DPP or any government department.[38]

West Mercia Constabulary had actually produced two

reports. The first one was sent to the DPP by Willison. Its title was 'Disorderly conduct by pickets at building sites in Shropshire on Wednesday 6th September 1972' (referred to as 'the police report'). It had been prepared by Chief Superintendent Fred Hodges and Detective Chief Inspector Colin Glover.[39] The report contained a summary of the picketing in Shrewsbury and Telford on 6 September 1972, the witness and other evidence that had been obtained by the police in the following months, and their recommendations for prosecutions. Accompanying the forty-six-page report were appendices and files containing 246 witness statements, photographs and other exhibits.

Willison's letter and other important documents are contained in a DPP file at The National Archives but neither the West Mercia nor the Gwynedd police reports are included in it.[40] My quest to find these reports is dealt with in Chapter 14.

A second West Mercia report, not sent to the DPP, was prepared by Hodges alone and addressed the complaints that the police had received from local building contractors, that policing of picketing on 6 September was inadequate. The report does not have a formal title. The front cover simply has a heading, 'Report file'. For simplicity, it is referred to as the 'complaints report'. It gave a detailed account of the actions of West Mercia police on the day and an explanation for the lack of any arrests or cautions. It is undated but appears to have been completed in spring 1973. It was produced for internal purposes, to provide the police with a script to answer employers, members of the police committee and others who might demand answers from them. In the event it has proven to be an invaluable source of information to understand the role of the employers and the Home Office in driving the prosecution of the pickets

Whose Conspiracy?

The police report contains a convoluted discussion of whether a charge of conspiracy could be made out. It had to establish *where* any conspiracy was hatched, *what* criminal enterprise was agreed and *who* took part. 'It was initially felt that the events of "Black Wednesday" were all deliberately planned and organised by the strike leaders at meetings held at Chester.'[41] This was the strike action committee meeting at the *Bull and Stirrup*, Chester, on 31 August: 'This resolution – and the vote taken on it – proved to be the blueprint for the serious disorder and widespread fear which subsequently took place on 6th September 1972.'[42] This was misleading. The evidence was simply that the Chester meeting had voted to support the Oswestry action committee in organising a mass picket of sites in Shrewsbury. That was the extent of any 'blueprint'.

The report then downplays any 'conspiracy' to commit a criminal offence:

> However, the evidence suggests that the events at Kingswood, followed by Shelton roadworks, were probably spontaneous, despite the explosive potential already present in the circumstances of the pickets' visit. There was a common intent to close the sites at Shrewsbury, but there was no clear-cut plan of action in being. When the men saw work continuing at the roadworks and on the building site, they simply erupted.[43]

It concluded that the 'decision to go to Telford appears to have been equally spontaneous and neither a majority of pickets nor the coach operators knew of this beforehand'. It then goes on to consider explicitly the law of conspiracy:

> 148. The only other main consideration again concerns the party leaders, and it is whether a charge of conspiracy should lie. It is a possibility, but evidence concerning the meeting at Chester is not strong and there are no admissions about it from those responsible. There were also many other persons at the meeting, as shop stewards on various sites – many of whom did not visit Shropshire on 6th September 1972. For these reasons, and taking account of the spontaneous element in the disorders, conspiracy is not strongly recommended.

Further evidence that the police could not prove a conspiracy among the north Wales building workers was the information that it had been gathering on them throughout the dispute. In the complaints report Hodges reported that police had a lot of intelligence but it wasn't shared between forces. At a police conference in Chester that West Mercia Constabulary arranged in autumn 1972,

> Gwynedd Constabulary proved to be well organised from the point of view of special branch surveillance. At the conference already referred to, it was found that they had a wealth of information about the strike and the intentions of the pickets – in some cases to the extent of verbatim records of what was said at meetings.[44]

The Political Analysis in the Police Reports

Although the two West Mercia police reports related to a criminal investigation into picketing incidents, they both highlighted the politics running through the dispute. There was an entire section of the police report headed, 'Politics', covering nine paragraphs. The final one began, 'One other person who has been of interest because of his political inclinations, is William Dominic REAGAN.'[45] This was Billy Reagan, the north Wales secretary of the Building Workers' Charter group. A fellow Communist Party member, Lou Armour, also featured. The role of the Building Workers' Charter group was discussed.

> Bearing in mind the recent disorders during the miners' and dockers' disputes, the Police service generally should have appreciated on a national basis that this type of militancy was liable to be produced in the building dispute ... References have been made elsewhere to political aspects in the miners' and dockers' disputes and in this connection the Communist-inspired Building Workers Charter, drawn up in April, 1970, was well known to Special Branch officers.
>
> The possibility of serious disorder was not a confidential matter as it had been predicted in the 'News Review', published by the Economic League, from the time the Charter was drawn

up. This publication had also commented from time to time on the increasing use of 'flying pickets'. Whilst accepting that the publishers may have a private axe to grind, much of what is written has the ring of authenticity and is therefore worthy of consideration.[46]

A further example of the focus upon trade union activists was Hodges's mention that DCI Glover had attended a security conference at Birmingham City Police Training School on 18 January 1973. During a session on 'industrial disputes in the building trade' the speaker, 'a Detective Sergeant in Birmingham, referred to a list of names of the militant organisers, all of whom are CP or IS members'.[47]

Throughout the report Des Warren was identified in several ways as being both a leader and someone who was to be selected for prosecution:

> The man WARREN deserves a special reference: he does not have the confidence of his union but appears to have a special knack in arousing workmen to militant action. He is strongly inclined to the Left and appears to eke a living somehow by spreading industrial disorder in the building trade. Certainly he admits (the only thing he did admit) to being 'blacked' on various sites and has to resort to pseudonyms to gain employment. As a result of a recent similar incident, Gwynedd Constabulary have put forward a suggested charge against him of obtaining the opportunity to earn remuneration by deception.[48]

West Mercia obtained information about Warren's background, most likely from the Home Office F4 Division, whom ACC Rennie was in contact with:

> In this connection, there does not appear to be any National liaison in Special Branch and it is interesting to note that one 'leader' in the present enquiry (Desmond Michael WARREN), who was active on the Barbican site dispute in the City of London, was 'lost' to New Scotland Yard after 1966 when he left the area.[49]

The police also obtained information about Warren's background from his own union. One source was probably the UCATT official for north Wales, Albert Prest, who knew him. In his unpublished memoir, Prest recounted a visit to Wrexham police station to meet with Glover and Salisbury, 'in connection with the dispute'.[50] He continued,

> I was pleasantly surprised, for the greater part of the time was spent in listening to the police officers, and looking through the books of photos showing pickets in action on various sites, with rings superimposed around the heads of the leaders. I gathered that the police were compiling information to make sure that the charges arising would stick, and their success was to be proved later in the year with the outcome of the Shrewsbury trials.

The authors of the police report foresaw more instances of flying pickets in the future:

> Bearing in mind the serious public concern in the area about these events and keeping to the fore the thought that such industrial disorders are an innovation of the recent past – and escalation an alarming prospect for the future, it may prove convenient to closely examine the type of considerations taken in the investigations [sic].[51]

The report recognised that the current law did not place any restrictions on the number of people who could attend a picket line. So instead the police referred to a speech by Attorney General Peter Rawlinson QC for guidance on the law that would justify taking legal proceedings against the pickets: 'it is very hard to see how the attendance of large numbers of pickets can possibly be justified in the name of lawful, peaceful persuasion.'[52] On that basis, the police report concluded that

> one point of view of the situation in Shropshire is that all persons present committed at least the offence of unlawful assembly, on the grounds that 250 pickets is an excessive number and therefore is, prima facie, unlawful picketing ... Even if not accepted

as being prima-facie unlawful, it is felt in some quarters that, once an affray is established, all persons proved to have been present commit that offence unless equally credible proof is given that they actively disassociated themselves from what was happening.[53]

This line of argument, which the police shared with the Tories, employers and judges, was an attack on the fundamentals of trade unionism. They acknowledged that there was no legal limit on the numbers of people who could attend a picket but were now seeking to retrospectively criminalise the north Wales building workers for their actions during the strike. What the Conservative government could not achieve through a change in the law in Parliament or in a code of practice with the TUC, they hoped to get through a decision of the unelected courts. The judges would be using the vagueness and the elasticity of the 'common law' to discover that the pickets had committed an offence simply by 'being there' in large numbers.

The West Mercia police reports and correspondence confirmed that they were under pressure to take action. But this was no different from agitation by employers in other towns and cities discussed in the previous chapter. The allegations made against the north Wales pickets were similar to those made against pickets in Yorkshire, the Midlands and the South East. So the decision to investigate and prosecute them was a calculated one. West Mercia police were given full political support and encouragement to build such a case. The discussion of the politics of the building workers' strike in the police reports, including the role of the charter campaign, indicates that the decision to conduct such a wide-ranging inquiry into the north Wales building workers was a political one. The case was now passed to the DPP, who had to decide whether the reports and evidence from West Mercia and Gwynedd police could support a successful prosecution.

8

The Prosecution 'Construct' a Case

The West Mercia and Gwynedd police forces had spent a considerable amount of time and resources on the investigation of the north Wales pickets. More, perhaps, than the combined efforts of all the other forces in England and Wales that had investigated picketing in their respective areas. Despite this, the West Mercia police report concluded that the evidence for a successful prosecution, particularly of any 'leaders', was weak. But three months of Home Office-inspired investigation was not going to go to waste. The government was subject to significant political pressure from employers and Conservative Party members to take conspicuous action against picketing. A trial was necessary regardless of the weakness of the evidence.

The West Mercia complaints report made clear that the West Midlands employers were demanding a prosecution of pickets as the price for dropping any complaint against the police. Hodges emphasised that putting pickets on trial was the NFBTE's priority, regardless of whether the evidence was strong enough to secure a conviction:

> Mr SMITH of the N.F.B.T.E. has intimated confidentially that the various building employers as a whole are very pleased with the fact that such a comprehensive investigation has been carried out. He has gone on to say that if a case comes to Court then, irrespective of the outcome, there would be no pursuance of any complaint against the Police.[1]

A conference to discuss the police reports took place on 29 December 1972 at the offices of the Director of Public Prosecutions, 12 Buckingham Gate, in the shadow of the palace. In attendance were West Mercia's Chief Constable Willison and two senior DPP representatives: the assistant director, Michael Jardine, and John Walker. In his letter of 18 December, Willison had outlined some of the difficulties in pursuing prosecutions: there were weaknesses in the police evidence, including the hearsay nature of many of the statements, there were difficulties with the identification evidence due to the lapse of time, and up to 200 witnesses would need to be called to court. Many of the alleged offences in the Gwynedd police report were minor and not appropriate for a Crown court trial. Willison warned that trade unionists might criticise any prosecutions for being politically motivated, whereas if the police did nothing or the pickets were acquitted it would encourage them to carry on.

Despite these misgivings the DPP decided to proceed and a file was opened after the conference, listing twenty-six names, beginning with Henry Winston Barton.[2] Eleven pickets were concerned with events at north Wales sites and fifteen with incidents in both north Wales and Shropshire.

The Attorney General Gets Involved

The DPP decided to seek an opinion of the evidence from a senior barrister, for which they needed the permission of the attorney general, Sir Peter Rawlinson QC. Copies of the two police reports were sent to him on 1 January 1973,[3] with a pro forma requesting the nomination of two counsel, 'to advise and, if necessary, conduct the prosecution in the case of Barton & Others at Shrewsbury ... for Intimidation – Affray – Conspiracy & Protection of Property Act 1875'.[4] The DPP form was signed by Walker and he had written the names of two counsel on it, Maurice Drake QC and Desmond Fennell.[5] Rawlinson endorsed Walker's suggestion on 16 January and instructions were sent to the two barristers to advise. Drake was Establishment through and through. Private schooling was followed by service in the

RAF during the Second World War, when he was awarded the Distinguished Flying Cross. After studying at Exeter College, Oxford, he began his career as a barrister in 1950, joining the London chambers of Quintin Hogg QC,[6] who was to become the Conservative Lord Chancellor in Heath's government. Drake himself was made Queen's Counsel in 1968.

Rawlinson Writes to the Home Secretary

No documents have been discovered showing any discussions about the two police reports between the initial conference on 29 December 1972 and a conference at Maurice Drake's chambers five weeks later, on 1 February 1973. But a remarkable letter was written by Rawlinson during that period, on 25 January. He wrote to the home secretary, Robert Carr, advising that charges should *not* be brought:

> The building workers' strike last summer produced instances of intimidation of varying degrees of seriousness in which I have had to decide whether or not criminal proceedings should be instituted for an offence against section 7 of the Conspiracy and Protection of Property Act 1875.
>
> A number of instances of this kind have been submitted to me recently in which the intimidation consisted of threatening words and in which there was no evidence against any particular person of violence or damage to property. In the circumstances Treasury Counsel, to whom the cases were referred by the Director of Public Prosecutions to advise on the prospects of securing a conviction, took the view that the prospects were very uncertain, and in the result I agreed with him and the Director that proceeding should not be instituted.
>
> In arriving at this conclusion, we have been considerably influenced by the fact that section 9 of the 1875 Act gives to the accused an unfettered right in a case of this kind to be tried by jury if he wishes. Past experience shows that, if proceedings were to be instituted against these men, they will almost certainly elect trial by jury.

One has therefore to consider the prospect of conviction by a jury, rather than by a magistrates' court, and you will appreciate that accordingly different considerations apply. Firstly, the delay in bringing the case to trial would lead to an air of unreality about the proceedings long after the strike has been settled, and this would be likely to work in favour of the accused. Secondly, juries tend to treat mere words more leniently than actual violence. Thirdly, a jury will be likely to be influenced by the political factor that conviction might revive a strike atmosphere.[7]

No documents have been discovered at The National Archives or elsewhere to clarify the ambiguities in this letter. We do not know the identity of 'Treasury Counsel' to whom the DPP had referred the cases, or of the agreement between Rawlinson, Treasury Counsel and the DPP. The 'number of instances' of alleged intimidation are not identified by reference to a town or city. What we know is that by 25 January other investigations into picketing during 1972 were closed, with one minor exception.[8] The only cases involving picketing that were known to have been submitted to Rawlinson in the weeks before he wrote to Carr were those involving the north Wales pickets. Walker had sent the two police reports to Rawlinson three weeks earlier.

It is not clear why the Home Office should have been seeking the views of Rawlinson about whether or not anyone was prosecuted for a criminal offence; that rested with the police, the DPP and the attorney general. Rawlinson's letter was not sent in his position as legal adviser to a government department about a matter within that department's jurisdiction. Rawlinson's letter to Carr was a political communication, explaining the decision not to prosecute.

What is also unusual is that the letter makes no reference to any previous correspondence or meeting between them that would explain why Rawlinson was now writing to Carr.[9] What it shows is the close involvement that Carr had with the prosecution of pickets. The Home Office was behind it from the start. Carr's role in pushing the investigation and prosecutions was confirmed in a remarkable handwritten comment on the DPP file, opened following the conference on 29 December 1972:

'The Home Sec is interested in this case.'[10] Carr repeated his interest in a letter to the prime minster on 8 February 1973: 'I have taken a close personal interest in this problem since I came to the Home Office and I have myself discussed it with the chief officers of those police forces which have had to deal with the most serious picketing.'[11]

This was the background to the letter that Peter Rawlinson sent to Carr on 25 January 1973. He advised against a prosecution of building workers under the 1875 Conspiracy and Protection of Property Act but several days later a decision was taken to go ahead nevertheless. The senior civil servant in Rawlinson's department, Tony Hetherington, spoke with John Walker at the DPP on 30 January 1973 to advise that the attorney general did not need to be consulted about charges that might be preferred against the north Wales pickets. Rawlinson was 'content for this to be left in the hands of counsel'.[12] On the same day, Carr's ministerial diary records that at 12:45 he had lunch with the NFBTE at the Dorchester Hotel, just after a Cabinet meeting.[13] No doubt he was able to give them some reassuring news.

Maurice Drake QC Advises in Conference

The meeting that planned the legal case against the pickets was a seven-hour conference on 1 February 1973 at Drake's chambers in London. In attendance with Drake were his junior, Fennell, four senior police officers (Rennie, Hodges and Glover from West Mercia and Detective Chief Inspector Salisbury from Gwynedd) and two civil servants from the DPP (Walker and Charles Hall). *The Times* carried a brief item the following day:

> Charges are to be brought against some of the 'flying pickets' who are alleged to have terrorized building sites in Shropshire and north Wales during the building workers' strike last year, Mr Alexander Rennie, Assistant Chief Constable of the West Mercia Police Authority, said yesterday.[14]

The *Shropshire Star* also carried a report and quoted Rennie: 'After obtaining legal advice in conjunction with the Director of Public Prosecutions we have decided to instigate proceedings against members of the flying pickets for alleged criminal offences committed in Shropshire and North Wales.' He added, 'We have a number of things to tie up so I am at present unable to say how many people will be charged and with what offences.'[15]

Drake was to produce a written opinion three weeks later but the crucial decisions had already been made at that conference. Eleven further names were added to the initial list of twenty-six defendants and some of the original names were dropped, leaving a total of thirty-two north Wales pickets who were to be charged.

Gwynedd Police Charge Pickets

Gwynedd police acted first and obtained summonses on 6 February against eight people for offences alleged to have been committed on sites in north Wales in August and September 1972.[16] They were charged with minor offences at several different sites on different days, including criminal damage, assault and intimidation, which could all be dealt with in a magistrates' court. For that reason, at this early stage, the police did not deal with the pickets at one court. On 2 April, four appeared at Llanwrst Magistrate's Court, one at Flint the following day and three at Mold on the 4th. They were all charged with at least one count of intimidation under Section 7 of the 1875 Conspiracy Act, which gave the accused the right to elect trial by jury in the Crown court. All of them, except Peter Westwater, decided that they had a better chance before a jury and were committed for trial to Mold Crown Court on all the charges they faced.

West Mercia Follow Suit

The legal process for West Mercia followed the day after Gwynedd police, with the swearing of an 'information' at Wenlock Magistrate's Court by Chief Superintendent Hodges on 7 February 1973. The first charge was that six pickets had conspired with others between 1 July and 31 October 1972 to intimidate those working on building sites in Shropshire and elsewhere with a view to compelling them to stop, 'Contrary to Common Law'.[17] In addition, each of the six was charged with a varying number of additional offences: John Carpenter with eight, John McKinsie Jones with eleven, John Llywarch with eight, Ken O'Shea with fifteen, Eric Tomlinson with eighteen and Des Warren with twenty-eight offences.

The police report had not identified those six as the leaders of any conspiracy; only Warren was highlighted, as someone of special interest. Two of the six, Carpenter and Llywarch, had not been on the original list of potential defendants when the DPP opened its file on 29 December 1972. The decision to select those six to be charged with 'conspiracy to intimidate' was arbitrary. Only three of them could be described as leaders: Warren, who had been active from the very beginning of the strike and was an experienced trade unionist; his colleague, Ken O'Shea, with whom he went picketing on many sites in north Wales between June and September; and Jones, who was an active trade union-ist and had been a shop steward for a number of years at the Shotton steelworks, where he worked for one of the contractors in the plant, Midlands & North West Painting Contractors Ltd.[18]

The other three pickets charged with conspiracy were not sea-soned trade unionists. Llywarch and Tomlinson were not union members when the strike started; they went on strike themselves from mid-August when the unions called an all-out national strike. Carpenter worked for Wrexham Council's building department and, although the unions did not call out members in local authority building departments,[19] he went picketing with the Wrexham Action Committee.

There was one common feature of the six that the prosecu-tion relied upon to justify charging them with conspiracy: they were either secretary, chairperson or treasurer of a local strike action committee and had been the steward of a coach that took pickets to Shrewsbury on 6 September.

According to Fennell it was Drake's idea to charge six with conspiracy (although it had been considered and dismissed in the police report[20]). A subsequent note in the DPP files about whether the attorney general was involved recorded that Fennell 'agrees that at no time did they see the A/G – Michael Jardine was the highest ranking [*sic*] man – Desmond did not favour conspiracy – it was really Maurice Drake's brainchild'.[21]

The police report had argued that although the police did not have evidence that the 'organisers and leaders' had committed particular offences, they ought to be made responsible for the actions of others:

> The evidence against several of the second group – the organisers and leaders – is not so strong. It mainly consists of the very act of organising their party's attendance, in circumstances where disorder on a large scale must have been foreseen, and the fact that they were present on the sites with the pickets without trying to restore order (or paying lip-service in that respect).[22]

Drake took up this position and proceeded on the basis that a jury could infer a conspiracy among the organisers of the pickets because they knew or ought reasonably to have known that fellow pickets were intimidating non-strikers and damaging property when they went onto a building site.

After the two police forces had obtained the initial summonses against several of the pickets, Drake held a further conference, with Hodges, Glover, Salisbury and Hall, on 8 February. He advised that twenty-four pickets be charged with offences arising from the events at Shrewsbury on 6 September. They would be divided into two groups: six so-called 'ringleaders' would face the most serious charges of conspiracy to intimidate and affray; the remaining eighteen would be charged with lesser offences. 'A decision was, therefore, made to deal with the 6 by arrest and the 18 others to be summoned, thereby indicating the distinction to the court.'[23] Following this conference, Hodges went back to Wenlock Magistrate's Court on 12 February and obtained summonses against the eighteen.

What was notable about the charges against the 'Shrewsbury 24' was that, apart from allegations relating to Shrewsbury and Telford on 6 September, they also included offences that were alleged to have been committed in north Wales. These were not going to be left to Gwynedd police to deal with. Drake wanted to maximise the air of criminality about the twenty-four by keeping the north Wales charges in the minds of a Shrewsbury jury.

Arrests and Charges, 14 February 1973

Out of the blue, the six 'ringleaders' were arrested at their homes on the evening of 14 February, Valentine's Day. They were charged and held overnight at the police headquarters at Wellington and then brought before Woodside Magistrates' Court, Telford, where they were bailed to attend court again in four weeks' time. At the same time, summonses were served personally on the other eighteen pickets to also attend the court on 15 March 1973 to answer charges. Warren recalled his arrest:

> Two plain clothes [sic] officers came for me in Prestatyn around 6.30pm ... I was driven to Flint police station, Ken O'Shea from Denbigh and Mackinsie Jones from Connah's Quay were already there. The three of us were taken to Wrexham where Ricky Tomlinson, John Carpenter and John Llywarch were picked up. Then on to Shropshire where we were locked up in separate cells in a police station ... The next day was even more bizarre. We were taken to court in a police convoy with motor-cycle outriders. Outside the court, police seemed to be all over the place. There were dogs and a host of press photographers. It was bewildering. Someone remarked it looked like the Kray gang were coming up.[24]

Although the six were understandably shocked at their arrest, the biggest surprise was the arrest of the three Wrexham men, two of whom were originally considered prosecution witnesses. Llywarch was one of the first north Wales pickets to be interviewed by West Mercia and Gwynedd police, on 3 November. Glover prepared a statement after their meeting for Llywarch to sign at a later date. Before he returned to the police station Llywarch rang the police to say that he'd been advised not to sign anything. He went back to Whitchurch police station on 30 November and confirmed that he was not going to sign the statement that Glover had before him. Only then did Glover caution him. The unsigned statement became a central part of the prosecution case (see Chapter 10).

Tomlinson was not mentioned anywhere in the West Mercia complaints report or in the political discussion of the Charter Group in the main police report. Nor was he one of the six pickets arrested for questioning in November 1972.[25] Later, he wrote that the police visited him at work after the strike had ended and asked him to be a prosecution witness against Warren and the other strike leaders. The police thought Tomlinson's National Front politics would have made him an obvious choice as a police witness to convict communist trade unionists. He refused and then became a target.[26]

Drake's Opinion, 21 February 1973

After a third meeting with police officers and the DPP at Drake's chambers, he summarised his advice, principally on the Shrewsbury cases, in a written opinion, 'Offences disclosed by the evidence'.[27] This gives an insight into the issues that had been discussed between them during the previous three weeks. In it he identified five categories of offence that the pickets should be charged with. First, all were accused of one or more counts of intimidation. Second, the six leaders would be separately charged with a 'conspiracy to intimidate', even though there was 'little or no evidence of any event agreement: but in respect of the 6 apparent ringleaders we think there is sufficient evidence to justify the inference of such agreement so as to support charges of conspiracy'. Drake acknowledged that the courts had held that, generally, a conspiracy charge should not be brought when someone has been accused of *committing* the actual offence. He answered, 'we think that the conspiracy goes beyond the sum of the individual acts of intimidation ... these 6 ringleaders had embarked upon a deliberate plan of campaign to intimidate non-striking building workers.'

The third category of offence was affray. The six had already been charged with this offence when they were arrested on 14 February. Drake originally decided not to charge the other eighteen with the offence to highlight the difference between them and the six 'leaders'. Drake had also hoped that some of the eighteen would elect for a summary trial in the magistrates' court for the offences that they were charged with. But he noted, 'Police information suggests that the 18 accused are likely to elect trial by Indictment', i.e. a jury trial in the Crown court.[28] As a consequence of this information, he changed his mind and recommended that all twenty-four be charged with affray throughout the day at all sites on 6 September 1972.[29]

Drake advised that if all twenty-four were charged with affray there would be just one trial, albeit a long one, with witnesses being called just once. The jury would then hear evidence from a lot of witnesses and this would create an overall picture of criminality that might persuade the jury to convict everyone, even where the specific evidence against a particular picket, if heard in isolation, was weak and would not lead to a conviction.

The fourth and fifth categories dealt with the more minor offences of threatening behaviour, common assault and criminal damage, for which the twenty-four pickets had already been charged.

Drake Adds Charge of Affray

After the 'long conference' on 21 February, Hodges returned to Wenlock Magistrate's Court two days later to obtain further summonses against all twenty-four pickets, charging them with affray in Shropshire. At this stage Gwynedd police had not been asked by Drake to bring a charge of affray against any of the pickets who were eventually tried at Mold Crown Court. This charge was only added later on, in May, when Drake gave further consideration to the upcoming cases at Mold.

The essence of the case against the Shrewsbury 24 was now

set and Drake wanted to ensure that they were all dealt with together at Shrewsbury Crown Court. He was aware that seven separate trials, involving offences at each of the seven sites visited on 6 September, would create its own difficulties:

> The evidence against many of the accused in respect merely of one individual site is extremely thin. In several cases it amounts only to an identification of the accused on or leaving the site with no evidence whatsoever of the part he played in the intimidation on the site.[30]

Drake decided to leave nothing to chance. Over the following months he would ensure that he took control of all the most important hearings so that any necessary adjustments could be made before the main trial opened in Shrewsbury in autumn 1973. The prosecutions at Mold were thought to be minor affairs in comparison, but they gave Drake valuable insights into how to deal with the later cases.

Notwithstanding that the prosecution of building workers was progressing, the employers continued to put pressure on the police to take a tougher stance against picketing. The chief security officer for Sir Robert McAlpine & Son Ltd, ex–Scotland Yard chief superintendent Hannam, wrote to the Metropolitan police (his former employer) on 26 February 1973 to remind them of the speeches of Carr, Shawcross and others calling for greater enforcement of public order law against picketing.[31]

The Shrewsbury 24 had their first collective appearance in court on 15 March at Shrewsbury Magistrate's Court. A demonstration of several thousand supporters was held through the town, organised by trade unions and the newly formed North Wales Defence Committee.[32] It was to play a vital role in organising support and funds for the pickets to cover their expenses and loss of earnings throughout the trials and periods of imprisonment. Both Drake and Fennell appeared for the prosecution and the pickets were all remanded on bail to return for a committal hearing on 25 April, when they would be expected to enter pleas to the charges. In the meantime, Drake and Fennell returned to north Wales on five occasions for hearings at the magistrates' courts in Ruabon, Llanwrst, Flint and Mold (twice). They now had the support of a second junior counsel, James P. Wadsworth, who had been Drake's pupil barrister at his chambers in London.

In the event, the committal hearing of the Shrewsbury 24 on 25 April did not take place because, the police reported, '1973 Criminal Justice Act statements were still being amended and signed, following Counsel's advice'.[33] Bail was extended until 18 May. This hearing did not take place on the later date either and the twenty-four finally returned to court on 15 June.

Among the cases that Gwynedd police were dealing with were charges of intimidation by three pickets at Brennig Reservoir on 9 September and one at Padewood on 7 August. The police had hoped that they would agree to be dealt with by the magistrates, but all four men elected for a Crown court trial. Among the Shrewsbury 24 were seven pickets who had also been charged with intimidation on the same sites and dates, five at Brennig reservoir and two at Padeswood. Drake decided that all pickets involved with these incidents should have their cases heard at the same time in Mold rather than at Shrewsbury. He arranged for the seven to attend Shrewsbury Magistrates' Court on 18 May and they were all committed for trial at Mold.

This changed the complexion of the Gwynedd cases. In February the police had originally forecast that the pickets would be dealt with in the magistrates' courts in North Wales.[34] But as most elected for a jury trial in the Crown court, Drake then upped the stakes and had all eight charged with affray.[35] This offence had not featured at all in the original Gwynedd police 'schedule of offenders and direct evidence'. Drake would use the Mold trials as a testing ground for both the affray and Section 7 intimidation offences, neither of which had been used against trade unionists for decades.

The Pickets Denied Union Legal Aid

The thirty-two building workers who were charged with offences were a diverse group, from different areas in north

Wales. There were many different trades spread among them including bricklayers, steel-fixers, scaffolders, roofers, plasterers and painters, together with labourers. They were employed by different contractors at different workplaces, the largest number being those who worked for the five firms that had contracts at the Shotton steelworks. There were huge communication problems among the pickets. Many people in 1972 did not have a home telephone, nor did they own a car. Many of the pickets who were arrested and summonsed did not know the names of the other people charged by the police; nor were they familiar with many of them. The twenty-four were not a cohesive group and, with the exception of 6 September, they had not gone to picket another site together in north Wales.

One of the few meetings they had was on 9 March 1973 at the Ship Hotel, Flint, called by UCATT's regional secretary, E. V. Hughes. The meeting was to discuss the charges that they faced and the support that they could receive from the unions. Hughes had prepared a letter for each picket to make a request for union legal aid. Most of the pickets signed up but Warren and two others refused, preferring to stay with Casson & Co., whom they had consulted after their arrest on 14 February. Warren was suspicious of the union and thought that if all twenty-four were represented by UCATT's London solicitor they would be sold out. He feared that the lawyers would make a deal with the DPP which the union would require them to accept, otherwise union legal aid would be withdrawn.[36]

UCATT's general secretary, Smith, had written the day before to the other three unions on the National Joint Council for the Building Industry to inform them that he had sought legal advice. He was particularly concerned about the charge of conspiracy as it was thought to be based upon decisions taken at the officially constituted North Wales Action Committee in Chester, which reported to the regional and national action committees. It raised the spectre that he and his fellow officials, indeed any union full-time official who attended a strike meeting, could be charged with conspiracy. On that basis he advised that UCATT's solicitor would be representing the pickets when they attended court in Shrewsbury on 15 March and Mold on 4 April.[37]

Less than a week later, UCATT reversed its position. The same union lawyer, John L. Williams, wrote to Smith on 12 March advising that the union should not provide legal aid to its members:

> My reasons were that the number of charges would involve pro-ceedings over about 6 months with potential costs in the region of £10,000 at least; that the charges involved assault, damage to property and personal intimidation which could not arise out of joint action committee decisions; that at least three of the men charges [sic] (particularly Warren, Tomlinson and O'Shea) who attracted about 40 charges between them intended to stay with Casson and Co., so that we could have no influence over the conduct of their defence; and that a defence by the organisation on matters such as assault and damage to property might imply condonation [sic] of attempts to do this.[38]

As an advice letter from a solicitor, it mixed up legal, tactical and political judgments. Williams was pre-empting the outcome of the trials. He implied that the fact that the pickets were charged meant that they were guilty and should not be given legal representation by the union as it might appear that the unions supported criminal behaviour, which had not yet been proven in court. This was contrary to the basic legal principle, the 'presumption of innocence', that an accused person is inno-cent unless and until they are proven to be guilty. It follows that every person charged with a criminal offence, regardless of its seriousness, is entitled to legal representation.

The lawyer's advice was that the nature of the charges meant that the pickets' behaviour was inconsistent with proper trade union activity and therefore was ineligible for legal assistance under any union's scheme. Smith wrote to Hughes summarising the advice and directed him to inform the pickets that union legal aid would not be granted. Copies of the letter were sent to the three other unions on the NJC. He also sent a four-page document to each UCATT branch for distribution to members explaining that the union's decision is that Union Rule 27, Clause 37, although providing legal aid to members in defending claims arising from an industrial dispute, does not allow legal aid for defence against criminal charges alleging misconduct in industrial disputes. Neither do the rules of any union.

... the union as such, by reason of its rules, could not be seen to offer indirect encouragement to acts alleged as criminal by making legal aid available wherever they were alleged, a common trade union attitude.[39]

An appeal was made to the union's general council on behalf of the UCATT members but it was defeated by four votes to ten. The main argument that Smith put forward was that the costs would bankrupt the union and the pickets could get state legal aid instead. The final resolution that was agreed, by ten votes to four, endorsed the decision of Smith and the executive council. It accepted the union solicitor's advice, that the nature of the charges and the costs of the defence were 'outside the scope of the rules of the union'.[40]

The stage was now set. The prosecution was being carefully planned, led by a team of three barristers, Drake, Fennell and Wadsworth; two representatives of the DPP; and two senior police officers from West Mercia and Gwynedd. The thirty-two pickets who were to face trial in Mold and Shrewsbury were not so cohesive or led. They were left by their respective unions to apply for state legal aid to obtain their own legal representation and organise their defence from the various towns in north Wales in which they lived.

9

The Mold Trials and the Lessons Learned by the Prosecution

It took the police and prosecution several months to settle on the structures of the trials. As late as 22 May 1973, Chief Superintendent Hodges confessed to the DPP, 'The administration of this case has been a little confused due to the initial intention to deal with certain defendants in North Wales and the remainder independently in Shropshire.'[1] The confusion was intensified by the stand taken by several of the pickets, who exercised their right to be tried in the Crown court rather than the magistrates' court for the offence of intimidation under Section 7(1) of the Conspiracy and Protection of Property Act 1875.[2] If found guilty of this offence in either court the maximum sentence was three months' imprisonment. Drake decided to turn their decision to his advantage by using the trials at Mold as a testing ground. Warren described the Mold trials in this way:

> These were of great importance and a dress rehearsal for Shrewsbury. What they meant was described to me by one solicitor: 'Like a West End impresario, the Director of Public Prosecutions used the Mold trials to cross out the faults in the production, prior to the Shrewsbury run.'[3]

Maurice Drake later agreed that the trials were a dry run for the Shrewsbury cases: 'When we got to Mold Crown Court we were "testing the water" so to speak.'[4] It was a test for the charges of affray and intimidation, which had not been used against trade unionists in a strike for over a century. Drake also wanted to test out the witnesses, particularly the non-strikers who were called for the prosecution. He needed to know whether they would stand up to questioning or downplay events out of sympathy for their fellow building workers in the dock.

Peter Westwater in the Magistrates' Court

The first 'rehearsal' was the trial of Peter Westwater at Mold magistrates' court, on 4 April 1973.[5] He was charged with just one offence, section 7 intimidation, allegedly committed at the Buckley sewerage scheme at Padeswood on 14 August 1972. He was a union shop steward on the site and had come out on strike. The site had been picketed successfully in the past but some men had returned to work. Westwater was reported to have said to them, 'If you go back to work there will be murder on the site.' He, unlike all the other pickets charged with intimidation, opted to be tried by the magistrates. This was a risk because most pickets took the view that magistrates were less likely to acquit than a jury. But in his case, 'the examining Justices found "no case to answer".'[6] The magistrates accepted that he did not mean the words literally and was simply expressing the discontent that would erupt if his colleagues went back to work.

The secretary of the 4/1107 Holst Branch of the Transport & General Workers' Union, D. A. Jackson, observed Westwater's trial and reported, 'I still look upon these proceedings as anti-Trade Union, for example it is not often a Q.C. (Mr. Drake) is sent to prosecute by the Director of Public Prosecutions before a magistrates' court.'[7] Jackson was right. It was remarkable that a QC should prosecute in a magistrates' court. Perhaps even more remarkable was that Drake also attended most of the preliminary hearings, with Desmond Fennell. This Queen's Counsel graced magistrates' courts in Ruabon on 23 March and 4 April,

Llanrwst on 2 April, Flint on 3 April and Shrewsbury on 15 March, 18 May and 15 June.[8]

The First Trial at Mold Crown Court

The prosecutions of the fourteen pickets at Mold Crown Court were dealt with at five separate trials. The court building was subjected to a high level of security when the first one started, on 26 June 1973. According to *The Times*, 200 police stood shoulder to shoulder around the building and a further 100 were on standby inside.[9] David Turner-Samuels QC complained that the police numbers gave jurors the impression that the court was 'under siege', but the judge replied that the security of the court was not his affair. The police had already put on similar shows of force when six pickets were arrested and charged on 14–15 February and when all twenty-four appeared at Shrewsbury magistrates' court on 15 March and 15 June. The show of force at Mold on the opening day of the trial was designed to influence jurors, as well as anyone reading the newspapers, that this was a major trial of serious criminals.

The first trial was the most significant, involving eight pickets: Derrick Hughes, Colin Kelly, Ken O'Shea, Michael Pierce, Gwyn Roberts, John Seaburg, Gwynfr Williams and Edward Leonard Williams. The case centred on events at Brennig Reservoir, Denbighshire, on Monday 11 September 1972. The site had been picketed in the past, including 23 August, but work had resumed and so a larger group of pickets went there to demonstrate that the strike was still on and was still strongly supported.[10] No one was arrested or cautioned. The first time any picket learned that they were to be prosecuted for any activity that day was six months later, in February 1973.

The indictment against the men contained seven separate counts. All eight were charged with affray (count 1) and intimidation of workers (count 2). Seven were charged with damaging a drill rig (count 3) and the remaining four counts involved individual acts of criminal damage. At the start of the trial three pickets pleaded guilty to one count of damaging or attempting to damage property. That left the most serious counts, of affray and intimidation, plus the remaining counts of damaging property, to be heard by the jury.

Drake, supported by Desmond Fennell, called seventeen witnesses, seven of them police officers. Although all seven counts that the pickets faced alleged criminal conduct at Brennig on 11 September, Drake made frequent reference to the events in Shrewsbury on 6 September. The police witnesses he called were asked to recount the interviews they had conducted with pickets. He read out sections of pickets' statements that the police had taken in November 1972, which referred to picketing elsewhere in north Wales. Drake tried to paint a picture for the jury that wherever the pickets went, including to Shrewsbury, they would use force to intimidate workers and stop them working, just as they did at Brennig. The pickets' case was that they went there in large numbers to demonstrate that the strike was still strongly supported and to inspire their fellow workers to join them.

At the end of the prosecution case the various pickets' barristers made submissions to the judge, Richard Chetwynd-Talbot, that there was no case to answer on the affray and intimidation charges. None of the prosecution witnesses had given direct evidence that a particular non-striker had been intimidated by a picket. The prosecution had to prove that for an affray to be made out the pickets had terrorised those still working on the site and not merely caused them apprehension. The defence argued that the prosecution evidence could not support such a charge. Despite this, the judge let the case proceed and all eight pickets and a UCATT official, Lou Armour, gave evidence in their defence. Yes, there were arguments between strikers and non-strikers on 11 September, as the pickets tried to explain the need for unity among building workers to end low pay and dreadful working conditions. But there was no fighting or other violent behaviour.

One remarkable feature of the trial was the frequent references to Des Warren.[11] In Chetwynd-Talbot's ninety-three-page summing-up of the evidence for the jury, thirty-four pages referred to picketing at Shrewsbury or to Des Warren, based upon the case advanced by Drake.[12] The judge mentioned Warren's name on seventy-three occasions in his summing-up, even though he was not on trial and had not given evidence as a witness. He was not present at Brennig reservoir on 11 September, but a number of witnesses mentioned him at the prompting of Drake. George Hallowes began his evidence by referring to the first visit of pickets to the site, on 23 August. He said that he spoke with the pickets' leader and later recognised him as Warren from his photograph in the *Sunday People* article.[13] James Hunter, a blasting engineer at the site, gave a similar statement to Hallowes. Warren attended several days of the trial, sitting in the public gallery, and wondered why he wasn't in the dock because his name was mentioned so often.

The jury retired at 10:20 a.m. on 12 July. After several requests for guidance in the afternoon the jury had completed its deliberations by 5:40 p.m. It pronounced not-guilty verdicts on all defendants on the first two counts, of affray and intimidation. O'Shea, Roberts and Seaburg were found guilty of one count of damaging property. They were fined between fifteen and fifty pounds.[14] Similar fines were imposed on the three pickets who had pleaded guilty to criminal damage at the start of the trial. On all the remaining charges of criminal damage the pickets were found not guilty. So the end result of a trial of eight men, lasting thirteen days, was £195 in fines.[15]

Four Later Mold Trials

The second Mold trial started on 11 July, overlapping with the end of the first trial. Drake and Fennell appeared again for the prosecution and Chetwynd-Talbot was the judge. The case dealt with picketing at a sewerage construction site, Padeswood, near Mold on 7 August 1972. The indictment was shorter, containing just three counts. Three pickets, William Hooson, William Hough and Arthur Murray, were each charged with intimidation (count 1). The other two counts accused Hooson and Murray each of threatening to cause criminal damage to the property of a non-striker at the site. After seven days, on 19 July, the jury found them all not guilty.

A similar result followed the third trial, on 19–20 July 1973. It involved a single picket, Peter Moroney, who was charged with intimidation and common assault at a Cefn Park housing estate, Penycae, Wrexham, on 7 September 1972. He was found not guilty. For this and the next trial Drake was not present, leaving the two cases to his juniors, Fennell and Wadsworth.

The fourth was a one-day trial of Kenneth Thomas, on 20 July. He was alleged to have intimidated building workers and caused damage at a site at Penrhyn Beach, Caernarvon, on 18 August 1972. He pleaded not guilty to intimidation but guilty to causing criminal damage, which was accepted by the prosecution. He was fined fifteen pounds.

The fifth trial, of Glyn Davies, did not take place until 2 April 1974. It had to be adjourned in July 1973 because a prosecution witness was unavailable.[16] The case was not related directly to the other Mold cases because it involved picketing on 28 October 1972, six weeks after the national strike had ended. Davies was charged with two counts. He was found not guilty of intimidation but guilty of common assault, for which he received a conditional discharge.[17]

Government Disappointed with the Outcome

A senior DPP official, Michael Jardine, wrote, 'The results of the trials so far are disappointing.'[18] The only convictions were for damaging property, many the result of guilty pleas. The prosecutions for the more serious offences of affray and intimidation had all ended in acquittals. These were the two main charges facing the Shrewsbury 24, whose trials were due to start in three months' time. Drake did not see it so negatively. There were a number of important lessons for them all, but otherwise they would continue with their preparations for the 'main event' in Shrewsbury.

After the Mold trials, a report was written by Charles Hall.[19] He was and continued to be a common thread for the DPP in planning the prosecution of the north Wales pickets, from the first conference with Drake on 1 February 1973 through to the final appeals in October 1974. He had attended the Mold trials as the 'instructing solicitor' to Drake, Fennell and Wadsworth. Another report was prepared by Inspector Hayes for the prosecution team. 'This contained points to watch and other observations.'[20] These reports would be discussed at subsequent meetings of the lawyers, DPP officials and the police so that they could plan their tactics for the conspiracy trial in October. The DPP obtained many documents from Mold as part of its preparations over the summer.[21] If the Mold trials were a dress rehearsal, the prosecution team used it to get their lines right for Shrewsbury.

The Defence Teams

The prosecution approach contrasted starkly with that of the defence, which was not as unified or well organised. Most of the pickets tried at Mold Crown Court were represented by a small firm of solicitors based in Salford, Casson & Co. The lawyer who worked on the case was a young partner at the firm, Campbell Malone. The uniqueness of the charges against the north Wales building workers meant that there were probably very few solicitors in England and Wales who had any experience of such a case, apart from a handful in London. For the first Mold trial, Malone had instructed six barristers to represent his clients to confront just two on the other side, Drake and Fennell.[22] This might seem an advantage to the defence but, as it turned out, it was actually a weakness. The defence did not have the same single-minded strategic direction and planning that the prosecution had. Each defence barrister was concerned, first and foremost, with their individual client.

Twelve of the twenty-four pickets tried at Shrewsbury were represented by a Chester firm, Walker, Smith & Way, but no one from this firm attended the Mold trials, so did not gain direct knowledge of how Drake was presenting the Crown's case in court. When I spoke with a solicitor from this firm about the coordination of the defence between his firm and Casson & Co., which acted for eleven of the pickets at Shrewsbury, he replied, 'We paddled our own canoe.' A third small firm of solicitors, Gwilym Hughes & Partners of Llangollen, acted for Derrick Hughes, who was tried at both Mold and Shrewsbury Crown Courts.

There was not the same level of coordination between these three solicitors' firms and with the many barristers they instructed, as existed with the prosecution. From the first Mold trial in June 1973 through to the third Shrewsbury trial in March 1974 the pickets were represented in court by a total of thirty-three different barristers. Warren's lead barrister, John Platts-Mills QC, was regarded as the most senior barrister at Shrewsbury, but he had not appeared in any of the Mold trials. None of the Shrewsbury pickets that I spoke with about the case could ever recall a meeting of all of them and the legal teams together in one room. It was compounded by the fact that the pickets were spread out all over north Wales. Half of them had a solicitor over fifty miles away in Salford, which was inaccessible for many.

The weakness of the pickets' legal defence was not due to a lack of money. They were all awarded state legal aid to fund their solicitors and barristers. The court records of the first trial at Shrewsbury show that the twelve defence barristers were paid a total of £74,505 and the three prosecution barristers were paid £25,620. In 2022 these figures would be £960,505 and £330,288 respectively. The three firms of defence solicitors would be paid from state legal aid on top of this.

The pickets were hamstrung by one of the principles of the legal profession, that a lawyer's first duty is to their client. If that meant following a path that implicated one or more of the co-accused, so be it. There was no authoritative figure from the unions or one of the solicitors' firms that could advise the pickets to act collectively, with just one firm and one team of barristers acting for them all, like the prosecution acted for the state. Ken O'Shea told me, 'We were just building workers. We went with the flow. They were lawyers and we thought they knew best.'

Lessons from Mold

The two main offences that Drake tested out at Mold were intimidation and affray. He learned lessons about both. At the first Mold trial, Judge Chetwynd-Talbot had directed the jury that the offence of intimidation was committed if the act of the accused picket was a threat of *personal violence* towards someone. During the second trial he was challenged about this definition. After hearing the opinion of both sides he gave a four-page judgment. In it he ruled that his direction to the jury about the meaning of 'intimidation' would include threats to *property*, if it could be shown that such threats were intended to cause a person to stop working.[23] Drake concluded that prosecution witnesses at Shrewsbury, where possible, should emphasise examples of threats to property that affected their willingness to continue working. Their written statements could not be changed as these had already been served on the defence when the twenty-four pickets attended Shrewsbury Magistrates' Court on 15 June to enter their pleas. But he could draw this evidence out of the witnesses when he questioned them during the Shrewsbury trials in the autumn.

Likewise, there needed to be a change in the emphasis of the witness evidence due to a development in the legal definition of affray. The House of Lords had given a decision in a case involving affray just before the start of the Mold trials.[24] It was emphasised by the law lords that, for an affray to be established, the conduct had to cause terror in the minds of those who were threatened or of bystanders. At Mold the defence pointed out that none of the prosecution witnesses said that they felt terrorised by the actions of the pickets, merely apprehensive or worried about damage to machinery. Again, Drake would ensure that witnesses at Shrewsbury would say that they felt terrorised by the conduct of the pickets.

Unlawful Assembly Added to the Charge Sheet

Drake was aware of the risks of losing the affray charge at Shrewsbury. After the not-guilty verdicts at Mold, he decided to add a new charge against the Shrewsbury 24, unlawful assembly. It had not been suggested in the West Mercia police report or at any of the conferences with the DPP and police earlier in the year. None of the pickets had been charged with the offence when they appeared at the magistrates' court on 15 June 1973 to be committed for trial at the Crown court. The addition of the charge was an example of the prosecution's power in being able to charge people with several different offences based upon the same event. Like conspiracy to intimidate and affray, unlawful assembly was a common law offence, not one found in an Act of Parliament. It was vague and did not require strong evidence. It was a case of simply being there. This proved to be a successful move by Drake because twenty-one Shrewsbury pickets were eventually convicted of this offence. For many it was the only offence for which they would be convicted.

The Prosecution Strengthens Its Case

It was not until 15 June that the Shrewsbury 24 made their second appearance in court, when the prosecution presented 227 signed statements to the magistrates. The prosecution's 'list of exhibits' included four albums of photographs and newspaper articles from the *Shropshire Star* and the *Sunday People*.[25] At the hearing each picket was asked whether they wanted to make any response to the charges; most of them declined. Renshaw was defiant, though: 'This is an attack by the Government itself where the Industrial Relations Act has failed. They've got Drake here – Danger Man just attacking Trade Unions, not 24 building workers. Sir Alfred MacAlpine [*sic*] has gone on cruise, £135000 on QE2.' Warren was equally combative: 'Police tactics will not deter strikers to achieve justice. We face charges. We are victims, not defendants. Conspiracy between Tories and Police.'[26] The pickets were then committed for trial at Shrewsbury Crown Court as *R* v. *Butcher and 23 Others*. At this stage there was no indication that Drake intended to split them up into three separate trials.

Over the following three months a number of steps were taken in preparation for the trials at Shrewsbury which highlighted the enormous power and advantage that the state had over the defence. Drake, the DPP and the police made a number of decisions to tip the scales in its favour.

The Trial Venue

The venue for the trial was crucial. The West Mercia police report had discussed this, noting that Mold was tier 1 and Shrewsbury tier 2, a reference to the seniority of the courts in dealing with offences. It indicated that Shrewsbury was not categorised as a venue for major criminal trials and therefore all the trials should take place at Mold.[27] Chief constable Willison had highlighted other considerations when he submitted the police reports to the DPP in December 1972: 'The venue may be thought important. Mold is a first-tier court but there is considerable unemployment in the district and Chester or Shrewsbury might be better alternatives.'[28]

Juries drawn from working-class towns and cities, particularly where unemployment was higher than average, were more likely to be sympathetic to pickets. Peter Rawlinson had highlighted the issue at a meeting of the Conservative Party Home Affairs Committee. He claimed that biased juries made it difficult to obtain a conviction of pickets – 'for instance in a recent case in Liverpool the jury came from a dock area and gave an acquittal.'[29]

The decision to try the north Wales pickets at Shrewsbury was opposed by their lawyers. On 27 July 1973, an application was made by the defence to move the trials from Shrewsbury to either Mold, Chester, Birmingham or Liverpool. The application was heard by Judge Mais, to whom the trial had been reserved.[30] The defence were represented by three counsel,[31] who put forward several grounds for moving the venue from Shrewsbury:

1 The jury would be influenced by the adverse reporting of the events on 6 September 1972 in Shrewsbury's local newspapers.[32]
2 Shrewsbury was approximately fifty miles from the pickets' homes in north Wales and they would incur significant daily

travelling expenses at a time when they would not be working. Lodgings would be expensive and Social Security would not cover these costs.

3 The trial could be held in Birmingham where suitable over-night accommodation could be found. The defendants had to be in court every day whereas witnesses need only attend on one, two or, at most, three days.[33]

The local newspaper for the Shrewsbury area, the *Shropshire Star*, which was likely to be read regularly by many members of the jury, reported each occasion when the pickets appeared in court. The 15 March 1973 edition had a front-page lead headlined, '800 police ring Salop court demo' to counter an estimated 3,000 protestors. There was similar publicity at the second magistrates' court hearing, on 15 June. In 1970s Britain the readership of local evening newspapers was far higher than it is today. There was no Internet and only two main television channels that had news programmes (BBC1 and ITV).

Desmond Fennell replied for the prosecution. He argued that the principle was that, unless there were very good reasons, a trial should be heard in the area in which the alleged offence occurred. He pointed out that the recent pickets' trials at Mold resulted in acquittals on the most serious charges, demonstrating that jurors there were not biased.[34] He claimed, without any evidence, that the passage of time meant that jurors drawn from the Shrewsbury area would not be prejudiced and were likely to have forgotten press reporting of events a year ago. The DPP's note of the hearing ended simply, 'Without hesitation Mr. Justice MAIS then said, "I am not persuaded that there have been any good reasons advanced for changing the venue." Application refused.'[35]

The Careful Choice of Judge

Just as the prosecution considered the trial venue to be important, so too was the right judge. Superintendent Glover commented in his post-trial report,

It was appreciated at an early date that there would be difficulty in obtaining a judge, the decision having been made that a senior red-robed judge was required for a case of this magnitude and with the obvious political undertones involved.[36]

Judge Hugh Mais was an unusual choice for a case that was expected to involve twenty-four defendants and last six months. He was not a 'senior red-robed judge' of the criminal courts, despite his age (he was sixty-six). He had been appointed to the High Court in 1971 but had not been awarded the customary title for senior, distinguished barristers, of Queen's Counsel. Throughout his career, Mais had appeared mainly in the lower courts and his specialism had been ecclesiastical law, not crime.[37]

David Altaras, a junior barrister at the trial, provided more detail of Mais's background in an interview with the CCRC in 2014. He recalled that Mais 'was not a very bright Judge. He had been on the County Court Bench. He had also been the Head of Chambers at a set in Manchester – he was very reactionary and did not allow any Jews or black people to become members.'[38]

Mais's behaviour in court left a particular mark on Altaras's recollection of the trial:

Given the fact that I regularly adjudicate criminal trials myself I have no hesitation in saying that, during the trial, the Judge's conduct towards the defence frequently crossed the line between permissible and impermissible behaviour and amounted to a display of obvious hostility towards the Defendants. He took particular exception to John Platts-Mills ... and to Des Warren himself. I vividly recall an occasion when Mr Platts-Mills was cross-examining a witness (probably a police officer) and the Judge took off his wig and threw it on the bench in irritation. I recall occasions when he threw his pen down and turned to face the wall when either a defendant was giving evidence or the defence were adducing evidence in cross-examination.[39]

Even Drake admitted much later that Mais was not suitable to preside: 'He was a bad judge for the case. Everyone realised it would be an unusual case. It had been known to Widgery LCJ that it needed a strong judge. Mr Justice Mais immediately volunteered for it.'[40]

Selection of Jurors: Moving the Goalposts

The right to trial by a jury of one's peers in England is a long-standing principle for serious crimes. But the unpredictability of trial by someone's equals has led the state, through the centuries, to restrict jury trials, the category of person who could sit on a jury and the right of the defence to challenge potential jurors.[41]

The defence had a long-standing right to object to up to seven jurors without giving an explanation, the so-called peremptory challenge.[42] At the Mold trials the pickets' lawyers had objected to any juror who listed their occupation as 'building contractor' because they were likely to be hostile to pickets.[43] This may have been an important factor in the pickets' being acquitted of the more serious charges of affray and intimidation. Drake also recognised the importance of the composition of the jury:

> One important issue was challenges to jurors. We had the occupations of jurors at that time. Each defendant was permitted 7 challenges to jurors by the defence without cause. They were always jumping up, for example if it was apparent a juror was a bank manager a defence advocate would jump up and challenge it. It was convention that the Crown would not challenge without giving a specific reason ... The jury at Mold Crown Court were heavily selected by the defence. I thought about this a lot in advance of the Shrewsbury trials in an effort to avoid what would be a huge number of challenges. I thought 'Could we limit it? Why don't we start interfering with jury selection by making challenges?' I discussed it with Desmond Fennell and remember asking Lord Hailsham 'off the cuff' about whether the Crown should interfere with jury selection in order to balance things up a bit.[44]

Drake was in a good position to have 'off-the-cuff' chats with Lord Hailsham as the latter had been head of Drake's chambers,

4 Paper Buildings, during Drake's early career as a barrister.[45] They knew each other well and Drake went on to head the same chambers before he became a High Court judge. They were both Freemasons and mixed in the same circles and networks in legal London.

In preparation for the Shrewsbury trials, Casson & Co. wrote to the court on 13 September to request a copy of the jurors' list so that they could identify jurors that they might want to challenge before the jury was sworn in. Unbeknown to the defence, the rules on juror lists had recently changed. In July 1973 Lord Hailsham, issued a direction under the Courts Act 1971.[46] His direction stated that, in future, the occupation of a juror was not to be published alongside the juror's name. Drake later admitted to the CCRC that Hailsham's direction was prompted by the upcoming Shrewsbury trial.[47]

The direction was criticised when news of it finally emerged. Hailsham had not conducted any prior consultation with the legal profession and other interested bodies, as was customary. The direction was issued at the start of the 'long vacation' in July when, traditionally, the higher courts do not sit and many judges and lawyers who might have questioned it were away on holiday. The pickets' regarded it as a deliberate step by a Conservative Lord Chancellor to change court rules so that the defence could not identify potentially hostile jurors.

Hailsham's decision was the subject of a critical editorial in the *New Law Journal*.[48] It questioned his motives when he changed the procedure without public consultation, 'the Home Secretary, the Attorney-General and a number of judges being the only repositories of the Lord Chancellor's confidence in this matter'. Although the journal did not state the source of this information, it is another example of Home Secretary Carr being involved in decisions that impacted upon the prosecution of the pickets. The editorial noted that the government claimed that the right of peremptory challenge was being abused, but the fact that 'a part, at least, of the Government's disquiet arises from "some cases with political overtones" will do nothing to lessen public concern or, more particularly, lawyers' concern in this matter'.[49] Hailsham's direction was also the subject of questions in the House of Commons on two separate occasions during the pickets' trial. Douglas Mann MP asked the attorney general,

> will he publish the terms of the administrative arrangement made by the Lord Chancellor in July under Section 32 of the Courts Act which deprives the defence of information relating to juror's occupations but leaves it available to the police and, consequently, counsel for the prosecution?

Rawlinson replied,

> if the direction has not been published – I think that it has – I shall see that it is published. However, it is wrong to think that information is denied to one side and not to the other. Neither the prosecution nor the defence now knows the occupation of jurors.[50]

The following month Stanley Clinton Davis MP took up the issue. In reply Rawlinson repeated, 'This information is now denied to both prosecution and defence. What the hon. Gentleman says may equally affect the prosecution.'[51] Notwithstanding Rawlinson's pledge to lodge a copy of the direction in the Commons library it is not available from there.[52] It was not published in the law reports (the *Weekly Law Reports* or the *All England Reports*[53]). There is no copy in the papers of Lord Hailsham at the Cambridge Churchill Archive or within the LCO series at The National Archives. There was no reference to the direction in the standard work on criminal law in England and Wales, *Archbold*, and only a brief mention of it is in the supplement to the thirty-eighth edition.[54] This vital change remains shrouded in secrecy.

Rawlinson stated that the effect of the direction was that the list of potential jurors given to the defence and the prosecution excluded a juror's occupation. Yet the prosecution papers at The National Archives included the names of all twelve jurors empanelled on 3 October 1973 and against each name was their occupation.[55] (The prosecution had the same advantage at the second trial. A list in the DPP's files showed the seating placements of the twelve jurors in the jury box together with their names and occupations, which included a civil engineering maintenance worker, a pipe layer and a building contractor.[56])

Fortification of the Shrewsbury Crown Court Building

The police were able to shape the jury's perception of the pickets through the preparation of the court building. Warren recalled, 'All ground floor windows were boarded up and the police line surrounding it was three deep.'[57] Arnison, a daily visitor to the court, described it as a massive show of police force, 'as if spies, mass murderers or train robbers were on trial.'[58] This was a continuation of the manipulation of the presentation of the case from the start.

At a pre-trial conference with Drake on 17 September 1973 the police discussed the issue of security for the opening of the first trial on 3 October, and did not expect any problems. 'The question of intelligence was mentioned but there was nothing to add to what was already known. It was felt that after an initial demonstration on the opening day any further activity would be ill-supported and sporadic.'[59] Despite this assessment the police ensured a large daily presence. An operational order was issued by Chief Superintendent Barnett on 1 October giving details of 166 police officers who were assigned to the event, led by him.[60]

The heavy security around the court building was not restricted to the opening day, as Platts-Mills recalled:

> Counsel, judge and jury had a similar experience, for ground-floor windows and doors near the courthouse entrance were all boarded up and remained like that throughout the two and a half months of the trial ... The idea can only have been to suggest to the jury that the accused and their friends were uncontrolled hooligans likely at any moment to hurl stones at every piece of glass in sight, or stink bombs at the judge and jury.[61]

The various steps taken before the start of the trial to strengthen the prospects of convictions highlighted the inequality of arms between the prosecution and the defence. The former, with the assistance of the police and court authorities, were able to prepare the trials to favour the Crown. The pickets were tried in a hostile environment that was strengthened by the siege-like arrangements of the court. The attempts by the defence to minimise the potential unfairness, by moving the trial to an alternative venue or to oppose jurors that might be prejudicial, were blocked by the trial judge and the Lord Chancellor respectively. The prosecution had prepared the groundwork and left nothing to chance, but they had not finished. The manipulation of the cases was to continue during the next five months at Shrewsbury Crown Court.

PART IV

The Shrewsbury 24 on Trial

10

The First Trial at
Shrewsbury Crown Court

A march of several thousand trade unionists was held through Shrewsbury on the opening day of the trial, Wednesday 3 October 1973, though solidarity strikes were limited. Holding the trials in a provincial English town like Shrewsbury downplayed the impact of the case. All twenty-four pickets attended, many with their wives and family members. Marlene Tomlinson recalled sitting in the public gallery on the opening day when Jimmy McAlpine came in and sat down in the row in front. She recognised him as he lived in the Wrexham area and was well known. He was chairman of Sir Alfred McAlpine & Son Ltd.

Nine months had passed since Maurice Drake QC and Desmond Fennell held their first conference with the DPP and police to plan the prosecutions. They had become a close-knit legal team and knew that they had the full support of the government. Drake had an arsenal of weapons to bombard the defence with. He had prepared the battle by selecting charges against the pickets that were simple to prove and difficult to defend. Detective Chief Inspector Glover gave him his ace card, John Llywarch's 'statement', which would prove to undermine the defence case and lead to the long prison sentences that were handed down.

The lessons from the Mold trials had been well learned. Drake had lost every case where pickets had been prosecuted for intimidation under Section 7 of the Conspiracy and Protection of Property Act 1875. But he knew that if he had succeeded, the pickets' maximum penalty under the Act was just three months in prison or a twenty-pound fine. Shrewsbury was to be the real showdown; the prosecution wanted convictions that would bring longer prison sentences. The charges which were laid against the six pickets in the first Shrewsbury trial were carefully selected, as was the evidence that was prepared to support them. Drake was determined to succeed.

On paper, the prosecution looked outnumbered. The Crown was represented by a QC and two junior barristers, Fennell and Wadsworth. They faced twelve counsel on the other side. The six pickets to be tried first were each represented by a senior barrister, usually a QC, and by a junior barrister.[1] This may appear to have favoured the defence but it disguised the control and understanding that the prosecution had in planning every aspect of the trials.

Defence Kept in the Dark

The twenty-four building workers had all been committed for trial on 15 June and knew that they were charged with 190 offences between them.[2] During the summer they were kept in the dark about the way that their trial was going to proceed. Casson & Co. complained to the DPP on 4 September that it had been a year since the alleged offences had occurred and they were still unaware whether the prosecution intended to proceed against six pickets first or all twenty-four, and which of the many charges they would face in court.[3] It was not until mid-September that the DPP informed them that there would be two trials (later three) and that the first trial, of the six so-called ringleaders, would be limited to just three charges. This was when the twenty-four also learned that Drake had added the offence of unlawful assembly.[4] This deliberate lack of cooperation by the DPP and Drake prejudiced each defendant. Until the pickets' lawyers knew the exact case that they had to face in court they did not know the extent of the preparations that had to be made for a trial that was to start in less than three weeks' time.

Drake's Selection and Presentation of the Charges

One of the enduring legacies of the Shrewsbury trials was the charging of trade unionists with conspiracy. Many believed that this was based upon the Conspiracy and Protection of Property Act 1875 and it led later to calls for the Act to be repealed. This was an understandable mistake because although all twenty-four were originally *charged* with intimidation under Section 7 of the Act, none of them was *tried* for it at Shrewsbury.[5] But charging them with all these offences had a propaganda value when reported in the local newspapers. It conveyed the impression to the public, including jurors, that the accused were major criminals.

> *Conspiracy and Protection of Property Act 1875, section 7*
>
> Every person who, with a view to compel any other person to abstain from doing or to do any act which such other person has a legal right to do or abstain from doing, wrongfully and, without legal authority –
>
> (1) Uses violence to or intimidates such other person or his wife or children, or injures his property ...
>
> shall, on conviction thereof by a court of summary jurisdiction, or on indictment as hereinafter mentioned, be liable either to pay a penalty not exceeding twenty pounds, or to be imprisoned for a term not exceeding three months, with or without hard labour.

Drake proceeded instead to prosecute the six for three *common law* offences: conspiracy, affray and unlawful assembly. This was judge-made law, which the courts had fashioned through a series of cases over several centuries. These were vague offences and allowed the prosecution to bring forward a mass of generalised evidence to paint a picture of criminality for which the six were to blame. It did not require specific eyewitness evidence against the six other than that they were present on a particular site.

Drake regarded the offence of 'conspiracy to intimidate' to be a free-standing common law offence that could be charged even if the 1875 Act did not exist. The offence he used was not a 'conspiracy to commit the Section 7 offence'. No reference to

Section 7 or any other part of the Act was necessary. Intimidation was a common law offence before 1875 and had not been expressly abolished by the Act. Therefore a 'conspiracy to intimidate' remained a valid charge against trade unionists when they picketed. It highlighted the hidden dangers of 'the common law'.

On the opening day of the trial the defence applied to have the count of 'conspiracy to intimidate' struck out because the six pickets were charged with multiple counts of committing the actual offence of intimidation under Section 7. Drake argued that the seriousness of the six pickets' behaviour could not be dealt with adequately by simply prosecuting them under Section 7 as the maximum sentence was limited to just three months. The sentence for a conviction for conspiracy was unlimited – it was whatever the trial judge thought was appropriate. Judge Mais dismissed the defence application.

Table 4 sets out the total number of charges that each of the six pickets faced. The wording of the three counts for which they were prosecuted shows how vague they were.

Count 1, conspiracy to intimidate, specifically that they

> on divers days between the 1st day of July 1972 and the 31st day of October 1972 in the County of Salop and elsewhere conspired together and with others not before the Court wrongfully and without legal authority to intimidate those working on building sites in the County of Salop and elsewhere with a view to compelling them to abstain from their lawful work.

Count 2, that they

> together with others not before the Court on the 6th day of September 1972 in the County of Salop unlawfully assembled with intent to carry out a common purpose in such a manner as to endanger the public peace.

Count 3, that they

> together with others not before the Court on the 6th day of September 1972 on divers building sites in the County of Salop unlawfully fought and made an affray.

Table 4: Summary of the type and number of charges against each picket in the forty-two counts of the first indictment

Offence	John Carpenter	John McKinsie Jones	John Llywarch	Ken O'Shea	Eric Tomlinson	Des Warren	Total of each offence
Conspiracy to intimidate	1	1	1	1	1	1	6
Affray	1	1	1	1	1	1	6
Unlawful assembly	1	1	1	1	1	1	6
Intimidation (Section 7 of the 1875 Act)	6	6	6	7	9	12	46
Damaging property	–	3	–	1	5	8	17
Attempting to damage property	–	–	–	–	–	2	2
Common assault	–	–	–	–	2	2	4
Threatening to damage property	–	–	–	1	1	1	3
Assault occasioning ABH	–	–	–	–	1	–	1
Using threatening words	–	–	–	1	–	–	1
Totals	9	12	9	13	21	28	92

Source: compiled from the indictment, TNA J182/9

The other charges were mainly *statutory* offences, based upon an Act of Parliament, such as the Criminal Damage Act 1971, and were much more specific. The defendant could understand exactly what they were being accused of doing, when and where they allegedly did it. These charges would be easier to defend, as they had been at Mold, particularly as the police report had stated that 'the evidence against the organisers and leaders was not so strong.' Drake did not proceed with these charges, though; they were left to 'lie on the file'.[6]

Common Law: Conspiracy to Intimidate

The wording of the conspiracy charge criminalised all the activity of the six in 1972 (1 July to 31 October) to build support for the strike and to persuade non-strikers to stop work. The implication of the conspiracy count was that any trade union official, whether shop steward, branch official or full-time officer, who organised any action where there may be disruption, allegations of intimidation or criminal damage, could be accused of conspiring to commit those acts even if they played no direct part in them personally.

The essential *act* of the crime of conspiracy is an *agreement*, but differing views were expressed by the police and the prosecution about the time, place and nature of that agreement by the pickets. It was alleged that it took place over a period of four months, but the main focus of the trial was the picketing in Shropshire on one day, 6 September, which had been organised at a meeting of the North Wales and Chester Area Strike Committee in the Bull and Stirrup pub. The police report had noted that

> the Chairman, LLYWARCH, raised the matter at Chester on Thursday, 31st August, 1972. At the same time, he produced and read a press item from the local 'Shropshire Star' newspaper in which it was said that 300 workmen at Shrewsbury were 'ready and waiting' to oppose any attempt by pickets to close the site.
>
> A vote was taken and the outcome was unanimous – that as many pickets as possible from the constituent Strike Action

Committees would attend at Oswestry on Wednesday, 6th September 1972, to picket Shrewsbury and 'stop the sites'. Telford does not appear to have been mentioned at that stage ...

This resolution – and the vote taken on it – proved to be the blueprint for the serious disorder and widespread fear which subsequently took place on 6th September 1972.[7]

It was argued for John McKinsie Jones that he could not be guilty of conspiracy to intimidate because he did not go upstairs to the meeting. He had decided to go home from the pub before the meeting started as he, as the committee treasurer, had just been given a sizeable collection from steelworkers at Shotton. Ken O'Shea did not attend the meeting either. The police accepted that they had no evidence that the pickets had hatched a plan at the Chester meeting or anywhere else to intimidate non-strikers in 'the County of Salop and elsewhere'. And the 'decision to go to Telford appears to have been equally spontaneous and neither a majority of pickets nor the coach operators knew of this beforehand'.[8] The police had concluded that, due to the weakness of the evidence about the Chester meeting, and 'taking account of the spontaneous element in the disorders, *conspiracy is not strongly recommended*'.[9]

Drake dealt with these reservations and objections in his opening speech to the court, highlighting the vagueness of the offence of conspiracy. He set out how he intended to prove his case:

The prosecution in this case will not bring before you any evidence of these six men, or any of them, sitting down or being present at some meeting where a formal agreement to terrify, to intimidate other workers was worked out. But you are entitled to see what happened to judge their actions and conduct and ask yourselves at the end is there not a compelling inference here that these men did at some time join together in one common accord?[10]

So for Drake, a conspiracy to intimidate was not formed at the Chester meeting from a discussion and an agreement between the strikers to go picketing. Instead, the conspiracy was formed through the knowledge that the six leaders had of the behaviour of many of the 250 pickets when they got off the coaches and went onto the building sites in Shrewsbury and Telford. Drake did not have to prove that the six 'ringleaders' had committed any specific act other than to lead the men. This approach would cover all the picketing throughout north Wales during the strike.

Drake just needed to call witnesses, lots of witnesses, to say that damage was caused and non-strikers were frightened by all these pickets. Although none of the police had written in their statements that they had seen any violence, they would be encouraged to say in court that the atmosphere on the day was menacing. The six would be held responsible for the conduct of fellow pickets, none of whom needed to be named or identified.

Warren's barrister, John Platts-Mills QC, argued that there was no planned violence and that any incidents were spontaneous and episodic by just a few pickets. In his later reflections on the case, he acknowledged that this was not enough to defeat a charge of conspiracy:

> It is the rarest thing to have direct evidence of a clandestine meeting to plot events. Once the events have taken place, and if they show a series of wrongful acts, it is easy enough to infer that they were agreed in advance. Mr Drake told the jury ... that to establish conspiracy he need not prove that there was a meeting or a decision of the wrong-doers. It was enough to show that the illegal events complained of had a common pattern and were done by men acting together. From this, a conspiratorial agreement could be inferred. 'A nod or a wink' would do, and you don't even need an independent witness to prove the nod or wink.[11]

The pickets and their witnesses emphasised that there was never any agreement at the Chester meeting or anywhere else during the strike that they were going to use violence. The purpose of a mass picket was to inspire the trade union members in the area and to persuade the non-members to support the strike.[12] During the most active period, August and September, Warren and others would visit sites to address the workers. He would speak with the site agent and persuade them to sign up to the terms of the national agreement. He would encourage workers to join a trade union, elect representatives and send delegates to the area action committee. Warren recognised that trade unionism could only flourish and become permanent if workers were persuaded of the case for combining and acting collectively. A single visit to a site that was just a show of force to stop people working for a day would not achieve that.

Warren denied that he had used violence or seen anyone else behaving violently or damaging property in Shropshire. It was a normal day's picketing. He claimed that Chief Superintendent Meredith had shaken his hand as he left Telford on 6 September. Platts-Mills later wrote of his cross-examination of Meredith on this point,

> He answered, 'Yes, I did go to Warren and shake his hand, as one would with any member of the criminal fraternity.' Whether he meant that this was his hopeful approach to receiving a bribe or that he expected a few stolen diamonds to fall from the cuff of any building worker was not clear. When I suggested it was an absurdity, he said that he had not really shaken hands with Warren. He had merely put out a hand to detain him.[13]

A major line of defence that Platts-Mills put forward for Warren was to contrast the alleged criminal actions of the pickets with the actions of building employers that caused the industry to have the highest rates of fatalities and serious injuries in the British economy.[14] He argued that lumpers were evading tax and much of their work was shoddy and in breach of the building regulations. It followed that the charge of a 'conspiracy to intimidate workers from following their lawful employment' was improper because the lumpers were not working lawfully. He also tried to appeal to the jury that the illegal activities of each lumper meant that 'other taxpayers pay more to make up for him.' Platts-Mills asked Warren about the speech he made to the building workers on the Brookside site about the vagaries of the lump:

DW: I pointed out the evils of the lump and at first what the men were concerned with was money. I pointed out it was more than money. The £30 for a 35 hour week was a slogan [*sic*]. You couldn't write on a banner all the evils of the lump. I pointed out, you know the housing problem, the millions of people living in sub-standard homes and pointed out that building workers had obligations to society, not just to themselves and their pay packet.

JPM: Did you point out any common denominator amongst all the lumpers that they had in common?

[DW]: Only one thing they have in common, that is greed.

MR JUSTICE MAIS: I told you in my view the lump was somewhat irrelevant to this case. I thought we had exhausted all the various matters about the lump again and again and again.

DW: It is far from irrelevant.[15]

A second line of argument was picked up by Charles Hall, the DPP's clerk at the trial, who wrote to Walker, 'Platts Mills QC who leads the defence team, is suggesting that the leaders of the pickets were acting on union instructions, and carrying out union policy, and it was a few extremists among the pickets who caused all the damage.'[16] This approach played into the prosecution's hands, even though Platts-Mills's client, Des Warren, denied that there was any violence or damage done by pickets. Warren repeatedly pointed out that there were no arrests or cautions on the day and no police officer complained to him about any damage caused by pickets.

Drake presented a very simple picture to the jury: 'lots of witnesses will say that property was damaged and they were threatened and frightened by pickets; that's not right, someone must be held criminally liable.' If the six leaders were admitting that this happened, even if it was done by a few, unidentified extremists, they were responsible for organising it all. It did not matter whether the unions condoned it.

Years later, Platts-Mills acknowledged that he might have been overconfident, though this offered precious little comfort to the six men who went to prison:

Throughout the trial, I had thought that the defendants would all get off. The evidence was poor and the jury was sensible. Towards the end, it seemed possible that with the judge's hostility and the over-vigorous presentation of the defence, we might have brought on our own conviction.[17]

The recollection of one of the opposing barristers, James Wadsworth, was that the prosecution was confident throughout the trial of obtaining guilty verdicts. In an interview with the CCRC in 2014 he told them, 'I felt that the defendants got nowhere near addressing what was a strong case against them.'[18]

The Prosecution 'Offer a Deal'?

Tomlinson later wrote that, just before the trial started, when the six men were downstairs in the interview rooms, his barrister, Keith McHale, came to tell them that the prosecution had offered a deal: agree to plead guilty and they would all be fined fifty pounds, which the unions would pay. 'He gave us each time to think about it, but I already knew my answer. We took a vote. Four of the lads were in favour of taking the deal. Dezzie and I were opposed.'[19] He stated that the four changed their minds when they saw how resolute their two co-accused were.

Tomlinson's trial had taken place thirty years before his book was written and some of his recollections may have been confused. The court records show that McHale did not attend the first day of the trial. During my interviews with two of Tomlinson's co-accused in the first trial, Ken O'Shea and John McKinsie Jones, I asked them about his suggestion that the prosecution had offered a deal. They had no recollection of such an offer or of participating in a vote on anything. Jones informed me that he had mentioned this to his trial barrister, Geoffrey Kilfoil, at a meeting in Chester in 2016, and Kilfoil likewise had no recollection that such a deal was offered to the six men at any time during the first trial. Neither Warren nor Platts-Mills make any mention of it in their autobiographies.[20] The solicitors from Casson & Co. and Walker, Smith & Way that I spoke with did not recall any deal being offered at the first trial either. McHale was interviewed by the CCRC on 17 March 2014 and made no mention of it; neither did his junior, David Altaras, who was interviewed on 19 May 2014. The police, the DPP and Drake had spent a year preparing for this case at great cost and were ready. It is unlikely that the government, which had supported the prosecutions politically and financially, was going to lose its nerve at this point and give it all up for £300.

Jim Arnison attended every day of the trials as a journalist for the *Morning Star* and had known Warren for many years. He wrote a book, *The Shrewsbury Three*, which was published in March 1974. It made no mention of a deal at the start of the first trial but in the postscript he does refer to a deal at the start of the second trial. This was offered to the other eighteen pickets, when they were aware of the fate of their six colleagues. A number of them agreed to change their plea to guilty of unlawful assembly to avoid a prison sentence and the remaining charges were left on the file. The state was willing to offer a deal at this stage because it had got what it wanted from the first trial, three pickets in jail.

Drake's Opening Speech

On the opening day of the trial, after defence objections to Drake's indictment were rejected by Mais, the six men entered their pleas to the long list of charges. The following morning a jury was sworn in and then, at 11:45 a.m., Drake got up and began his opening address. He continued for the rest of the day and into the next,[21] spending five hours outlining the prosecution's case to the jury. A report in the following day's *Times* was typical of many, headlined 'Terrifying display of violence by "flying pickets" at building sites, prosecution says.'[22] According to Drake, the pickets moved across Shropshire like an 'expeditionary force'. He told the jury that witnesses would describe the pickets as like 'a mad horde, a bunch of Apache Indians – a frenzied mob'. Once Drake had painted this colourful picture, he would argue that the six leaders were responsible for the 'mob', even if it was not their intention to create a 'terrifying display of violence' or take part in such alleged violence themselves. He even introduced the common caricature of a conspiracy known to every British schoolchild:

> One thinks of Guy Fawkes, as we are approaching November, and gun-powder, treason and plot, conspiring in some dark cellar, there round a table hatching the plot. But it is not as complicated as that. A conspiracy in itself is no more than an agreement, a common consent between two or more people.[23]

John Llywarch's Damning 'Evidence'

Towards the end of his opening address to the court, Drake pulled his masterstroke. He had John Llywarch's unsigned statement distributed to the twelve jurymen and then he proceeded to read out the whole nine-page document, word for word.[24] Llywarch's barrister, Sir Arthur Irvine QC, raised no objection to this.[25] Two weeks later Llywarch sacked him and two junior barristers represented him from then on.[26] Irvine's decision not to raise an objection was a serious mistake as the statement was to have a devastating impact upon the pickets' case. It was a focal point throughout the trial, as Llywarch's presence in the dock alongside his five co-accused was a daily reminder to the jury of what he was alleged to have told the police. In answer to later cross-examination Llywarch agreed that '95% of it is true'.[27] The parts of the statement that Llywarch disputed were the comments made about named pickets.[28]

According to Arnison, Llywarch's 'statement to the police … was one of the most damaging pieces of evidence against Warren and Tomlinson'.[29] Llywarch had been interviewed on Friday 3 November 1972 as a potential prosecution witness by two senior officers, Detective Chief Superintendent Hodges and Detective Chief Inspector Glover. Afterwards Glover prepared a nine-page witness statement from his notes, which he planned to get Llywarch to sign at a later date. In the intervening period Llywarch had heard of the questioning of his fellow pickets, including the arrest of six of them. The union was advising all its members not to sign any statement or document from the police. Llywarch telephoned the police and told them he was not going to sign anything. He returned to the police station on 30 November, when Glover read out the typed statement to him in the presence of Inspector Powell. Llywarch maintained his stance and would not sign it. Only then was he cautioned and then questioned by the two officers for an hour.[30] Glover wrote at the end of the statement that Llywarch 'agreed with its accuracy but refused to sign'.[31]

Llywarch had not been cautioned before the start of his interview with the police on 3 November and was not advised of his right to have a solicitor present. He was not aware of the risk of self-incrimination when discussing the events of 6 September.[32] Despite being cautioned on 30 November he was not listed as a potential defendant when the DPP opened its file on the pickets a month later. In court Glover claimed that when he first interviewed Llywarch he did not have any reasonable grounds for charging him.[33] It was only at the conference with Drake on 1 February 1973 that a decision was taken to charge him.

Drake was able to read out Llywarch's purported statement because Glover would be giving sworn evidence in court that the document had been written by him from the information that Llywarch had volunteered on 3 November. (This was in the days before routine tape recording of interviews.) The statement recounted the incident at the first Shrewsbury site, Kingswood, where a contractor pulled out a shotgun from his car, which the pickets took from him and broke in half. It then continued, 'After this gun incident, the pickets went really beserk. There were windows smashed, machines smashed, scaffolding pulled down, and a lot of obscene shouting. I cannot identify anyone responsible.'[34] In describing the pickets at Brookside the statement said, 'They swarmed across it like a load of madmen and I've never seen anything like it in my life, I saw walls pushed over and scaffolding pulled down. I don't know which coaches these madmen got off, but it was the same crowd the whole time.'

In his evidence in court Llywarch maintained that Warren was not a violent man and did not threaten anyone. Llywarch was asked about his police interview and whether Glover showed a particular interest in Warren. Llywarch replied,

> He [Glover] said that he knew that he was one of the ring leaders and that he would find some way of getting him put away.
> Q. Was it suggested that it might do you good to help put him away?
> A. Yes. I was told that if I said what they wanted me to say I would not even be charged.[35]

Drake's questioning of him included the supposed reasons why he would not sign the statement. He referred Llywarch to his interview with Glover and Powell on 30 November where they said he told them that if he signed it there were men on the Wrexham bypass site who would have him off the site and he would end up in hospital.

The use of Llywarch and his purported statement was one of the most manipulative acts of the prosecution at the trial. By placing him in the dock next to his five co-accused the jury were given a daily reminder of the statement that the police claimed that he made to them. It did not matter whether Llywarch was convicted or not as he was not the main target of the prosecution. The police report did not identify any evidence that Llywarch had committed any specific offences.

Well-Hung Game

While the prosecution had consistency, the pickets' representation was less-so. Drake and Fennell attended every single day of the first trial; Wadsworth missed just five of the fifty-five days that the court sat. Three defence QCs, Platts-Mills, Turner Samuels and Owen, missed the opening three days of the trial. The latter, representing Ken O'Shea, did not arrive until the afternoon of Monday 22 October. Keith McHale QC, representing Tomlinson, missed twenty-two days of the trial, mostly at the start.

The confrontations that took place in court between the two legal teams over many weeks disguised the harmonious relationships between them. Peter Hain, who defended himself at an Old Bailey trial in 1972 on a charge of conspiracy, had experienced such behaviour:

> One of the specific problems from the defendant's standpoint is what appears to be an unhealthy close relationship between prosecuting and defending counsel ... As spectators at their trials defendants realize that their defence counsel have more in common with the prosecutors than with them. Indeed, they can be seen having a smoke together during an adjournment or chatting intimately together over lunch! In a political trial, what is to the defendant a 'war' seems merely like a game to the barristers, which also means that the latter are very reluctant to press the political cause of a defendant.[36]

This culture was confirmed in Platts-Mills's recollections of the trial. Disagreements between the two sides and with Judge Mais were not going to interfere with the etiquette of the Bar:

> I have not before seen a judge sulk. In spite of that, relations between Bench and Bar remained normal and in every other way there was total courtesy on both sides in the courtroom. The judge had counsel to lunch and to supper at his lodging; we had him to dine in mess.
>
> One of our more distinguished counsel was Tom Rhys-Roberts ... he would occasionally invite all counsel, including the prosecution, to a feast at a convenient hotel. It was based upon some delicacy such as venison or wild swan or hare from his family estate in Wales. The meat was hung to the point where it dropped from the hook and each feast was presided over by Mrs Rhys-Roberts ... The trial proved to be a long one, but for us it was shortened by these interludes.[37]

Witness Evidence: Prosecution Blitz

On the eve of the trial the DPP served a list of 246 witness statements that it intended to rely upon. In the end 157 witnesses gave evidence for the prosecution. The penultimate witness was Chief Inspector Glover, who took the stand at 12:10 p.m. on Monday 12 November and finished at 11:50 a.m. the next day. Through four and an half hours of questioning by Drake and the pickets' barristers he was able to wrap up the prosecution's case: that Shropshire had been invaded by a bunch of violent pickets from Liverpool and north Wales, terrorising the hard-working folk of Shrewsbury and Telford, organised and led by the six in the dock.

The defence did not reply in kind. Each of the six accused pickets took the stand except Ken O'Shea, who was advised by his lawyers that the prosecution evidence against him was so thin he didn't need to rebut it on the stand. Apart from their own evidence the pickets relied upon just three other witnesses: Alan Abrahams, UCATT North West Regional Council member and chairman of the North West Regional Action Committee during the strike; Peter Moroney, a T&GWU member and a labourer on the Wrexham bypass site who had been acquitted at the third Mold trial; and Barry Scragg, a UCATT shop steward, employed by a contractor at the Shotton steelworks.

Not surprisingly, Drake was hostile to Abrahams. He asked him why he had been demonstrating outside the court on the opening day of the trial, to which Abrahams replied, 'To bring the maximum public attention to the fact that six building workers had been arrested and charged with Conspiracy.' He reinforced the pickets' case, that the meeting at the Bull and Stirrup was a normal trade union meeting that had decided to send pickets to Oswestry. Abrahams then went on to emphasise the sinister aspect of the prosecution:

> I know that trade unionists attended a meeting in Chester during a national official dispute, they were asked to picket and they did so on behalf of the union … The result of being involved in picketing on an official strike is that they were charged with conspiracy when they attend[ed] an official Trade Union meeting.[38]

In one part of Abrahams cross-examination, he explained that the decisions of the action committees on where to picket were not clandestine, but often shared with the local police: 'Wherever possible we informed the police that we would be picketing. It was a tactic that was used during the strike that would normally double the size of the picket.' He went on to clarify this: 'I am saying that the police doubled the number of pickets. If they had 200 and we had 200 there, there would be 400 in total. Q. You were using the police as pickets? A. Yes.'[39]

It has been claimed that one of the pickets in the dock at the first Shrewsbury trial was a police informant, but my extensive research has not located any evidence to support this allegation.[40] Abrahams open evidence at the trial showed why the police often had a presence at building sites that the pickets visited – it was union policy to inform them.

It was not as if the defence was short of other witnesses. A number of the remaining eighteen men had offered to give evidence, as had other building workers who had gone picketing in north Wales and Shropshire during the strike. Ted Hughes, Wrexham and Oswestry district secretary of the T&GWU, made a statement on 20 September 1973 in support of his two members and said he'd be willing to attend the trial to give evidence. The defence could have called several dozen witnesses to rebut the prosecution case, but chose not to do so. Instead, the jury were left to believe that the pickets on trial had few people to support them on the witness stand.

John McKinsie Jones vividly recalled to me his frustration at not being listened to by his lawyers. During the trial he frequently sent notes to them challenging the evidence that was being given by prosecution witnesses. He was told by his counsel that although the information was important it was best that he did not raise any issues of clarification as it put the spotlight on him. His barrister's view was that every day John's name was not mentioned, the better it was for his case.

Destruction of Initial Witness Statements

When Chief Constable Willison had sent his reports to the DPP in December 1972 he had highlighted a problem with witness evidence: 'The officers are in no doubt that there may be some difficulties in identification after this lapse of time.'[41] His assessment was based upon the interviews that his officers had conducted in which many witnesses could not give a clear description of any particular picket. What was unknown to the defence at the time, and was only discovered by me in The National Archives in 2013, was that the police had later revised the witness statements that had been taken originally during their investigations in autumn 1972. (My find proved to be the crucial evidence that was to lead to the quashing of all the pickets' convictions nearly forty-eight years later.) A letter for Desmond Fennell, who could not attend a conference with Drake and the police two weeks before the start of the Shrewsbury trials, included a two-page summary of the issues that had been discussed. Crucially, paragraph sixteen reported,

> So that Counsel would be aware it was mentioned that not all original hand written [*sic*] statements were still in existence, some having been destroyed after a fresh statement had been obtained. In most cases the first statement was taken before photographs were available for witnesses and before the Officers taking the statements knew what we were trying to prove.[42]

The destruction of original handwritten statements was improper as it deprived the defence of sight of the initial recollections of witnesses.[43] It is a fundamental principle of evidence that a person's immediate memories of an event are superior to any later attempts to recall what happened and what any particular person looked like or said.

The West Mercia police had amended statements after they 'knew what we were trying to prove'. This confirmed that the police, after their initial evidence-gathering, did not have a case against any of the pickets, just like their counterparts in other parts of England discussed in Chapter 6. The police therefore decided to construct a case by reinterviewing witnesses and steering their evidence with the use of photographs taken by *Shropshire Star* journalists and police photographers.[44] The police put numbers and arrows on the photographs and then questioned the witnesses again. According to Warren, 'Platts-Mills later succeeded in getting James to tell how police had shown him photographs of myself and other pickets and pressurised him to make allegations against us.'[45] James had complained that his interview with the police, when they were trying to make him identify pickets in photographs, was like being interviewed by the Gestapo.[46]

Warren wrote that the prosecution witnesses were coached to identify him, to support the police narrative that he was the leader of pickets terrorising non-strikers. Just before each witness entered court to give evidence the police showed them marked photographs of the pickets on trial to 'refresh' their memories and gave them copies of their statements that they had made months after the events in question.[47]

On a number of occasions, when the pickets' lawyers asked a witness about the existence of earlier statements, they were led off the scent by Drake and Judge Mais.[48] On one occasion Mais, after a lengthy exchange in front of the jury, criticised the questioning of James: 'Mr Turner-Samuel, it is a most outrageous suggestion, isn't it, to suggest this man's statement has been altered without his consent.'[49]

When PC Jones was being questioned, Drake intervened to say, 'It is true, all the witness statements which the defence are not [sic] entitled to see we have said that they are made available.'[50] Drake was aware that 'earlier statements', which the police had destroyed, could not be made available, but he kept that from the judge and jury. The prejudice that the pickets faced was in not being able to question witnesses about the evidence they had just given in court compared with evidence that they had given when they had first been interviewed by the police.

These points were not lost on the police witnesses at Shrewsbury. Drake's questioning allowed them to embellish their written witness statements, none of which stated that they had seen any acts of violence by any picket. But in court they emphasised that they felt terrorised by the behaviour of the pickets. Keith McHale questioned DCI Lewis about his statement, in which the police officer had recalled the pickets shouting 'Out, out' at the Mount site. Lewis agreed but then added, 'mingled with: "Kill, kill, kill." That was another expression I heard.' McHale challenged him about these additional words as they were not in his original statement. Lewis agreed but replied, 'It is apparently omitted from my statement.'[51]

Earlier, Platts-Mills had an exchange with Sergeant Hartland, who had told the court, in answer to questioning by Drake about the pickets at Brookside, 'Their whole attitude frightened me ... They just ignored us, they brushed us aside as though we were not there.' Platts-Mills asked whether he was frightened at being ignored, to which Hartland replied, 'No ... I was frightened for my own safety and the safety of my fellow officers.'[52] This was also used by the police to justify why they did not arrest anyone on the day. They were too frightened! The mettle of West Mercia police was in sharp contrast to other police forces in Britain in 1972, when arrests were made by a handful of officers from among a group of several dozen pickets.

Clifford Growcott: Prosecution Star Witness

The allegations of Clifford Growcott were central to the case against the pickets. He was a general labourer on the McAlpine site at Brookside in Telford. He was anti-union, a lump worker with no interest in either health and safety or his fellow workers. He featured in articles in the *Shropshire Star* and the *Daily Mail* in September 1972.[53] Subsequent newspaper reports and speeches by Conservative MPs would often make reference to a building worker who, variously, lost an eye, lost the sight in one eye or suffered damaged vision.[54] This was even repeated by Tom Breakell, president of the electricians' union (the EEPTU), when speaking at the TUC Congress in September 1975.[55]

Prosecution photographs of the Brookside site showed police standing at the back of a meeting of pickets and non-strikers that was addressed by Warren and others. Growcott is pictured standing in the crowd listening to the speakers, along with many other building workers. The scene appears peaceful, a typical outdoor mass meeting at a workplace. Growcott claimed that he was struck by mud and pulled down from the scaffolding on which he was working. At the end of the mass meeting all the site workers went home. Growcott was in a works Land Rover when Chief Superintendent Meredith spoke with him and offered to take him to the hospital. At first he agreed to go and walked with Meredith to a waiting police car. 'When he saw the police car he immediately turned back and stated that he was not going to hospital and did not want to be involved with the police.'[56] Crucially, in Growcott's statement and his evidence in court he could not identify that any of the six pickets on trial were the persons who had hit him.[57]

The *Shropshire Star* report of 7 September 1972 noted that Growcott 'has been told that damage to his eye, which was hurt when he was hit on the head with a brick and then kicked, is not permanent'. Growcott was quoted as saying, 'I was getting very worried, and although I may have to wear glasses for a while it's better than not being able to see out of the eye at all.' The medical evidence presented at the trial gave a more accurate picture. Dr Mario Galvao was a casualty officer on duty on 6 September at the Royal Salop Infirmary when Growcott was brought in. He confirmed that there were no internal or external signs of head injury and that he could not find any neurological signs of head injury. He agreed that he had to rely upon Growcott's self-reporting of having a severe headache and from that Galvao concluded that he had suffered a head injury. He could not find signs that Growcott had suffered an eye injury.

Another doctor who treated Growcott was a house surgeon, Julia Garden. She was interviewed at Copthorne Hospital on 1 December 1972. In her statement, she recalled that Growcott was admitted to the hospital from the Casualty Department on 6 September following a head injury. He was discharged a week later. She noted, 'An ophthalmic opinion was obtained but it was said that there was no clinical abnormality and his condition improved over the next week.'[58] Growcott was in no rush to leave hospital when he had had a visit from a Fleet Street journalist and photographer. His employer, McAlpine, said, 'He will be treated as a member of the permanent staff and be paid his average weekly earnings.'[59]

In his evidence, Growcott, speaking a year after the event,

stated, 'I have been told that my sight will return. I am nearly sure that I am registered 5% disabled.'[60] Later in his evidence he admitted, 'The doctor said, yes, that they couldn't find anything at all wrong with my eye, that was about, let's see, that was at the time of the accident.'[61] The objective evidence about Growcott indicated that he suffered a temporary disturbance to his vision from which he was expected to make a full recovery. Yet this was not the conclusion of Conservative MPs or of press reports, which instead spoke of someone suffering loss of sight.[62]

When John Bithell, a labourer, was interviewed by Inspector Powell and DC Jones outside Flint British Legion Club on 16 November 1972, he told them that he had been on an official picket on 6 September but had nothing more to say without a solicitor. He did tell them, though, 'The only damage I saw was done by lumpers. That chap GROWCOTT who I read about in the Liverpool Post as being injured, he caused all the damage on that site, he was throwing bricks at us.'[63] Neither Bithell or any other picket was called by the defence to give evidence for the six on trial to describe the behaviour of the lump workers on the Brookside site and elsewhere.

Red under the Bed

Drake concluded the prosecution case on Tuesday 13 November 1973. On that day the television listings section in the *Shropshire Star* highlighted a programme that was to be shown on ITV that evening, *Red under the Bed*.[64] It was made by Anglia Television and presented by former Labour MP Woodrow Wyatt. The film argued that the Communist Party and various Trotskyist organisations were trying, covertly, to win influence within trade unions and workplaces to achieve their goal of the overthrow of the government.

The programme was broadcast at 10:30 p.m. It opened with a sweeping shot of police lines outside the Shire Hall, home to Shrewsbury Crown Court and the magistrates' courts, taken on 15 March 1973, when the twenty-four pickets appeared at the magistrates' court for the first time. The film included footage of picketing during the building workers' strike and other disputes. At the end of the programme most ITV regions broadcast a thirty-minute studio discussion of the film. The panel of five included Wyatt, Alan Fisher (general secretary of the National Union of Public Employees), Lord McCarthy (an industrial relations academic) and two MPs, Barbara Castle (Labour) and Geoffrey Stewart-Smith (Conservative). The latter, publisher of the anti-communist *East–West Digest*, was given the last word in the discussion. He made explicit reference to the involvement of communists in the area action committees of the building workers' trade unions:

> The violence in the building strike was caused by a group, the Building Workers Charter, operating in defiance of their union leadership, indulging in violence and flying pickets, and this is an example of these people operating, opposing free trades unions, opposing the Labour Party.[65]

The day after it was shown the defence made an application for the two television companies to be summonsed to court to answer a charge of contempt, as the programme was an interference in the proper course of justice. The application, in the name of John Carpenter, claimed that the programme prejudiced the fair trial of the case and wrongfully influenced the jury, because sections of the programme showed

a   Warren and Carpenter
b   the Shrewsbury Crown Court
c   violence and damage alleged to be caused by pickets on building sites during the National Building Strike of 1972
d   violence and damage alleged to be caused by pickets during a recent coal strike and during a recent dock strike
e   commentary containing allegations of a communist conspiracy to infiltrate a number of Trade Unions including the Building Trades unions
f   commentary containing allegations that official strike Action Committees formed for the purpose of the said building strike were all controlled by communists.[66]

The film showed four of the six pickets on trial at the head of the demonstration, walking towards the court buildings. The jurors had been attending the trial for six weeks and would now be very familiar with the court building and the six on trial.

A summons was served on Barry Milne of Anglia Television to attend court and to produce a copy of the film. The application could not be heard until Thursday 15 November as Judge Mais and the jury were on a visit to the building sites in Shrewsbury and Telford, following the route taken by the pickets on 6 September. Remarkably, none of the pickets attended, on the advice of their lawyers. The junior prosecution counsel, James Wadsworth, remembered the visit for producing one of the lighter moments of the trial, though unreported: 'I recall that on a site visit the jury put a sign out of the back of one [sic] the coach they were in that said "The Flying Jurors". I recall the judge was not very impressed.'[67]

When the trial resumed Mais viewed the film in chambers and considered Carpenter's contempt application. Afterwards he dismissed the defence's application without any recorded explanation. Crucially, the jury were not asked whether they had seen the programme. There was no inquiry with them about the possible impact that the film might have made. According to Glover, Mais was annoyed at the application: 'The film was shown in chambers and the Judge expressed some displeasure at this action of the Defence.'[68]

Carpenter's lawyers had prepared a witness statement in his name in support of the contempt application. It ended, 'There followed an uneventful discussion about the programme described above.'[69] This was a gross misjudgment, though the lawyers did not have the benefit of tape or digital recording in 1973 to review the programme before drafting the contempt application. 'Uneventful' was not the view of those who were behind the making of the programme. I secured the release of a file of documents about the programme, compiled by the Cabinet Office,[70] beginning with an internal Information Research Department memo from T. C. Barker to the head of the IRD, Norman Reddaway:

We had a discreet but considerable hand in this programme ... In February Mr Wyatt approached us direct for help. We consulted the Department of Employment and the Security Service through Mr Conrad Heron's group ... With their agreement, Mr Wyatt was given a large dossier of our own background material. It is clear from internal evidence in the programme that he drew extensively on this.[71]

Barker referred to cuts that the Independent Broadcasting Authority had made to the film, principally opinions expressed by Wyatt as part of the narrative. Arguments about these cuts had held up the transmission of the film, which had been scheduled for broadcast on 1 May 1973. Barker claimed that the IBA's cuts 'left the ending of the film rather formless' and to balance this several ITV regions asked Wyatt to take part in a discussion programme after the film was broadcast. Barker observed that this was to their advantage because Wyatt 'was able to make many of the points excised from the film'.

The significance of Wyatt's programme was noted at the highest level of government. The prime minister's principal private secretary, Robert Armstrong, wrote to Heath, 'You may like to glance through this transcript of Woodrow Wyatt's "Red under the Bed" TV programme.' Heath's scribbled response said, 'We want as much as possible of this.'[72]

An attempt was made to rebroadcast the programme during the final week of the trial. The head of Anglia Television, Aubrey Buxton, wrote to the heads of the regional television companies on 17 December 1973, 'It would seem highly opportune to repeat Red under the bed this week. Hope you agree.'[73] 'This week' was the week that Mais concluded his summing-up and the jury were to be sent out to consider their verdict.

The government attached considerable importance to programmes like *Red under the Bed* in shaping public opinion about picketing. It was actively involved in the making of the programme through the IRD. The broadcasting of the programme at any time during the pickets' trial would be prejudicial to the defence. It made explicit references to picketing during the building workers' strike as a central part of Wyatt's theme, that militant extremists were destroying British democracy. Yet Judge Mais dismissed the programme as irrelevant to the jury's consideration of the evidence. He would not hold the television companies in contempt or order a retrial with a fresh jury.

Summing-Up by Judge Mais

The prosecution had taken twenty-nine days to present its case, calling 157 witnesses. The defence took just eleven days and only three witnesses were called, finishing on 4 December. There followed six and an half days of summing-up. Drake went first followed by leading counsel for each of the six, Platts-Mills, Turner Samuels, Rhys-Roberts, Garrett, Owen and McHale. Before Judge Mais began his summing-up on Thursday 14 December, applications were made for the six to remain on bail. This was only granted for Jones and O'Shea, the other four being remanded in custody until the jury gave their verdicts on 18 and 19 December. This sent a signal to the jury in the final few days of the trial, that these pickets were guilty of a serious criminal offence. There was no indication that the pickets would have absconded. They had attended court each day for eleven weeks.

Mais's summing-up of the evidence to the jury bookended Drake's opening speech at the beginning of October. It started at 10:15 a.m. on Friday 14 December and finished at 10:40 a.m. on Tuesday 18 December, covering 211 pages. Like Drake, he also made many references to evidence relating to Llywarch, including fourteen pages devoted to Llywarch's statement, reminding the jury of how frightened Llywarch was of his fellow pickets.[74] Mais referred to alleged threats that Llywarch faced at work on the Wrexham bypass after the police had interviewed him on 3 November 1972. Mais said to the jury that no doubt they would reread Llywarch's statement while they were deliberating. Throughout, he emphasised the evidence of prosecution witnesses who spoke of fear.

Misdirection of the Jury

After almost eleven weeks of evidence, speeches from the various barristers and a summing-up, the jury were sent out to consider their verdicts at 10:41 a.m. on 18 December. The court records show that the jury reported back at 4:14 p.m. that day. They had reached unanimous verdicts on most of the counts. They found all six guilty of unlawful assembly. On the affray count they found Jones, Tomlinson and Warren guilty, and the other three not guilty. But the jury could not agree unanimous verdicts for four of the pickets on the first count, conspiracy to intimidate.[75] They had found unanimously that Carpenter and O'Shea were not guilty of this charge.[76]

Judge Mais informed the members of the jury that he would accept a majority verdict of at least ten to two and sent them out again. They returned at 5:35 p.m. to report that they could not agree majority verdicts either. He asked them whether they might reach majority verdicts if they were given a bit more time but the foreman replied that it was unlikely. He continued that some of the jurors had had enough for the day and wanted a break. It was clear that they were deadlocked. As it was late, the jury were sent to a hotel overnight before returning to court the next day, as was the practice at that time. Before sending them away Mais said, 'I think the court should now adjourn and that you should go to the accommodation which has been prepared for you. Arrangements will be made for your reception, *and I suggest that possibly you continue your deliberations there.'*[77] His last comments were improper. He had failed to direct the jury *not* to continue their discussion about the case; instead he did the opposite. The need for this was later described in the case of *R v. Thakaran:*[78]

> The dangers inherent in deliberations continuing in a hotel ... are obvious. Unless the jurors are all together in one room, rival camps may be formed. If a jury is divided then obviously some are taking one view and the remainder are taking the other view. There is a clear danger that pressure may be brought to bear on

individual jurors in the opposite camp at a time when they are not acting as a collegiate body.

One of the strengths of the jury system is that they do act as a body, and if there is disagreement then individual jurors can look to others of the same view for support. If they continue their discussions outside the jury room, then those of a weaker disposition may be open to persuasion without having the support of others of the same mind.

The jury returned to court at 10:00 a.m. and gave their verdicts at 10:55 a.m. Like the jurors in the *Tharakan* case, the Shrewsbury jury returned majority verdicts within an hour of returning to the court from their overnight hotel stay, suggesting that there had been unsupervised discussions at the hotel. The foreman announced that a sufficient majority, ten to two, had found Jones, Tomlinson and Warren guilty of conspiracy to intimidate. Llywarch was found not guilty of the charge.

The Intervention of the Court Usher

Just after the pickets were sentenced a claim was made that there had been interference with the jury's deliberations. It was said that the court bailiff, who would have been present with the twelve men throughout their stay at the hotel, had spoken with them late on Tuesday 18 December when they were deadlocked. He was alleged to have informed them that if the remaining pickets were found guilty by the jury, they would only be fined. Warren's wife, Elsa, recalled that a juror approached her outside the court. 'He told me that the jury had been told that the defendants would be fined, would not receive a custodial sentence and if the jury had taken any longer over the verdicts "they would be there over Christmas."'[79]

Platts-Mills also recalled the discussion:

Outside court, the distressed foreman told the wives of the defendants what had happened. The jury wanted none of the accused to go to prison, but one juror claimed to know the law and had insisted that this could not possibly be the outcome. They were eight/four for nearly twenty-four hours. Finally, two gave way on the basis of the argument, 'You can't keep us here forever.' The jury bailiff confirmed a lot of this to counsel. The foreman had stood firm throughout against the conspiracy charge and was crying as he spoke to the wives.[80]

The Pickets Are Sentenced

The six men were given the opportunity to speak before sentencing. Four declined. Although Warren and Tomlinson were expecting to go to jail they decided to speak out, making speeches from the dock before Mais pronounced. Tomlinson spoke first. Warren knew the risks but began,

> I have spent a week in jail, and people in there and various other people, not including my counsel, have told me that it was always a mistake to make a speech from the dock, because whatever you are going to get will be doubled.[81]

Mais interrupted him during the speech and warned Warren, 'You must not use this opportunity as a political platform.'[82] But Warren continued regardless, stating his belief that the trials had been politically stage-managed by the state.

Carpenter, Llywarch and O'Shea were each sentenced to nine months' imprisonment, suspended for two years. McKinsie Jones was sentenced to nine months in prison on each count, to run concurrently. The shock of this caused him to collapse and he had to be helped down to the cells. Paul Foot wrote,

> Mais relished his job. He positively enjoyed sending down John McKinsie Jones, a man almost Christ-like in his innocence. He enjoyed the fact that John suffers from a chronic fear of enclosed spaces. He set no store by the fact that Mrs Jones was due to have a baby at any time.[83]

Tomlinson was sentenced to two years on each count, to run concurrently. When this happened the foreman of the jury stood up and struck another jury member before storming out of the court.[84] According to Platts-Mills,

At this point, the foreman of the jury shouted, 'I'm leaving this court.' We all turned to look and there he was, forcing his way out past the crowded knees in the jury box. He shouted, 'It's disgraceful,' and kept on shouting until he disappeared through the jury door. Another juror followed, showing his anger by slamming the door of the jury box. Everyone was astounded. I had never seen the like, and I don't think any of us had.[85]

The incident was also noted in a report to the DPP:

It was a majority verdict 10–2 – whilst sentences being passed 2 jurors left the Jury Box – the foreman and one other – believed to be the dissenters – and one (?the foreman) [sic] remarked he was annoyed that custodial sentences were being passed. Judge did not refer to this outburst but indicated that they should return to the Jury Box and this they did.[86]

Mais left Warren until last:

So far as you are concerned, you took part in violence, and violence is far too prevalent in this country today ... I regard you as arrogant, vicious, and prepared to impose your views upon others by violence if need be. You have the power of speech and the power of leadership which you apparently used to ill purpose.

He then sentenced Warren to three years on each count, to run concurrently.

The protest at the length of the prison sentences by the foreman and another juror was surprising given that they had voted earlier with their ten fellow jurors to find three of the pickets guilty of affray and all six guilty of unlawful assembly. These were serious charges and those guilty verdicts, particularly for affray, could have been enough to send them to prison for a lengthy period.

These draconian sentences sent a shock wave through the trade union movement. It was 19 December, six days before Christmas. After fifty-five days in court Des Warren, John McKinsie Jones and Ricky Tomlinson were taken down to the cells and transferred by prison van to HMP Shrewsbury to begin their sentences, not knowing when they would be seeing their families again.

With the court emptied of defendants and jurors it just left Mais to convey to Drake his gratitude for the organisation of the proceedings:

> I would wish to be conveyed to the Chief Constable the Court's appreciation of the excellent arrangements made in this Court throughout the trial by the Shrewsbury Division of the West Mercia Constabulary, and in particular by Chief Superintendent Barnett and Inspector Needham and also that the attention of The Chief Constable should be drawn to the work done by Mr Rennie, Mr Hodges and Superintendent Glover.[87]

They got their rewards: Hodges was promoted to assistant chief constable the following year. Alex Rennie was promoted to chief constable on 1 January 1975 on the retirement of Willison. Glover, who had been a chief inspector when he co-authored the West Mercia police report in December 1972, was now a superintendent.

11

The Prosecution on a Roll

The Pickets Left to Their Fate

The eighteen remaining pickets were dealt with in the same way as their six colleagues. The charges were similar, though significantly no one was charged with conspiracy to intimidate. They were not going to be tried as ringleaders but as followers of those leaders in Shropshire on that fateful day, 6 September 1972.

On 3 January 1974 the DPP informed the pickets' lawyers that all the men must attend court to plead to the fifty-three charges that they faced between them. It also warned them that after the pleas they would be split into two groups, as eighteen men in the dock would be too unwieldy. Both trials were heard by Judge Chetwynd-Talbot, who had dealt with the cases at Mold. They would be tried for just two of the counts on which they were charged, affray and unlawful assembly. The first trial would be of Malcolm Clee, Derrick Hughes, Dennis Morris, Arthur Murray, Michael Pierce, Roy Warburton, Thomas Bryan Williams, Gary Davies and Alfred James.[1] Like the first trial, all twelve jurors were men.

The Second Trial: Pickets Fear the Worst

On the opening day of the second trial, 14 January, Drake made an application to amend the wording of the original charges of affray and unlawful assembly.[2] The eighteen were now accused of 'fighting and causing an affray' on the Brookside site only, not throughout Shropshire on 6 September. The count of 'being an unlawful assembly' was also revised. Each picket was now accused of being part of one on several separate occasions that day: at Brookside (count 1), at Kingswood (count 1a) and at Shelton roadworks (count 1b).[3]

To everyone's surprise, when the eighteen men attended court together a deal was offered to them: plead guilty to unlawful assembly and they would not go to prison. The remaining charges would be left on the file or dismissed. The jailing of three pickets after the first Shrewsbury trial had had a chilling effect. Clee, Hughes and Morris decided to plead guilty to the charge of unlawful assembly (Morris at the start of the trial, the other two at the close of the prosecution case).

The offer of a deal was not a sign that Drake had lost his nerve. He used his four-hour opening address in the same way as he had done the previous October, alleging that the accused had been violent and had put people in fear of their safety, which had nothing to do with lawful picketing or trade unionism.[4] He told the jury to disregard the reports that they may have read of the first trial, but this was a reminder to them that it had happened. At the end of his speech Drake informed the jurors that those now on trial 'are not put forward as the organising ring leaders of what happened that day. Those organising ring leaders have been dealt with in a separate proceeding'.[5] This was a further reminder to the jury that pickets had been jailed just before Christmas for their part in the events in Shrewsbury and Telford. During the case Drake repeatedly tried to associate the men in the dock with the 'ringleaders'. On one occasion he showed a photograph of the Brookside site to the jury and remarked, 'You may think it not insignificant – it is a matter for you to say – the position of some of these men in the dock right up among the leaders addressing the crowd, uttering their threats plus promises at that stage.'[6] This was guilt by association.

The use of photographs and witness statements that referred to numbered photographs, caused great confusion for the jury. They sent a note to Judge Chetwynd-Talbot asking,

Many statements refer to photographs by letter and the persons by number. Some of the statements have the name in the margin of the identified person. Some statements do not have a complete name of the identified person. Is it possible to have the other photographs forwarded to the jury for proper identification of persons[?][7]

The prosecution called ninety-seven witnesses over a period of eleven days. They had already had experience of giving evidence in the first trial. At the end of its case two pickets decided to plead guilty to unlawful assembly, leaving six for the jury to decide. Four of them gave evidence – Davies, Murray, Pierce and Warburton – whereas James and Williams declined to do so. The only additional witness listed for the defence was John Batterbee, the treasurer of the Oswestry Strike Committee, who was called to give evidence in support of Davies.

Drake re-created the same impression for the jury as he had done previously. An enormous number of prosecution witnesses were called to describe a catalogue of terror, fear and damage to property. They were aided by press and police photographs that enabled them to point to the men in the dock as the ones responsible. This was countered by just five building workers who tried to explain, during three days of giving evidence, that what they were doing that day was lawful picketing in furtherance of their strike. Again, the lack of witnesses on the defence side weighted the scales hugely in favour of the Crown. It seems that no lessons had been learned by the defence from the first trial.

The case concluded on 13 February and the jury went out for five hours. Murray, Pierce and Thomas Brian Williams were found guilty of affray and unlawful assembly. They were each sentenced to six months' imprisonment for the former and four months' for the latter, to run concurrently. Warburton and James were found guilty of unlawful assembly but not guilty of affray. They were sentenced to four months' imprisonment, suspended for two years, as were the three who had pleaded guilty to unlawful assembly earlier in the trial. Gary Davies was found not guilty on both counts, the only one of the twenty-four to be acquitted.

This was the second time that Drake had succeeded in securing convictions and prison sentences against pickets. He was on a roll and approached the third trial with a high degree of confidence.

The Third Trial: The Fear Level Increases

The third trial had the fewest men in the dock as most of the pickets accepted Drake's deal. Graham Roberts, Peter Sear, Bryn Thomas and Thomas Bernard Williams pleaded guilty to unlawful assembly. They were sentenced to four months' imprisonment, suspended for two years. Kevin Butcher was adamant that he was not going to plead guilty to any major charge but was terrified at the thought of going to prison as he was a married man with children. Drake added a lesser charge against him, count fifty-four, charging Butcher with threatening behaviour at Brookside. Under pressure, he decided to plead guilty to it. Not-guilty verdicts were entered in relation to the other charges that he faced. He was given a sentence of three months' imprisonment, suspended for one year.

Only four of the final nine pleaded not guilty to all charges: William Hooson, Terry Renshaw, John Seaburg and Edward Leonard Williams. Just before the start of their trial on 26 February, no evidence was offered by the Crown against Hooson and he was discharged straight away as the prosecution thought its evidence against him was too weak. He joined Gary Davies as the only two of the twenty-four not to be convicted. The trial proceeded against the remaining three, who were charged with unlawful assembly and with affray at Brookside. Drake added two additional charges against Renshaw, affray and unlawful assembly at Woodside.[8] Despite Drake upping the stakes, Renshaw was adamant and still refused to plead guilty to any of the charges.

Renshaw had broken his leg on 12 February and was in a plaster cast. Chetwynd-Talbot was not going to make any concessions despite Renshaw's treating doctor writing to the court to confirm the position.[9] He had to use crutches when he attended court two weeks later. His co-accused, Kevin Butcher, despite not needing to attend following his guilty plea, drove Renshaw each day from Flint to Shrewsbury. He had to remove the front passenger seat from his car to allow Renshaw to sit in the back with his leg stretched out.

Ninety-two witnesses were called by the prosecution, showing that Drake was not letting up. The three accused pickets gave evidence and two others appeared for them, Barry Scragg and Fred Walker. On 22 March the jury went out for over three and an half hours. Renshaw believed that the additional charges that he faced made him a marked man and he expected to go to prison if he was convicted. In the event, the jury found Renshaw and Williams guilty of just one count, unlawful assembly at Brookside, and not guilty on the others. They were each given suspended prison sentences of four months. Seaburg was convicted of both affray and unlawful assembly at Brookside. He received suspended sentences of six months' and four months' imprisonment respectively.

The Government Celebrates Its Success

The day after the six 'ringleaders' had been sentenced by Judge Mais on 19 December 1973, the law lords upheld the conviction of a UCATT official, John Broome, for obstructing the highway while picketing.[10] The government and its supporters welcomed the outcome of both cases. The *Sunday Telegraph* reported,

> Resolute action to curb the menace of violent strike picketing can be expected from the police, with Government encouragement, following last week's gaoling of three members of a flying picket for conspiring to intimidate building workers into joining the national stoppage a year ago.
>
> Police powers for dealing with peaceful pickets were also strengthened last week when the Law Lords ruled that strikers have no right to delay people entering strikebound premises if they wish to do so.
>
> The verdict in the 'violent picketing' case swept away fears that existing laws were not strong enough to deal with terror

tactics in strikes. It also followed Government pressure on Chief Constables to abandon their reluctance to act in industrial disputes because of anxiety about the political consequences.[11]

The outcome was a vindication of the position taken by the Conservative government during the past two years: 'The jury's verdict demonstrated that, contrary to what many people believed, new laws do not seem necessary to deal with violent picketing.'[12] The *Daily Mirror* reported the result with the triumphalist headline, 'Police chief's elite corps ... smash pickets'.[13]

The government was pleased with the result of the two cases. Home Secretary Carr wrote to Edward Heath to discuss the public statement that Carr had been due to make about the government's review of the law on picketing. It had been delayed pending the outcome of the *Broome* case. Carr indicated that if he was questioned in Parliament about the review he would state 'that the Government has no intention of proposing any change in the law on picketing in present circumstances'. Heath agreed and advised Carr to draw attention to the House of Lords judgment and the reference in Carr's letter to 'the heavy sentences recently passed at Shrewsbury on some of the organisers of the picketing during the building strike'.[14]

The message that the government sent out to the police at the start of 1974 was that they should be more willing to use the existing law to arrest and prosecute pickets. Heath's government was facing a second national strike by coal miners and possibly other challenges to its pay policy. On 4 February, Rawlinson advised colleagues at a Cabinet subcommittee meeting of the advice that needed to be sent to the National Coal Board and others that were faced with industrial action:

> The decision whether to take legal action was of course entirely for employers, and it was not open to the Government to give them instructions. But advice could be given; and employers should also be asked to hand over to the police as soon as possible any evidence suggesting that serious criminal offences, including picketing, might have been committed.[15]

At the same meeting the usefulness of a charge of conspiracy was highlighted in a discussion on contingency planning:

> In discussion, it was suggested that the police should be encouraged, like other public organisations, to forward to the Director of Public Prosecutions any evidence, in the form eg of leaflets, which suggested that a serious criminal offence, *such as conspiracy*, might have been committed.
>
> The police should also be readier than they had been in the past to ensure by immediate arrest and prosecution that pickets who infringed the law were seen to suffer the consequences, even though this might be difficult if pickets were present in large numbers. Summary proceedings were desirable – procedure by way of indictment was much slower, and would lead the public to think that no action was being taken.[16]

Overall, the various tactics adopted by Drake, the police and the DPP were a success. The enormous resources that the state put into the trials of twenty-four building workers resulted in the conviction of all except two. Six were jailed and sixteen received suspended prison sentences. The failures at Mold had been reversed because the trials at Shrewsbury were built upon the lessons of the earlier cases. Drake's inventive use of conspiracy, affray and unlawful assembly showed the availability and flexibility of the common law to weaken trade union action. But nothing was left to chance and every aspect of the trials that could be influenced in favour of the prosecution was manipulated in its favour.

The joint author of the West Mercia police report, Fred Hodges, now an assistant chief constable, wrote in his letter of thanks to the Shrewsbury court staff, 'This has been an unusual, and in many ways, history-making case. That apart, it has done much to clarify the law relating to picketing and to some extent, I think, established the rule of law.'[17]

Conservative ministers such as Carr and Rawlinson had made speeches arguing that a mass picket of any kind was intimidation. The message from the trials was that trade unionists could not demonstrate their collective strength without the risk of being declared an unlawful assembly. The organisers of any such picket could be tried for conspiracy if a non-striker claimed that they were intimidated from going to work because of the number of pickets, even if those pickets stood silently at the side of a workplace.

The Trade Union Response

UCATT's executive committee issued a five-page statement at the end of January 1974,[18] followed by a short pamphlet.[19] The latter was based upon an opinion of its solicitor, John Williams. His advice was contradictory and misleading. He suggested, wrongly, that the Shrewsbury pickets were convicted of assault, criminal damage and intimidation. He failed to address or understand the seriousness of the three charges that the six men had faced, which allowed Drake to obtain convictions, literally on the basis of 'guilt by association'. After explaining its decision not to give legal, financial and political support to the pickets from the point of arrest through to their convictions, UCATT was left simply to call for the pickets' sentences to be reduced and agreed with the T&GWU to set up a hardship fund for the pickets' families.[20]

Support for the Pickets

The three men who received suspended prison sentences at the first trial – O'Shea, Carpenter and Llywarch – threw themselves into campaigning for their three co-accused who were now in jail. They made themselves available to the North Wales Defence Committee, which had been raising funds and support for all the men on trial in Mold and Shrewsbury. They also spoke at public meetings organised throughout Britain by the International Socialists and other left-wing groups.

In the absence of any lead from the national trade unions, the organisation of a campaign to have the pickets released fell to grass-roots bodies. The left was united in working to free the

six: the charter group, the Communist Party, various Trotskyist groups and many rank-and-file networks across the trade
union movement. Resolutions were sent to union national executives and to the TUC calling for action. Lobbies of Parliament
were organised calling for the pickets' release. The TUC held
a number of meetings with the newly elected Labour government in 1974 but was told that there was nothing it could do
while appeals were outstanding. Building workers on Merseyside, including Alan Abrahams and Bill Jones, worked tirelessly
in UCATT and through their trades councils to get support for
the men in prison. They had both known Warren for many years
through their activities in the union and the charter movement.
They knew that only mass industrial action of the type that
freed the Pentonville 5 would release the Shrewsbury pickets.

The TUC held further meetings with the government later in
the year. On 18 December 1974 Prime Minister Harold Wilson
and his advisers had a meeting with fourteen members of the
TUC general council and senior TUC staff. The union delegation said that it was speaking with the unanimous backing of
the general council. NUM President Joe Gormley pointed out
that miners involved with the 1972 and 1974 strikes could have
been in the same situation as the north Wales pickets. At the end
of the meeting Wilson told the trade union delegation that the
issue of a pardon was a matter for the home secretary. But Roy
Jenkins had already expressed his opinion and did not move
away from it in the following months:

> The rule of law and the independence of the courts would be
> seriously undermined if the opinions of Government were sub-
> stituted for the decisions of the Court, and in advising on the
> exercise of the Royal Prerogative the Home Secretary must take
> every care not to usurp the functions of the courts.[21]

The North Wales Defence Committee remained the focal point
for organising financial and moral support for the pickets. It had
evolved from the North Wales and Chester Action Committee
that had been formed during the strike. When the pickets were
arrested and charged in February 1973 it began a nationwide

appeal for support for the men. The Shrewsbury archive at the Working Class Movement Library in Salford holds files containing hundreds of letters from trade union branches and political organisations throughout Britain enclosing donations and offering support. Its treasurer, Mike Williams, was a joiner and was responsible for distributing funds to the pickets and their families; he kept meticulous records. He was well respected and nicknamed 'the vicar' on sites because he never swore. He informed me that the defence committee ensured that none of the pickets on trial had to pay travel expenses to Mold or Shrewsbury and were given loss of earnings while at court or in prison. The committee made sure that the pickets' families were looked after and did not fall into debt. This type of support, so often downplayed or overlooked, was crucial for the pickets.

The plight of the imprisoned pickets was raised on many occasions in Parliament by members of the left-wing Tribune group of Labour MPs, principally Martin Flannery, Tom Litterick, Dennis Skinner and Stan Thorne. Warren kept up a regular correspondence with them.[22] Their interventions with the Home Office and prison governors kept the spotlight on Warren and Tomlinson and prevented their treatment in prison being worse that it would have been. Several of the MPs also wrote often to Elsa Warren to maintain her morale. Litterick had no illusions about the majority of his Labour colleagues, though:

> We, the labour MPs who tried to help, are part of the general failure of the labour movement to help its own people when the crunch comes; it's grimly ironic that the London dockers were able to do more for their people when a tory government was in power than we could for you with a labour government [sic].[23]

Solidarity meetings and conferences were held throughout the country but the pressure for industrial action had dissipated by the end of 1974. The leadership of the trade union movement, having got rid of a vicious Tory government, did not want any action that would jeopardise the position of the Labour government, which in October had won the second general election of that year, though with only a majority of three seats. Ken

O'Shea told me that he sensed a change in mood as the year progressed. He and the others found that all attempts to get the trade unions and Labour Party nationally to take up the pickets case was like 'swimming against the stream'. The pickets only other hope of release was their appeals.

12

The Court of Appeal

The Pickets' Last Hope for Justice

The six pickets convicted at the first trial immediately announced that they intended to appeal their convictions and sentences. Jones, Tomlinson and Warren had been sent to Shrewsbury prison, where they spent Christmas, away from their families.[1] It was particularly hard for McKinsie Jones as his wife was due to give birth to their second child at any time.

At the first preliminary appeal hearing, before Lord Justice James, Platts-Mills highlighted Judge Mais's biased attitude: 'plainly in this case he conceived a personal dislike for my client Warren and he expressed it in the plainest terms. The jury responded to it in a manner I hope never to see again.'[2]

There were two sets of appeals. The first dealt with legal issues about the validity of the charges that the six pickets had been tried on. The second, which did not take place until October 1974, concerned the fairness of Mais's handling of the trial, in particular his summing-up of the case to the jury.

First Appeal: Charges Were Unlawful

The first appeal was heard on 19 and 20 February 1974 before three judges: James, Mr Justice Kerr and the most senior judge in England and Wales, the Lord Chief Justice, Lord Widgery. The main grounds of appeal were:

A Judge Mais should not have allowed Drake to bring a charge of *conspiracy* to intimidate when each of the six men had been charged at least once with the actual (substantive) offence of intimidation, contrary to Section 7 of the Conspiracy and Protection of Property Act 1875.

B The wording of the affray charge was improper because the evidence to support it suggested that there had been several separate affrays; each should have been charged separately. This legal error is known as *duplicity*.

C The same argument, duplicity, applied to the wording of the charge of unlawful assembly that the six had faced.[3]

At the end of the hearing on 21 February the court immediately rejected the appeal on ground 1 but needed time to consider grounds 2 and 3. It reserved its judgment on them and gave full reasons for rejecting ground 1 at the resumed hearing.[4]

Improper Count of Conspiracy to Intimidate

On 4 March, at the resumed hearing, Lord Justice James gave the court's full decision for rejecting the appeal on the charge of conspiracy to intimidate:

> The question whether a conspiracy charge is properly included in an indictment cannot be answered by the application of any rigid rules. Each case must be considered on its own facts. There are however certain guiding principles. The offences charged on the indictment should not only be supported by the evidence on the depositions or witness statements, but they should also represent the criminality disclosed by that evidence. It is not desirable to include a charge of conspiracy which adds nothing to an effective charge of a substantive offence. But where charges of substantive offences do not adequately represent the overall criminality it may be appropriate and right to include a charge of conspiracy.[5]

James said that the conspiracy count was necessary, as otherwise 'the Crown case could not be adequately presented in the interests of justice by preferring a small number of charges of substantive offences of intimidation ... No material misdirection, confusion or unfairness resulted from the inclusion of this count.'[6] The unfairness for the defence was, as Platts-Mills argued, that the Crown had a much lower threshold to overcome to prove a conspiracy than to prove the individual counts of intimidation against any of the six pickets. Evidence that would not be allowed if the pickets were tried for intimidation was admissible if they were tried for conspiracy to intimidate.

James declared that the evidence showed that the pickets had intimidated workers on a number of occasions and that charges under Section 7 were not enough to deal with that, even though Parliament had set the limits. This was despite the fact that there was no evidence against Warren, Tomlinson and McKinsie Jones that they had intimidated anyone, as confirmed in the police report. James approved Drake's decision to find another law, from the deep reservoir of the English common law, that would sidestep Parliament's intentions. The Court of Appeal's decision showed the great flexibility of the English common law system for the state. It allowed the prosecution and the courts to ignore the statutory offence in the 1875 Act and instead use judge-made law to apply a more draconian punishment.[7] Drake just needed to persuade a jury that the behaviour of various unnamed pickets on 6 September 1972, in the vague words of public order laws, 'endangered the public peace' or 'created fear amongst the public', or that 'reasonable people might be frightened or intimidated'.

The Appeals against Affray

The appeal against the convictions for affray was successful. The pickets had been charged with fighting and causing an affray all day, uninterrupted. At the appeal their lawyers said that this was preposterous, although they did not deny that there had been affrays: 'It is submitted that there was more than one affray on the 6th September, 1972, in Shrewsbury and Telford, and that the Learned Judge was wrong to allow a multiplicity of alleged offences to be dealt with in only one count.'[8] The Court of Appeal agreed. It accepted that the evidence at the trial showed that the pickets went to one site, caused an affray with the workers there, left and moved peacefully to a different site on their coach or stopped and ate chips in Shrewsbury town centre at lunchtime. When they went to another site, they started a new and separate affray. Each affray should have been charged individually, as occurred in the second and third trials. It was open to Drake to have alleged seven separate affrays against Warren et al. – one at each site the pickets visited on 6 September. The pickets' lawyers had argued at the start of the trial on 3 October that this is what Drake must do, but Judge Mais had rejected it. The Court of Appeal decided that Mais was wrong, ruling that Drake's wording of the particulars of the charge was too broad.

The decision of the Court of Appeal to quash the convictions of Jones, Tomlinson and Warren for this offence was therefore based upon a legal technicality. It explains why the pickets convicted of affray at the second and third trials did not appeal their convictions. Drake had changed the wording before their trials began so that they were charged with causing an affray, at just one site, Brookside in Telford.

The Count of Unlawful Assembly Was Lawful

The appeals against the count of unlawful assembly were rejected. All six remained convicted of this offence. The Court of Appeal recognised that, logically, the same argument that applied to the appeal against affray would apply in the appeal against unlawful assembly. But whereas affray involved fighting, which clearly had not been going on all day on 6 September, unlawful assembly involved 'being or coming together'. The three appeal judges ruled that at no time during the day did the pickets stop being one assembly, from the moment they boarded coaches in Oswestry to head to Shrewsbury, then when they picketed sites, ate chips and finally moved on to sites in Telford. The appeal court also accepted that when the pickets had assembled on

6 September they had an unlawful intent – to picket in such a manner as to 'endanger the public peace'.

An application by the six men for permission to appeal to the House of Lords against the conviction for unlawful assembly was heard on 22 March 1974 before the same three judges. It was rejected.[9] That ended the appeals of Carpenter, Llywarch and O'Shea. They had withdrawn their appeals against their suspended prison sentences at the hearing on 4 March.[10]

The three pickets jailed after the second trial – Murray, Pierce and Williams – did not appeal their convictions. Drake had changed the wording before the second trial started to make them 'appeal-proof'. Only Murray appealed against his sentence. Hall reported to the DPP, 'but this can only be regarded as a gesture by the defence.'[11] It was dealt with by Lord Justice James on 20 April, when he dismissed it, writing, 'The sentence is correct in principle and not too severe.'[12]

Bail Granted: Free at Last, but Not for Long

The appeal court still had to consider Tomlinson and Warren's second main ground, which dealt with Mais's conduct of the trial. This required copies of the trial transcript, containing the questioning of witnesses and Judge Mais's summing-up. The prosecution and defence counsel agreed a list of the witnesses whose evidence they wanted for the appeal, but it was going to take several months for it to be transcribed. Applications were made for Jones, Tomlinson and Warren to be released on bail, but these were refused at the hearings in February and March. After several months, it was clear that the transcript would not be available until the autumn.[13] An application for bail pending appeal was heard on 3 June 1974 and granted.[14] Tomlinson and Warren would be free for the next four months. Jones did not apply for bail as he was due for release later that month, having served two-thirds of his sentence. He did not want to take part in any further appeal.[15]

The October Appeal against Convictions:
The Bias of Judge Mais

The second part of the appeal was heard between 24 and 29 October 1974. The main grounds were that Judge Mais had displayed bias, particularly towards Warren; had failed to put the defence case to the jury in his summing-up; and had given partial and confusing interpretations of the evidence and the law.

At the hearing Tomlinson and Warren were represented by the same legal team as at their original trial, respectively McHale and Altaras and Platts-Mills and Rumbelow. Their adversary, again, was the team of Drake, Fennell and Wadsworth. The defence referred the three appeal court judges to pages and pages of transcript to highlight how Mais had failed to control the proceedings properly and had shown bias towards the men on trial. It was argued that Mais equated the organising of picketing on 6 September by Warren and others with a conspiracy, simply because it happened. Mais had said,

> There must be some organisation behind the managing of 300 men back into 5 or 6 coaches ... The prosecution say here that in effect it is not credible that all this should have happened with no planning, no organisation, no leaders, nobody in charge, and they say that the conclusion is irresistible that this was a conspiracy as alleged in the indictment.[16]

After informing the jury of the prosecution case Mais had directed them, 'The first thing you have got to consider here, it seems to me, is was there a conspiracy, was there an agreement? Could this all have happened without there being any organisation, any agreement, and no agreement and no anything?' This confused the issues. Mais failed to ask the jury to decide what was supposed to have been agreed. There was an agreement: to book coaches to travel from north Wales to Shrewsbury and to picket certain sites in Shropshire and in north Wales during the strike. But it did not follow that the accused had also agreed to intimidate anyone.

Lord Justice James gave the appeal court's judgment and swept away the defence's objections. He accepted that, in the summing-up of such a lengthy trial, 'some room for criticism' of Mais was inevitable. But James concluded that Mais had not been in error because, 'Looking at this summing-up as a whole, the defence was put time and time again.'[17]

The Appeals against the Draconian Sentences

Jones's appeal against his sentence of nine months had been dealt with at the appeal hearing on 4 March. It had been argued that it was excessive, given his previous good character, his family connections and that he had a job to which he could return. In response Lord Justice Widgery referred to Mais's sentencing remarks to reject Jones's appeal, '"You took an active part on the 6th September … but I do not regard you as being in the same category as Warren and Tomlinson" … (We) see no reason to depart from the judge's assessment of the correct sentence in this case.'[18] Jones had not been found guilty of threatening behaviour, or of criminal damage or violence towards anyone. He only stood convicted of conspiring to intimidate and of being part of an unlawful assembly. The sentencing remarks of Mais were not based upon the charges on which the jury had found him guilty

The appeals put forward for Tomlinson and Warren in October 1974 were equally unsuccessful. Platts-Mills and McHale both argued that, since the convictions in December 1973, there had been no further mass picketing in the building industry and that things had quietened down, thereby reducing the need for a deterrent sentence. Widgery gave the obvious response: that industrial peace had existed since that time precisely because of the deterrent sentences. To reduce them now on appeal would send out the wrong message. Widgery ruled, 'We are of the opinion that this was a classic example of the type of case in which the punishment inflicted must be such as will actively discourage others from following suit.'[19]

Behind the Scenes, Drama in Government

An editorial in the *New Law Journal* considered the sentences to be of 'swingeing severity' and pointed out that they had not been imposed to reflect the *conduct* of Tomlinson and Warren but to deter others.[20] It argued that at the time of the appeal, two years after the strike had ended, there was no evidence of intimidatory mass picketing that needed to be deterred. Lord Chief Justice Widgery's comments were supported by a Conservative lawyer, Ivan Lawrence MP, who produced a paper for the party about the trials. In criticising the editorial in the *New Law Journal* he wrote, 'This ignores the obvious point that the crisis may have only been temporarily averted because of these deterrent sentences and a reduction of the sentence might lead to a reactivation of the crisis.'[21]

Bolton's *Panorama* Programme

The government and prosecution were put under the microscope again in March 1975 when Roger Bolton, a young producer on the BBC current affairs programme *Panorama*, wrote to the DPP, Rawlinson, and West Mercia police. He asked a series of questions about the trials for an edition of the programme that was to be broadcast the following month. Bolton asked the DPP,

1. Why was there a six-month gap between the incidents at Shrewsbury and Telford on 6th September 1972 occurring and charges being preferred?
2. Who took the decision to use the charge of conspiracy?
3. Did the D.P.P. consult the Attorney General's office and/or the Home Secretary about the prosecutions? If so at what stage?
4. Did the D.P.P. receive a communication from either the Attorney General's office or the Home Office urging that prosecutions against illegal picketing or associated acts be stepped up, or that the picketing laws be more stringently enforced? If so, when?[22]

The DPP's deputy director, Michael Jardine, prepared a reply which included 'Q.3 The A.G was consulted'.[23] He sent the draft to Tony Hetherington at the Attorney General's Department. The latter suggested that 'it would be more accurate to say that the conspiracy charge was preferred by Counsel instructed by the D.P.P. This is a point which Peter Rawlinson made when I was talking to him on the telephone the other day.'[24]

Hetherington's comment was classic British civil service. He wanted to ensure that the formal position was put: counsel is instructed by the DPP, and not by the attorney general. This avoided any mention of discussions between officials in the two departments and with the Home Office. Rawlinson was so keen to distance himself from the case that, according to Hetherington, 'certainly Peter Rawlinson tells me that he does not remember anything about the case at that stage, and indeed does not remember nominating Counsel.'

Bolton asked Rawlinson similar questions. The latter drafted a reply, which he sent to the DPP, Sir Norman Skelhorn QC.[25] They were all keen to make sure that they were getting their story right.[26] In his reply to Bolton on 8 April Rawlinson's answers also included a warning:

> Since you are considering a programme I think it right to tell you I consider that to attribute to a Law Officer political motivation of the kind to which you refer could be defamatory. For it reflects necessarily upon his professional integrity. Accordingly I would be obliged if I could be advised in advance of the date of the proposed programme, and also be provided with a transcript of the broadcast after it has been presented.[27]

In the final version of Jardine's reply to Bolton he wrote, 'Neither the Attorney General nor the Home Secretary was consulted about the prosecution.' This was not strictly accurate, as the attorney general was sent the police reports from West Mercia and Gwynedd constabularies when asked by the DPP to nominate counsel. The completed nomination form was not sent back for two weeks, suggesting that the attorney general spent time considering them.

At the time, Bolton was clearly keen to make the *Panorama* programme, which was to be broadcast on 21 or 28 April. He wrote to Barry Scragg, secretary of the North Wales Defence Committee, to arrange for up to four members of the campaign, including two pickets, to be interviewed by Denis Tuohy on film in Connah's Quay Labour Club on 10 April 1975.[28] One of those who recalled being interviewed was John McKinsie Jones. But by the time the film crew returned to London, Bolton had received replies from the DPP and Rawlinson. He wrote to Jardine on 17 April, 'We have decided to postpone our planned programme. Should we decide to transmit it later on we will of course let you know.'[29] Nothing was ever broadcast.

Was the Length of Sentences for Conspiracy Unlawful?

There was another objection to the sentences imposed on Jones, Tomlinson and Warren that was not pursued by their lawyers at the Court of Appeal. Were the sentences that Mais imposed upon them for conspiracy to intimidate – three years, two years and nine months respectively – lawful? At the first appeal hearing Widgery informed the men's lawyers that if they wanted to argue that the maximum sentence that Mais could have imposed for conspiracy to intimidate was limited to three months, as it would be for actual intimidation, they had to raise it quickly.[30]

Remarkably, it was not pursued by Platts-Mills or McHale. A note by an unidentified author in the DPP files pointed this out:

In fact on 21st February 1974 in the course of the appeal proceedings the Lord Chief Justice specifically inquired whether counsel for any of the appellants who had been convicted on a conspiracy count wished to argue that as a matter of law the maximum sentence was restricted to three months. It seems however that, after they had had an ample opportunity to consider the point during an adjournment of some days [*sic*] duration, counsel did not think it worthwhile to attempt to take this any further.[31]

The issue was highlighted a year later by the Law Commission, which had been examining the general law of conspiracy. In its draft report it discussed the position of Warren and Tomlinson, though parts of this section were removed from the final published version.[32] The draft report noted that the pickets' case 'furnishes another example of the imposition of a higher penalty for conspiracy than would have been available for the substantive offence'.[33] It then discussed various interpretations of the Conspiracy and Protection of Property Act 1875, including examining the speech of the Lord Chancellor, Lord Cairns, when he introduced the proposed law on 26 July 1875. The Law Commission then concluded,

> We do not think that there can be any doubt that parliament intended that the punishment for a conspiracy to commit an offence under section 7 of the Act should be subject to the same maximum penalty of three months' imprisonment as was provided for the substantive offence.[34]

The message from this collective view of legal academics and lawyers at the Law Commission was that Mais had acted unlawfully. But the clear wording was not allowed to stand and was dropped from the final report. Although the final report recommended changing the law, it comforted the legal establishment: 'Nothing in the rules we propose would curtail the power of the court to impose the sentence which was imposed on the unlawful assembly count in *R* v. *Jones*.'[35] In other words, even though the affray conviction had been quashed and he should only have received three months for conspiracy to intimidate, Warren's three-year sentence for unlawful assembly could safely stand. This was despite the fact that such a long sentence was unprecedented for being part of an unlawful assembly.

Lustgarten Ruffles Feathers

The issue was also raised by a Warwick University law lecturer, Laurence Lustgarten, in an article in the *New Law Journal*.[36]

It caused a stir when it was circulated within several White-hall departments while Warren was still in prison.[37] There was concern that Lustgarten's arguments would be raised by Labour MPs in the Commons during discussions on the Employment Protection Bill.

Norman Atkinson, as chairman of the left-wing Tribune group of Labour MPs, had campaigned consistently in support of the imprisoned pickets.[38] On 5 February 1976 he wrote to the Labour attorney general, Sam Silkin, enclosing a copy of Lustgarten's, article and asked for his views. An official, J. G. H. Gasson, wrote to Jardine at the DPP asking whether Lustgarten's argument had any merits. A three-page analysis of the article was prepared. It argued that the limit of three months' imprisonment did not apply to a conviction for conspiracy to intimidate, but the author, Pearson, concluded, 'If I am wrong, since the matter was at one time raised before the Court of Appeal, though it is not clear whether it was properly argued, it ought possibly to be referred back to them by the Home Sec-retary.'[39] Pearson's note was praised by a senior official, who was adamant that the sentences imposed for conspiracy 'were wrong in principle'. He agreed with the proposal that the home secretary, Roy Jenkins, could refer the point to the appeal court but suggested to Jardine that the issue be referred first 'to Senior Treasury Counsel (Tudor Price?), after which the Attorney could call Drake to a conference'.[40]

Jardine did not follow their advice when he replied to the Attorney General's Department. He informed Gasson that they had contacted Drake and Fennell, who confirmed that Platts-Mills and McHale had not pushed it at the appeals in February and March 1974. And, in any event, the argument could not have had any merit because, 'Furthermore, I have no doubt that had the Court of Appeal thought it had any substance they would have *insisted* on it being argued.'[41] A broad spectrum of people had thought that the lengthy sentences for conspiracy to intimidate were unlawful: junior counsel who drafted the pickets' appeals in January 1974, the Law Commission in its draft report, Lustgarten, and Dowling at the DPP. The purpose of raising it on appeal was precisely because the issue was not clear-cut. The opportunity to have Jones, Tomlinson and Warren released sooner, if the point had been argued and had succeeded in March 1974, was lost.[42] Two years later, when Warren was still in prison, a further opportunity was missed when the issue was buried by civil servants.

I sent copies of all these documents to Laurence Lustgarten in 2013. He noted that 'Mr Dowling advocated, and Mr Pearson suggested, that the matter could be referred to the Court of Appeal. It is therefore extraordinary to learn that nothing further was done'. Lustgarten pointed out that if the sentence for conspiracy to intimidate had been reduced on appeal to three months, the court could also be asked to review the sentences for unlawful assembly.[43] The three years that Warren received for the offence 'was *more than twice* the longest reported sentence'. Lustgarten concluded, 'This failure to act, to have the matter fully argued in open court and in the public eye was … a failure of justice.'[44]

The common law offence of conspiracy was finally abolished, with minor exceptions, by the Criminal Law Act 1977. Labour brought it in to implement many of the Law Commission's recommendations. It is still in force. Under Section 3 of the Act the maximum penalty for a *conspiracy to commit* an offence cannot now exceed the maximum penalty for *actually committing* the offence.

The Pickets Pick Up the Pieces

After the trials many of the pickets were shell-shocked and simply tried to put it behind them. Several told me in recent years that they had never told their families about the trials. It only came out when the Shrewsbury 24 Campaign achieved a growing profile and pickets joined the campaign to get their names cleared. All of the pickets' names were placed on the Economic League blacklist and they all had difficulty finding employment in the building industry.[45]

John McKinsie Jones served his sentence at Ranby prison in Retford, Nottinghamshire. He was the only one of the six imprisoned pickets who spent his whole sentence in a closed prison. He was denied special leave to be with his wife when she gave birth in January 1974, one of the most traumatic memories he still holds of his time in prison. He told me, 'Those were the worst days of my life. My family were devastated. None of us have ever got over the terrible way we were treated. Like a lot of the other pickets, I had never been in trouble in my life. We were completely innocent of these charges.'

When John was released, he returned to Shotton steelworks to ask for his job back with his former employer, Midlands & North West Painting Contractors Ltd. He was told that he could not come on the site as he had been sacked, so he went home, totally demoralised: he had a prison record, he was blacklisted and he had a young family. But later that day he got a phone call from the union convenor at the site who told him to report for work at 8:00 a.m. the next day. John was sceptical that he would get his job back after spending six months in prison. Nevertheless, he reported for work and found that his job was waiting for him. He was told that management backed down when they learned that the convenor was ready to organise a walkout, which would shut down the furnaces if John wasn't reinstated.

Ken O'Shea, despite being on trial at Mold for three weeks and Shrewsbury for twelve weeks, was offered his job back by his employer, Monks. He was particularly affected by the way Warren had been treated as he had showed such leadership in north Wales. They had picketed throughout the Denbigh area during the strike and sat together in the dock at Shrewsbury for twelve weeks. Ken always used to remind us at later meetings, in case anyone doubted that Warren had been the leading picket and most experienced among them, that 'Dessie was the man'.

Michael Pierce served his sentence at Sudbury open prison. He told me that while there he received unexpectedly kind treatment from one of the prison officers. This was especially surprising as Michael is mixed-race and prison staff had a reputation for right-wing politics and racism. Several years later, at his father's funeral, Michael answered a knock at the door. Standing on the step was the prison officer. Michael was astounded and alarmed in equal measure as he wondered how the man knew where he lived. It turned that he was Michael's uncle! He explained that he could not let on to Michael in prison for obvious reasons but he did what he could to make sure that he was OK.

Michael had worked for the same employer as Ken O'Shea and when he was released, he went back to work on the Monday morning. He was told that he had been sacked for breach of contract. O'Shea called a meeting on the site, explained the situation and called for support to have Michael reinstated. It was agreed unanimously. Ken then went to see management, and Michael got his job back.

Thomas Brian Williams, who served his time in the same prison as Michael Pierce, told him that his wife was so distressed that she felt she could not visit him in prison. When Brian was released, he would never speak with her about it as he did not want to cause her further unhappiness. Although he told Michael in 2012 that he wanted to put his name to the application to the CCRC with the rest of the pickets, he said that he would not do so as it would upset his wife.

Arthur Murray returned to his trade as a joiner and later opened his own joinery business.

Terry Renshaw, the youngest convicted picket, continued his trade as a painter. He became active in the Labour Party and was elected a local councillor for Flint, serving on the county council for many years. He served two terms as mayor of Flint. Terry remained an active trade unionist, UCATT branch secretary and full-time officer before becoming a TUC tutor, specialising in health and safety at work. He became a founder of the Shrewsbury 24 Campaign. 'We were not guilty of any crime or misdemeanour. Any fair-minded person looking at the evidence would conclude there has been a miscarriage of justice.'

Kevin Butcher returned to work as a scaffolder and remained a committed trade unionist. He was a consistent supporter of the Shrewsbury 24 Campaign. He told me that the memory of what happened to him and his fellow pickets had haunted him throughout his life. He felt helpless and could not understand why they were so let down by the unions. Kevin wrote to me shortly after we had travelled to the CCRC in Birmingham to deliver the pickets' application in April 2012, 'As I look back to that terrible time it wasn't only us, the Shrewsbury 24, that was affected. It also had a big impact on our wives and children as the detectives came to each of our homes to question our wives as well as us.'

Bernard Williams had been told by his employer that if he supported the strike in 1972 he would never work in the building industry again. He was blacklisted after the strike and never got back to his old job.

Ricky Tomlinson was freed from Leicester prison on 25 July 1975, after serving one year and eleven weeks in jail. Advance notice of his release was reported in *The Times* on 10 July and in a back-page piece in *Socialist Worker* under the headline 'Ricky Tomlinson out next week'.[46] Peter Carter and a group of family and supporters were at the prison gates when he stepped outside. Also present were television cameras and reporters, including Paul Foot.

Two months later he attended the TUC Congress in Blackpool and berated the platform from the balcony for failing to back Des, who still had another year to serve. Work in the building industry was blocked for Ricky and any jobs that he got were casual, so he turned to the work he had done throughout the 1960s, when he had earned a living at weekends as an entertainer in Liverpool pubs and clubs and as an agent for acts. He now made this his full-time work and also moved into acting and voiceovers for television commercials.[47] The rest is history.

Prison Protests

Throughout his time in jail, Des Warren would not accept that he was a criminal. He served his sentence in eight different prisons, plus two in London while his appeals were being heard. He was moved around at short notice, causing great distress to Elsa and the children when they tried to plan visits.

Des and Ricky had agreed to protest against their imprisonment. While in Wormwood Scrubs prison in February 1974, waiting for the outcome of their first appeal, they went on

Des Warren's wife, Elsa campaigning with their children to demand his release.

hunger strike, demanding to be recognised as political prisoners. When they returned to Stafford after the unsuccessful appeal, they continued with the hunger strike for a total of twenty-two days. They ended it when Des received a request to stop from the chairman of the Merseyside joint construction unions, who had just attended a lobby of Parliament with 3,000 trade union-ists.[48] A Labour government had just been elected and there were great hopes for their release.

Des and Ricky tasted freedom for a short period when they were released on bail on 3 June 1974. The trade unions in Liverpool obtained work for them for eight weeks at a site refitting the C&A store in the city centre. When the appeal failed in October, they were returned to Sudbury open prison, where they agreed to a new protest on Christmas Eve 1974. They refused to wear prison uniform any longer, which meant they could not mix with other prisoners or do work. They would be 'on the blanket' in solitary confinement for the next three months. They were both moved to closed prisons on 4 February, Des to Lincoln and Ricky to Leicester. Despite being split up they had made a pact not to wear prison clothes and accept the label of common criminal. In the event they would not see each other again for nearly twenty years.

Both men were considered for parole in the usual way but knew that it was unlikely to be recommended if they persisted with the protest.[49] Then Ricky changed his mind and decided to end his. He agreed to start wearing prison uniform again and wrote to Des on 18 March 1975 advising him to do the same.[50] At the same time he wrote to Des's wife, Elsa, to inform her of his decision. Des, however, was stunned and cut off all communication with him.[51] He later wrote of Ricky,

> I had never heard his name before the building workers' strike. I met him first at an action committee meeting at the Bull and Stirrup in Chester. Before the meeting we got into an argument. I overheard what he was saying to a group of building workers and I gave a derogatory fascist salute ... He had left the National Front but still put forward their racial views ...
>
> He was not active in the union until the 1972 dispute, which he had disagreed with at the outset. After involving himself, he worked hard at picketing – he was the leader of the Wrexham pickets. ... He and I were caught up in a situation where we were forced to fight together.[52]

Des Warren and Ricky Tomlinson were totally different characters. They were the only two of the twenty-four who had been politically active before the strike, but from different ends of the spectrum. Des had been an active member of the Communist Party for a number of years and Ricky an active member of the National Front, standing as a candidate for them in the Liverpool council elections in 1969.[53]

Although Des eventually agreed to wear prison clothes, he spent the rest of his sentence still challenging the prison authorities about conditions, the treatment of himself and fellow prisoners, and the corruption he witnessed among prison officers and by contractors.[54] His treatment was dependent upon the ebbs and flows of support for him outside prison. For example, at the end of July 1975, he went on a fourteen-day hunger strike in Nottingham prison as he was denied suitable footwear and had lost fourteen days' remission.[55] However, he received a morale booster when Amnesty International adopted him as a prisoner of conscience in that month, but after behind-the-scenes lobbying by a Labour Home Office minister this status was removed in November.[56] This left him demoralised, alone and exposed to all the hardships that the prison system could throw at him.

Des served a total of two years, twelve weeks and six days of his three-year sentence, including eight months in solitary confinement.[57] He had lost significant remission for the stands that he had taken. When he walked through the gates of Leicester prison at 8:00 a.m. on 5 August 1976 there was no fanfare or welcoming party.[58] He made his way home alone to north Wales using the rail travel warrant given to released prisoners. He had lost two stones in weight and, according to his wife Elsa, was a shadow of his former self when she met him at Rhyl station. Des was aged just thirty-eight.

On the day he arrived back at Henllan two visitors turned up at his house, Harry Chadwick and another building worker from Wigan. The door was opened by Elsa, who told the two men that she had a surprise for them. No one knew that Des had just been released. The pair had a bike for Des's eldest son, Nick, that they had bought from collections on building sites in the town. They had been involved in solidarity marches in 1975 for the 'Shrewsbury Two', from Wigan to London in February and later from Hull to Liverpool. Harry got to know Des very well over the following years, visiting him on many occasions. He was a founding member of the Shrewsbury 24 Campaign in 2006 and became its chairperson from 2011.

Elsa had campaigned tirelessly to gain Des's release. She had travelled from north Wales with the children to visit him in far-flung prisons and spoken at countless meetings calling for his release. Elsa now hoped that she and their five children could make up for lost time. Des felt that his task was to campaign for a public inquiry into what happened to the north Wales pickets. He was blacklisted throughout the industry and beyond, which denied him the opportunity to work ever again. He wrote two pamphlets about his experiences and continued to write to Labour MPs seeking their support for a public inquiry. Des went on to leave the Communist Party and joined the Workers

Revolutionary Party, which assisted him to write his book, published in 1982. When the WRP split up in the mid-1980s it coincided with the worsening of his health and he ceased being active in politics.

Des sued the Home Office for the damage to his health caused by the drugs he was given in jail by the prison doctor. The Home Office settled the action out of court.

Des Warren died prematurely on 24 April 2004 from Parkinson's disease, which he attributed to the drugs that he was given in prison. He was sixty-six. The most fitting tribute to him is the words that he wrote from prison for a Charter conference in 1975:

> From the day I was sentenced, in one way or another I have frequently found myself in a position which, as a political prisoner and a representative of the trade union movement, I could not accept. So, I've challenged the regime in various prisons, not fearlessly and without trepidation, in fact sometimes I have felt embarrassed because of the tremble in my voice, but I've always had my say and made my protest. The source of what has been termed my 'courage' throughout this ordeal is the support and encouragement I receive from the mass movement; the personal messages I receive from ordinary people who just drop me a line or a postcard; the struggle being put up in Parliament by Tribune MPs and their solidarity and visits; but most of all, the support I have had all along from my wife Elsa.
>
> What I'm trying to say is that I'm just like any other ordinary trade unionist caught up in an extraordinary situation, with ordinary strengths and weaknesses.[59]

PART V

The Campaign for Justice

13

The Shrewsbury
24 Campaign

Unfinished Business

History never really says goodbye. History says, see you later
Eduardo Galeano

On a bright Saturday morning in July 2006 an old friend, John Bohanna, a former T&GWU deputy convener at Ford's Halewood car plant, called to our house for a coffee, chat and catch-up. He had done this on many occasions for over twenty-five years. John asked me if I would attend a meeting at the Casa (the Liverpool dockers' club) to discuss the setting up of a campaign. Its aim would be to put pressure on the government to establish a public inquiry into the convictions of the Shrewsbury 24 pickets thirty-two years before.

John knew that I was familiar with the case and he thought that I would be interested in getting involved. The meeting had been arranged by a group of retired trade unionists and socialists based in the North West. John explained that the premature death of Des Warren in 2004 had acted as the catalyst for the launch of a campaign to clear the pickets' names. As we spoke about it the memories of the early 1970s came flooding back to me. I had never forgotten the sense of anger and disappointment felt by trade unionists at the time. The case of the Shrewsbury pickets was unfinished business.

The Launch of the Campaign

John and I sat together at the inaugural meeting on the afternoon of Saturday 5 August 2006. To me it was eerie as I knew
that this was the thirtieth anniversary of Des Warren's release
from prison. The Casa's big room was packed. The chairperson
explained that the purpose of the meeting was to campaign for
a public inquiry as they firmly believed there had been a miscarriage of justice. It ended with an agreement to set up a steering
committee. A clipboard was circulated, asking for people to
sign up if they wanted to participate. John did, but was surprised when I declined. I explained to him that I was involved
in a long-running equal-pay claim for forty dinner ladies in St
Helens and would not have the time to commit to the campaign.
I did not want to be a passenger who would just turn up to
meetings but never do anything. John understood and agreed to
keep me updated.

Eighteen months later John told me that the campaign
committee was desperate for a treasurer and they wanted me
to do it. He urged me to join as my skills and trade union
experience would be invaluable to the campaign. My involvement with the equal-pay case was coming to an end and I
agreed to do it.

The Campaign Committee

I understood that raising funds for the campaign was not going
to be an easy job but I was prepared to get stuck in and was
excited to be part of such a worthwhile cause. The committee
gave me a warm welcome when I attended my first meeting at
the Casa. I was told that the campaign was trying to secure a
public inquiry into the trials. Apart from John and myself there
were seven others in attendance: Harry, a joiner and UCATT
member; Ed, a retired car worker; Joe, a criminology professor
and UCU member; Richard, a part-time worker in an arts collective; Mick, a retired scaffolder; Frank, a retired labourer; and
Terry, the only convicted picket on the committee, who remained

an active UCATT member and was a TUC tutor. Apart from me, there were no other women on the committee.

I learned of the progress that had been made since the launch, and at the end of the meeting the secretary, who had also been the treasurer, asked me for a quiet word. He was friendly and gave me a bag full of old receipts and scraps of paper, then said, 'Thanks, luv, for agreeing to be the treasurer but you don't need to attend any further meetings. Your role is to raise funds for the campaign. You can do that from your house. We don't expect you to be involved with any of the campaign's activities.' I was a little taken aback, but responded with a smile and said, 'Let's just see how it goes.' He left the campaign in 2011.

I had been given a campaign bulletin dated 8 March 2008. It reported that the committee had decided to instruct a solicitor to prepare an application to the Criminal Cases Review Commission (CCRC), but this was going to cost a lot of money. Now I understood why they wanted a dedicated treasurer. I realised that there was no handy manual for setting up and running a campaign. There are no terms of reference; it is nearly always a case of trial and error. What keeps supporters together is their shared desire to achieve the objectives of the campaign. Ours was made up of different personalities, who were all involved in the committee on a voluntary basis. It was therefore quite natural for people to join and leave for their own reasons.

The campaign had reached a watershed in its development. It had organised well-attended public meetings in Shotton in 2007 and in the Welsh Centre, London, in October 2008, but they were 'one-offs'. The campaign needed to firm up its aims, objectives and direction. It had produced a campaign bulletin for its members but no regular leaflets to distribute to trade unionists, nor did it have any plan to broaden support. In March 2009 the campaign held a lobby of Parliament and a meeting in Committee Room 8, chaired by Jeremy Corbyn MP. It was an important milestone as the main speaker was Alan Ritchie, the general secretary of UCATT. He gave a passionate speech during which he apologised for the fact that UCATT had not supported the pickets in their hour of need in 1973–74:

The Shrewsbury pickets were not criminals; they were political prisoners. The leadership in my union at the time had a lot of failings. I am the first to hold my hand up and say that we failed the pickets at the time ... We are committed to right this injustice.[1]

The Criminal Cases Review Commission

A solicitor, Campbell Malone, had been advising the committee informally for several months. He had represented eleven of the twenty-four who were tried in Shrewsbury all those years ago and therefore knew about the case. Early in 2008 he told the committee that if the pickets wanted to make applications to the CCRC he would have to be formerly engaged to act on their behalf. Campbell was a criminal lawyer who was now working for Stephensons solicitors in Wigan. He was in his mid-sixties and winding down his career, working reduced hours, two or three days a week. Although on the verge of retirement he agreed to help the pickets as much as he could and would prepare a CCRC application for a fixed fee.

We received Campbell's first draft of a submission for the CCRC in August 2009. He apologised for the delay and explained that he was working part-time and that drafting the application for such a complex case was not straightforward. The committee's knowledge of the CCRC was limited, to say the least, so I decided to learn exactly what its function was and the powers it had. I discovered from its website and from various articles that it was a public body answerable to the Ministry of Justice, which dealt with claims of miscarriage of justice. It had the power to refer a person's conviction to the Court of Appeal if their first appeal had been unsuccessful. The most important point I discovered was that the CCRC would only consider an application if the convicted person had 'fresh evidence'. This meant evidence that the defence did not have or know about at the original trial.

Campbell's draft application was seventeen pages long, detailing the political and economic conditions in 1973–4 and the strikes that occurred. It also described the pickets' arrests, trials and convictions and the unfair treatment of the men at the time. Unfortunately, it did not contain any fresh evidence. The committee had concerns but was reluctant to upset Campbell after the work that had been put into the draft. After discussing the content in detail, we wrote to him itemising a number of issues. He accepted our comments and set about preparing another draft, but when we received it, it did not take us any further. We decided to refer it back to Campbell for a further look. We were conscious that we could ill afford to get the pickets' hopes up by lodging an application that we knew had little chance of success. We also realised that it was too big a task to expect Campbell to recall the details of what happened at the three trials after such a long period of time. We decided to assist him and obtain the services of a researcher whose job would be to look for fresh evidence to get us past the gatekeepers at the CCRC.

No Money, but We Need a Researcher

Due to the historic and political nature of the pickets' case we knew we would need an experienced researcher. We learned that we would have to pay in the region of £50,000 to do the job thoroughly and then there was no guarantee that any fresh evidence would be discovered. At that time, we had the princely sum of £1,500 in the bank so paying for a researcher was a complete non-starter. We had no choice but to try and find the fresh evidence ourselves. This task was made more difficult when, in 2008, the Labour government turned down our request for information relating to the Shrewsbury trials. The committee had asked Peter Kilfoyle, MP for Liverpool Walton, to ask the government to release such documents, but his repeated requests fell on deaf ears. After protracted correspondence between Kilfoyle and the Cabinet Office he eventually received a letter from Jack Straw, the lord chancellor and secretary of state for justice, refusing to release the documents under Section 23 of the Freedom of Information Act, dealing with national security:

The purpose of retaining Section 23 information is to protect the space within which the security agencies operate. In cases where the department has determined that the information ought not to be sent to TNA by virtue of the fact it falls within the scope of Section 23, I am satisfied that this falls into the category of 'other special reason' under the Public Records Act. As such the security and intelligence 'blanket' clearly applies. The department therefore has my consent to retain this information.[2]

Straw's attitude was in complete contrast to that of the next two Labour Party leaders who each agreed a commitment in Labour's election manifestoes for 2015, 2017 and 2019 to release all documents relating to the trials. I was confident that if Labour had succeeded on any of these occasions in forming a government, particularly under Jeremy Corbyn, they would not have hesitated in ensuring that all retained documents were released for public scrutiny.

At the time the Public Records Act 1958 obliged governments to release documents to The National Archives at Kew after a period of thirty (now twenty) years. I was soon to learn that there are exemptions that governments can use to retain any 'secret' information in perpetuity.[3]

Notwithstanding the earlier suggestion of the campaign secretary, that it was unnecessary for me even to attend the meetings, I volunteered to take on the task of campaign researcher as well as continuing with my treasurer's role. I had never done this type of work before but I was willing to have a go. My gesture was welcomed by most of the committee. The die was now cast; I had the responsibility of finding the fresh evidence that was needed to overturn convictions from thirty-five years ago. At the same time, I was acutely aware that I had the responsibility of raising funds to keep the campaign going. We desperately needed trade union and political support to put our campaign on the map. Our chairperson, Terry, hit the nail on the head when he said, 'We have got a mountain to climb.' We knew that without fresh evidence to present to the CCRC we were going nowhere. Thus my endeavours to search for the truth began.

Funds Needed

I made some changes to fundraising when I became treasurer of the campaign. I made it a policy that the pickets were not to be asked to make any contribution towards the legal costs. They had already paid a heavy price all those years ago. This did not go down well with some of the committee members as they argued that one of the pickets was a millionaire. But I pointed out that this man had gone to jail and we should not ask him to contribute to the legal costs, and indeed he never did.

In 2007 the committee had raised funds through donations and loans to have Des Warren's book, *The Key to My Cell*, reprinted. I was told that this was to be sold to raise funds and spread awareness about the case. They also had campaign T-shirts printed. The problem was that it takes time to sell books and T-shirts. We had pressure on us to pay legal fees and campaign expenses. The task was daunting. Who was going to donate to a campaign for 24 'criminals' who had been convicted decades ago? I thought, 'no pressure, Eileen'. I have always had confidence in the trade union and labour movement. My view is that workers' organisations stand for the abiding principle of solidarity, 'an injury to one is an injury to all.' I believed that if we told the story about what happened to the Shrewsbury pickets and explained what we were trying to achieve then we would get the support we needed.

An important first step came in 2007 when campaign supporters in UCATT successfully proposed a resolution calling for a parliamentary inquiry into the trials and jailing of the pickets. The resolution was taken to the TUC Congress in the autumn, where UCATT had it adopted as policy by the whole trade union movement. This was a significant platform for the campaign. I decided to build upon this by producing an affiliation sheet for trade unions, trades councils and Labour Party branches, who were our natural supporters. There was opposition from some committee members to my proposal to seek support from trade unions in this way. They regarded the trade unions as 'sell-out merchants' that had deserted the pickets the first time around. They argued that we could take their money, but have nothing to do with them! Terry responded for the majority of us, 'We cannot beat them with sticks and then put out our hand for money.' It was eventually agreed that I go ahead.

When a union branch parts with funds it naturally wants to know why. I prepared an information sheet that described the aims of the campaign. It also included a brief history of the strike and trials. In truth, the first one I wrote was like a chapter from *War and Peace*, a sharp lesson learned. Make it short and interesting. Throughout the following years we revised the information sheet regularly to keep it up to date.

When I joined the committee, I was told that Ricky Tomlinson had been approached in 2006 and asked to support the campaign. It was thought that his celebrity status would attract support for us. He agreed but explained that his involvement would be subject to his commercial interests. He had recently become a partner in the Green Room, a new cabaret club in Liverpool city centre, and he was keen to make a success of it. He also had a number of acting roles and personal appearances lined up. Ricky said he would not be able to attend any committee meetings due to his busy work schedule. He was absolutely honest and up-front with us; the committee was just grateful that he was involved. I did not know Ricky at all but was aware that he had served time as a Shrewsbury picket and deserved justice.

Research Begins

When my quest began, the campaign involved just four pickets: Terry Renshaw, Des Warren (through his son Andy), Arthur Murray and Ricky Tomlinson. I was keen to get more pickets involved. My view was that this was a campaign for justice for all twenty-four, not just for a handful. I proposed that we should try and contact all the pickets and ask if they wanted to become involved. One or two on the committee disagreed on the basis that 'the main pickets are involved, so why bother?' but the rest of the committee agreed with my suggestion. Terry immediately offered to try and find them. He had lived in Flint all his life and had been a Labour councillor for many years so he knew a lot of local people. Terry warned us that it would not be easy as the twenty-four pickets had been a diverse group. Most of them did not know each other before the strike and certainly had not met up as a group since then. They lived in different areas in north Wales, had different trades, worked for different companies and had belonged to two different trade unions. The only single thing they had in common was that they were prosecuted in one of the three trials at Shrewsbury Crown Court in 1973 and 1974. It was clear that Terry had his work cut out. In the event, we ended up with ten pickets to make an application to the CCRC.

Meeting the Pickets

As the former legal officer of the Liverpool, North Wales and Irish region of the General Municipal and Boilermakers Union I was experienced in talking to members, gathering evidence and taking statements for cases. But this was different. I was to meet people whom I had heard about for many years but not met. Over the next year I was to listen to their accounts, which for some had brought about prison sentences and for others suspended prison sentences and fines. I felt a real sense of responsibility to these people to ensure that I gathered as much information as possible so that we could submit a strong application to the CCRC on their behalf. They had not been interviewed by anyone about these events since being questioned by the police in 1972 and their lawyers in 1973.

First, I contacted Des Warren's son Andy and travelled to his home in Chester. He was still at primary school when his dad went through the rigours of a twelve-week trial and a long jail sentence. Andy was very friendly and welcoming and we had a long chat about the campaign and what we hoped to achieve. I asked if his dad had any papers that he felt he could share with me. He replied that I could have all his dad's archives. True to his word, he turned up at my house in Liverpool in his pickup truck with two suitcases, a holdall and a number of bags. He had a smile on his face and said, 'Here you go, Eileen. I told you my dad kept everything.' I was absolutely delighted and hugged him. Up to that point I did not have a crumb of information that would steer me in the right direction.

I knew that the pickets themselves would be a challenge. I decided that my first meeting with each of them would be informal. I was acutely aware that I am a Scouser and a woman! These men, with the single exception of Ricky Tomlinson, were all building workers from north Wales. I organised a timetable to meet them at their respective homes in trial order: first trial, John McKinsie Jones, Ken O'Shea and Ricky Tomlinson; second trial, Malcolm Clee, Michael Pierce and Arthur Murray; third trial, Kevin Butcher, Bernard Williams and Terry. All of the pickets were friendly and tried to assist me with as much information as they could remember. I also spoke with their wives to gain an insight into what they experienced during that time. I soon discovered that the pickets, understandably, had limited memories of their particular part in picketing on 6 September 1972 and of their trials. Most of the pickets were old-fashioned gentlemen, courteous, open and honest in their answers to my questions. Without doubt the picket who stood out with the sharpest memory was John McKinsie Jones.

When I reviewed all the information from my discussions with the men and their families a common theme flowed through all of their statements: that they had been 'set up' by the police. Fear had been commonplace among them, particularly after the first trial. Many of them explained that they had never been involved with any form of strike action prior to the national strike. Ricky Tomlinson had not been in a union when the strike started and he received a two-year jail sentence!

Elsa Warren and Marlene Tomlinson

I had read that at the end of the first trial at Shrewsbury, while Judge Mais was handing down his sentences to the pickets, there was a disturbance in the jury box and that two jurors had walked out in disgust. Outside the court a juror had approached Elsa

Warren and later Marlene Tomlinson and complained about the sentences. They each recalled that the juror told them that a court usher had spoken with the jury when they were deliberating their verdicts. He had assured them that if the pickets were found guilty, they would just be fined.

I needed to speak with both of them and, if they agreed, take a statement and pass it to the CCRC as further evidence to support the pickets' case. I discovered that Elsa lived in Chester and she agreed to see me. It was a pleasure to meet her. She is astute, wonderfully warm and a good historian. She had played a very prominent role during Des's imprisonment, organising child minders for their five children when she went to speak at meetings up and down the country. She would appear at demonstrations and lobbies of MPs at the House of Commons, and wrote countless letters to government ministers for the release of her husband.

Elsa confirmed to me that outside the court a juror had approached her and informed her, 'The jury had been told that the men would be fined, would not receive a custodial sentence and if the jury had taken any longer over the verdicts they would be there over Christmas.' I made a note of what she said and passed it directly to our solicitors.

Arrangements to talk with Marlene Tomlinson were complicated. She had divorced Ricky in 1986, and it had not been amicable. I contacted her through their daughter, Kate, who was friendly and helpful. Marlene was very ill and lived with Kate, who looked after her. She agreed to see me but this was subject to Ricky not being involved. I visited her on 29 October 2013. She was a lovely lady, a bit nervous at first, but soon got into her stride. She reminded me very much of my late mum, which made an impact on me. She reiterated that she was talking to me to support all the pickets because 'what was done was so wrong.' Marlene told me that she had two young baby boys when her husband went to prison. She said that she had always been a quiet person, but she had supported him by going on demonstrations, attending conferences and speaking at meetings.

Marlene, like Elsa, told me that when she had attended the last day of the trial, she had gone to the foyer of the court to smoke a cigarette and was approached by two men whom she recognised as jurors. One of them said to her, 'You are Tomlinson's wife, aren't you?' She replied that she was. The man then said to her, 'He should not have gone to jail. We were told they were going to be given suspended sentences or a fine.' She vividly remembers the discussion as, at that point, she did not know that Ricky had been sentenced to two years' imprisonment. The news stunned her.

I thanked her for meeting me and said I would love to visit her again. She held my hand and wished me well. I sent her statement on to our solicitors. Sadly, I was never to see Marlene again as she passed away in February 2015.

For many years the pickets had experienced dreadful indignities. They were blacklisted and ostracised by their communities, and their children ridiculed in the school playground. Their wives, sisters and girlfriends had been insulted when they went to work or out shopping. As a result, they had all kept their heads down over the past thirty or more years. Even then, a couple of the families asked me not to mention their names when writing about the campaign, or to display photographs of them. One picket only told his grown-up children of his trial five years after becoming involved in the campaign. They had carried the shame of their prosecutions throughout their lives.

The conversations I had with the pickets revealed a rich seam of unknown information about their experiences in 1972–4. It was also the start of a long friendship with many of them and their families. But sadly, those talks did not produce the fresh evidence that we needed for the CCRC.

Serendipity

The committee were informed that Campbell Malone was retiring from practice. He suggested that we keep the case with the Wigan firm and that another experienced solicitor would handle it. The committee discussed it and the general feeling was that, owing to the complexities of the case, we should instruct a firm that had a track record of human rights cases. Our link with

Campbell would be coming to an end and we thought that it would be a good opportunity for a fresh mind to consider the case. But who?

I had an appointment to meet Ken Loach, at his London office. He had agreed to provide a spoken introduction to our fundraising CD, *Whose Conspiracy?* He asked me how we were getting on and I explained our dilemma in trying to find a new firm of solicitors. Without hesitation he said, 'I have got just the firm for you.' He picked up the phone and called Stephen Grosz, senior partner at Bindmans, a distinguished London human rights law firm. He explained to Stephen who I was and passed the phone to me. After listening to me, Stephen said that a Bindmans lawyer would be in touch. Our campaign can never repay Ken for helping us when we needed it. It was pure serendipity meeting Ken at that particular time in the campaign's history. We went on to instruct Bindmans to work with us and to lodge and pursue the application with the CCRC on behalf of all ten pickets. The firm stayed with us over the next ten years through all the legal ups and downs until we achieved victory.

On the Road to Find the Truth

An old friend, Laurie Flynn, contacted me and said how delighted he was to hear that the convictions of the Shrewsbury pickets were being challenged. He had a distinguished record as an investigative journalist and had written two pamphlets on the case at the time of the trials. Laurie told me that he had a large number of documents and agreed to send me copies. Twenty ring binders arrived! He also sent a long letter of explanation and many ideas, which were most welcome. I transformed the upstairs study in my house with two desks, two printers, a desktop computer and a filing cabinet. Extra bookshelves were put up to hold files, newspapers and other material that grew from my discoveries over the following years.

The documents so generously given to me by Laurie set in motion a number of changes to my thinking about researching the case. There were many documents that I did not understand or know how to analyse properly. Laurie made an inspired suggestion to me, that I should apply to study for a PhD. I was stunned as I could not for a second understand his logic. He explained that if I was serious about researching the case, it would be useful to have the legitimacy of being a postgraduate student. It would give access to archives that are not generally available to the public and would assist me in persuading people to be interviewed about the case. It seemed a crazy idea as I was snowed under in campaign work but I said I would think about it.

I began to make inquiries and approached known left-wing academics at universities in Manchester, Keele, Bristol and Stirling whom I thought might be interested in supervising me in writing about the Shrewsbury pickets' case. None of them were. Then I discovered the ideal person right on my doorstep. I was speaking with Joe from our committee about Laurie's idea and he immediately suggested Dr David Whyte, a lecturer in the Criminology Department at the University of Liverpool. Joe arranged for me to meet David and it turned out to be one of the best things that could have happened for our campaign. He was totally supportive and helpful, and understood the issues straight away. I discovered that he was an authority on corporate crime and had written a thesis about the Piper Alpha disaster in the North Sea.

David recommended that I study first for a master's degree in research, which would be a one-year full-time course. He also said that I would need two referees to support my application. It had been thirty years since I had studied for a degree at Liverpool Polytechnic but I still kept in contact with two of the main lecturers, Professor Sam Davies and Ron Noon. Both were staunch trade unionists and socialists who lived nearby, so off I went to see them both. They were delighted to hear what I was planning and wrote the most glowing of references. They became supporters of the campaign and went with us to Birmingham when we handed in the pickets' applications to the CCRC in 2012.

At the time, I knew what information I was looking for but not how to develop a methodology to analyse and cross-reference the information I had. David was crucial for teaching me this and I was fortunate that he was my tutor on the master's course. In tandem with attending the master's course I would carry on my campaign work, raising funds, seeking speaker requests and affiliations, and looking for documents.

The main assessment for the degree was a 30,000-word dissertation, which I had to research and write in the final three months of the course. It could be on a subject of my own choosing and I decided that it had to be something that was central to the campaign. The title was, 'The Criminal Cases Review Commission: the key or the lock to the door for wrongful convictions?'. By time I had completed it there was nothing I did not know about the organisation. This knowledge proved to be invaluable for us when dealing with the CCRC over the following years. I was awarded the Masters degree in 2011 and then moved on to the big one.

The theme of my PhD thesis mirrored the research that I was doing for the campaign: 'Trade union action and the criminal law: the case of the Shrewsbury pickets'. I completed it in 2017. It enabled me to discover and use far more information about the case than simply the 'fresh evidence' that the CCRC was concerned with. I was awarded my doctorate in 2018.

The Committee's Activity

As the treasurer I gave serious thought to the ways we could raise money to support the pickets' legal case. There was nothing to be lost, I adopted the old adage 'always go for the biggest first', and hopefully it'll get easier after that. In this instance it was the national trade unions and I wrote to all of them. By 2012 we had fourteen national unions affiliated to the campaign, including the Professional Footballers' Association and the Musicians' Union. On the back of this success, we looked to regional and local trade unions to affiliate to us. These small annual affiliations from branches were the lifeblood of the campaign, providing a source of grass-roots support from which information about the pickets' case could be spread. I ensured that all our affiliates were acknowledged and kept up to date.

The campaign gained tremendous support from Shropshire & Telford Trades Union Council. In 2009 our chairperson liaised with two of their officers, Mike Edwards and Brett Davies, who pulled out all the stops to organise a successful march and rally in Shrewsbury town centre on 5 July. We hired a coach from the North West and other supporters travelled from north Wales, the Midlands and London. The march ended at Lord Hill's column outside the Shire Hall, scene of the trials in 1973–4. There were hundreds of enthusiastic people, including Des Warren's sisters, who heard speeches from Ricky, Arthur Scargill and Rob Williams. It was a good day, enjoyed by all. The following year the committee secretary wanted us to have another rally in Shrewsbury and asked the Trades Union Council to organise it for 3 July. Once again, Mike, Brett and other council members did all the work for us and arranged for the general secretary of the National Union of Rail Maritime and Transport Workers (RMT), Bob Crow, to be the main speaker, together with Janice Goodrich, president of the Public and Commercial Services Union (PCS).

We did not attract the same level of support from the North West and elsewhere as we had the previous year. We realised we could not expect our supporters in Shrewsbury to take on the responsibility for organising this every year, especially as they, like all trade unionists, were now becoming heavily involved in campaigning against the newly elected Tory–Liberal coalition government. We decided not to organise another rally, but to concentrate on broadening the support for the campaign in other ways. The trades council remained solid supporters and friends of the campaign.

Harry and the Warwick Archives

My interviews with the pickets gave me rich insights into their experiences of the strike and trials but they had no knowledge of the legal issues and no papers. I decided to look for documents in various libraries and archives around the country. First in line were the employers. I learned that the archives of the NFBTE were held at the Modern Records Centre, University of Warwick. I asked Harry Chadwick if he would like to come with me. At first, he gave me a funny look, then he said in his broad Bolton accent, 'Ay, alright then.' But I could tell he wasn't keen. Harry is a joiner, who had been on strike and picketed in 1972. He is a quiet and unobtrusive man, but beneath the veneer is an astute experienced trade unionist who has a sharp political mind. Harry became a friend of Des Warren after he came out of prison in 1976 and would often visit him at his home in Chester. He offered to drive me to Warwick, for which I was grateful as I had not been there before. He said that he had just one problem, a slipped disc! He assured me that he was fine driving, but walking was difficult. It was only when we reached Warwick that I realised what he meant. I had to help him from the car and into the archives, arms linked; we must have looked like a pair of drunks!

Harry sat down at one of the large tables in the archives, took his coat off and got comfortable. I then registered and confirmed my pre-order of documents with the librarian. Harry began to look worried. I was concerned that he was in pain and asked if he wanted painkillers. 'No, but I do have a problem. I've never been to a place like this before. I don't know what I'm supposed to be looking for.' I replied, 'Harry, you'll have no problem, you'll know as soon as you spot it.' I split up the files and gave him about half a dozen. No sooner had he opened the first one when I heard an almighty shout. 'Have you seen this, Eileen, what those bastards were doing and we didn't know!' The whole library came to a halt. I put my finger on my lips and whispered, 'We have to be quiet.' With that he turned around to face the room and in a booming voice said, 'Sorry about that!' We had a really good day at Warwick and among some interesting documents we found the important NFBTE 'dossier' of reports of picketing during the strike. Harry never hesitated again. He became an expert in spotting little gems of information. He absolutely loves the Working-Class Movement Library in Salford.

Kew – What a Revelation

The most important source of documents I discovered was at The National Archives in Kew. I was able to look through the catalogue online to try to ascertain what documents might be buried there. There is no big red arrow pointing to the files that would tell me who the decision makers were who planned the fate of the Shrewsbury pickets. It is a brilliant repository for the country's archives but the onus is on the visitor to find what they are looking for. Nothing is straightforward; lateral thinking is the name of the game. My first visit, in March 2012, involved two days familiarising myself with the systems and the best way to search for relevant files. It was very productive as I discovered the letter that the attorney general, Sir Peter Rawlinson QC, had sent to the home secretary, Robert Carr, on 25 January 1973. This was a revelation as it showed that Rawlinson had considered a number of picketing cases that had been referred to him and he advised against prosecutions. At last, we had some fresh evidence. This letter and a number of other documents I found on that first visit were incorporated into the submission that Bindmans made for the pickets when their applications were put in four weeks later.

I would return to Kew on many other occasions over the following five years. It was on a visit there in October 2013 that I found the crucial evidence in a file of the Director of Public Prosecutions. It contained scores of documents about the trials including the one that, in 2021, led the Court of Appeal to conclude that the pickets' convictions were unsafe and must be quashed. It was the letter from West Mercia police to Drake's junior barrister, Desmond Fennell, sent just a couple of weeks before the first trial began, advising him that they had destroyed original witness statements. The National Archives is a tremendous resource and I would advise everyone to visit.

Presenting the Pickets' Application to the CCRC

Terry Renshaw and I had a meeting at Bindmans' office in Gray's Inn Road, London, to discuss the applications to the CCRC with

Rhona Friedman, the criminal law solicitor who was to handle the case. She was very helpful and advised us that she was going to ask Ben Newton, a junior barrister at Doughty Street Chambers, to help. I gave Rhona the fresh evidence that I had discovered at Kew together with other background documents, including one of Campbell's drafts. I appreciated that Rhona knew nothing about a case that was nearly forty years old and involved three trials and multiple convictions. She informed us that she had experience with applications to the CCRC and was happy to take it on. We agreed a set fee for lodging the application and that Bindmans would work on a reduced rate for any future costs. After the meeting, Terry and I took a taxi to Euston in silence. We boarded the train and sat down in our seats. Then we just looked at each other, shook hands and smiled. No matter what was going to happen, we were on our way.

The bill from Campbell Malone and Bindmans' initial bill to prepare the submission to the CCRC had completely wiped out our funds. There were other costs coming in, so, with the agreement of the committee, I asked Ricky Tomlinson for a loan of £10,000 and promised to pay him back in three instalments. He agreed and this tided us over until we had raised more money through our campaigning work. It was really good of him to help us out at this point. We were able to repay the loan to him in three tranches, starting with £3,000 in February 2013, another in June and the final payment of £4,000 in June 2014. We stayed true to our word, that no picket would be asked to pay from their own pocket towards the campaign to get them justice.

Handing in the Pickets' Application to the CCRC

We were all delighted with the progress we had made. I knew we would need more evidence to support the case and told the committee I was prepared to continue to research. We were gaining trade union support and had become established as a legitimate and credible campaign, and were ready to lodge the pickets' application with the CCRC. I suggested that instead of simply sending it in the post we should make an occasion of it. We would all travel to the CCRC office in Birmingham and hand in the applications. This should be a celebration; the first time the pickets had had the opportunity to fight back. On 3 April 2012 we set off from the Green Room club, Liverpool, for the journey down the M6. The minibus was full of members of the committee, pickets and supporters. Although it was just after breakfast time the atmosphere on the bus was heady. There was a lot of laughter and singing of songs; there was a strong feeling of solidarity.

We were met in Birmingham by our friends from Shropshire & Telford TUC, headed by Mike, Brett and Jackie, together with many of their delegates and their union banners. UCATT's general secretary, Steve Murphy, and members from Birmingham were there, as well as John McDonnell MP, whom I had met the year before and who has given our campaign so much help over the years.

I had contacted the CCRC to let them know we were going to deliver the applications by hand. They were ready for us. The head of communications, Justin Hawkins, came outside to receive the applications on the steps of the CCRC. It was warm and sunny, and we had lots of photographs taken to mark the occasion. From there we walked around to Unison's West Midlands regional office, where we had been invited for sandwiches and tea. The day held so much promise, hope and friendship.

The following month, Terry, Ricky and myself travelled to London for a meeting at Bindmans. We then went to the House of Commons to see John McDonnell MP. He made us welcome and was very supportive, as always. He was delighted that the campaign had made such progress and asked how he could help. I asked him for advice on the direction of the campaign. He confirmed that it was crucial to have trade union support and a voice in Parliament. It was also vital to continue to obtain as much evidence as possible as he could not see the Tories releasing any information to the campaign. He said we had made such a good start that it was important to maintain the momentum and never give up. I have never forgotten and remind John of his wise words when we meet.

A couple of months after meeting John, myself, Terry, Ricky and Harry had a meeting at the TUC in London with Frances O'Grady, the newly elected general secretary, and Paul Nowak, the assistant general secretary. We received the warmest of welcomes and they both listened carefully to the case I laid out on behalf of the pickets. I was a little nervous meeting them both as there was a lot riding on their response. I need not have worried. From that first meeting on 11 July, they never hesitated in offering their help. Even when the going got tough for us there were always words of support from them. The pickets' applications had now been lodged with the CCRC and the campaign was on its way, even though we had a long way to go.

14

The Campaign Gets Going

When we lodged the pickets' application with the CCRC the campaign moved up a gear. My research had confirmed that there were a large number of documents about the Shrewsbury trials that were still being withheld by the government. I had made applications to the Cabinet Office and the Home Office under the Freedom of Information Act but these had been rejected under Section 23, 'Information supplied by, or relating to, bodies dealing with security matters'.

EDM and e-Petition

In July 2012 John McDonnell had sponsored an Early Day Motion in the Commons welcoming the pickets' application to the CCRC and the support it had received from UCATT, Unite and other unions. It noted the government's refusal to release documents about the trials under Section 23 and called 'on the Government to release forthwith all such papers for public scrutiny'.[1] The EDM attracted sixty-two signatures from MPs. At the same time the campaign decided to launch a 'Downing Street e-petition'. This had been one of the innovations of the coalition government of David Cameron a year earlier. If a petition attracted more than 10,000 signatures a government department would make a written response, and if more than 100,000 signed it would be considered for a parliamentary debate by the House of Commons Backbench Business Committee.

The campaign now made use of its own e-resources to publicise the petition. Richard Grove from Bristol Radical History Group volunteered to help. He designed, set up, and maintained our website, Facebook page and Twitter account. These platforms proved to be indispensable in promoting our campaign and communicating with supporters. We used them to send a link to the government's e-petition website. We quickly reached the 10,000 mark and on 20 September 2012 the government put a statement on its website.[2] It simply repeated the response I had received when I had requested the documents under the FOI Act: it baldly stated that there were only a few documents that the Cabinet Office was withholding, which all related to the intelligence agencies. That was not going to put us off.

The Fortieth Anniversary of the 1972 Strike

To keep the campaign in the public eye and to obtain and retain trade union support I suggested that we have a celebratory social on the fortieth anniversary of the strike. We could also use the occasion to raise badly needed funds. Some members commented about the amount of work it would take to organise such an event, which might come to nothing if we could not attract sufficient people. Their points were valid, but I just felt it was an opportunity too good to miss. To show how serious I was, I said that I would organise it and would also prepare a talk about the campaign, using slides on a big screen to show the documents I had uncovered at the Kew archives. I was relieved when the committee decided to support it. I approached Ricky Tomlinson and asked if the campaign could have the Green Room for the event; it would be on a Sunday afternoon when the club was closed. He readily agreed and said that some of the artists on his agency books would do a turn onstage for us. I wrote to every trade union contact we had and invited them to book tables in advance. I must admit my heart was in my mouth worrying about the attendance.

We turned up at the club at 10:30 a.m. on the Sunday morning and prepared it for the event. Ann Dobie and Harry Chadwick worked their socks off moving the tables around, placing the chairs, hoovering up after the frivolities of the previous night's cabaret. We set up the screen and laptop for the presentation, while my son Alex organised a display of photographs and large campaign information sheets. He also arranged a merchandise table. When we finished the nerves crept in while we waited for our supporters to arrive. But we need not have worried as they turned out in style. There were five union general secretaries, an MP, four local councillors and many shop stewards from the CWU, the RMT, ASLEF, Unite, USDAW, the PCS, Unison, the NUJ and the UCU. There was a delegation of former Ford workers and dockers, and many people whom we had come across over the years, as well as many relatives and friends. But the most satisfying for us was that some of the pickets attended with their families. I was also delighted that Laurie Flynn travelled from Edinburgh to be with us.

The speeches were extremely good, full of warmth and solidarity. On behalf of the campaign, I explained our progress and everyone was eager to see the documents that I had discovered. Ricky's artists lightened the afternoon, particularly the magician who mesmerised us with the disappearing twenty-pound note and a piece of toast. The scouse that we served went down a treat. The event was an absolute success. We were all shattered but relieved that it had gone so well. It was another milestone for the campaign. We were able to capture the occasion with pictures taken by our photographer, Chris Gregory, who had been taking photographs of pickets, campaign members and our activities since 2009. It has left us with a permanent record of our achievements.

Chris Grayling: Conservative Secretary of State for Justice

In October 2012, Terry Renshaw had approached his local MP on behalf of the committee to ask him to write to Chris Grayling MP, the secretary of state for justice, to request that he release all documents relating to the Shrewsbury trials. Grayling replied that a year earlier the government had reviewed the decision of various departments to withhold documents under Section 23 of the Freedom of Information Act, the national security exemption.[3] On 19 December 2011, his predecessor as Lord Chancellor, Kenneth Clarke, had signed a new instrument giving his approval for the retention of records. Grayling wrote that the information relating to the Shrewsbury trials was covered by this security instrument, which would be in force until 31 December 2021. We discussed the letter at our committee meeting and decided to make it public. The government was making these decisions behind closed doors and we needed to highlight the way in which they were obstructing us in achieving justice for the pickets. I set about organising a press conference in Portcullis House, London, an office building for MPs opposite Parliament. Here we could be sure to attract media coverage and get the message out to as many trade unionists as possible.

Portcullis House: Another World

I had never been to Portcullis House but was aware that meetings are held there by people who wanted to lobby and brief MPs. This was the so-called 'Westminster bubble'. John McDonnell booked a room for us for 23 January 2013 and worked very hard to encourage as many MPs as possible to attend. I contacted trade unions and the media, both press and television. I asked if any of the pickets would like to attend with our committee members. We were also hoping that the publicity would assist us with the e-petition that we had started six months earlier as we needed 100,000 signatures by June. John once again pulled out all the stops; among those in attendance were Frances O'Grady from the TUC; the general secretaries of UCATT, Steve Murphy, and Unite, Len McCluskey; MPs Dennis Skinner, David Anderson and Steve Rotheram; Lord Doug Hoyle; and Ken Loach. They all spoke passionately in support of our campaign and pledged to help us in any way they could. Ricky spoke and I said a few words about the research and the documents that I knew existed but were being deliberately retained by the government.

It was an excellent meeting and we obtained a lot of much-needed media coverage. One of the MPs who attended was David Anderson. Although we did not know it at the time, he was to play an important part in our campaign later on.

Jim Kennedy

In 2012 I asked Terry Renshaw to contact UCATT's head office and ask if I could have access to their archives dealing with the strike and trials. The person responsible for them was their national political officer, Jim Kennedy. He invited us to London for a chat about it. Jim was genuinely interested in what the campaign was trying to do and I explained to him the information I was looking for in their archives. Jim was understandably cautious as he didn't know me until I explained that I was a former legal officer of the GMB in Liverpool. He then told me he was a former postman and union activist and we discovered that we had a mutual friend, Billy Hayes. Billy was from Liverpool and I had known him for over thirty years. He was now general secretary of the CWU. Jim never hesitated after that and took us to the top room in the building where the union's records were stored. He said in his broad London accent, 'If you find anything that's going to be useful, let me know and you can photocopy and take it with you.' He wished me well and left us to it.

From e-Petition to Paper Petition

We had done an enormous amount of work during the latter months of 2012 promoting the e-petition, and were encouraged by the response we received. But it never reached the magic number to get it referred to the House of Commons Business Committee. We monitored the numbers on the government website daily and noticed that the number of signatures on the petition would fluctuate. Some days the total would go up and then some days the total would go down. I contacted the government department responsible for e-petitions but never really got a satisfactory explanation. It was a very frustrating time. I did not want to give up the petition as it was a brilliant way to reach people and to get a debate in Parliament. So we decided to launch our own paper petition and went onto the streets, attended meetings and conferences and sent petition sheets through the post to trade union branches.

Durham Miners' Gala

The campaign was now going out to all the national trade union events on the calendar to promote the pickets' case and get signatures for the petition. On 13 July 2013 we organised the first of what was to become an annual visit to the Durham Miners' Gala. I knew there were always thousands of trade unionists at the event and it would be an ideal place to get support. A minibus was hired and one of my son's friends, Neil, drove us there. Ricky also agreed to come and we arranged for him to speak on the platform.

The day was glorious even though it was an early start from Liverpool. We had to be there for the assembly of marchers and brass bands around Old Elvet Bridge before the traditional parade past the Royal County Hotel, where we showed off our banner. The sun shone and everyone was in good spirits. When we arrived at the Racecourse Ground, we had a stand to use as a base. We split up and circulated among the crowds of trade unionists and their families throughout the day. We ended up with sunburnt faces and sore feet but we got thousands of signatures and gave out hundreds of information sheets. Many at the gala knew little, if anything, about the Shrewsbury pickets, but it did not take them long to pick up the gist of the pickets' plight. There were thousands of ex-miners who had suffered through the 1984–5 strike and had experienced at first hand the viciousness of a Tory government. We have attended the gala every year since to promote the campaign and show our support and solidarity for the miners, who had worked in such a tough industry and were treated so badly.

David Anderson MP

I met David Anderson again at the Durham Miners' Gala, when we were gathering signatures for our petition. I told him that we had collected tens of thousands by hand to supplement the e-petition and we wanted to present it to Downing Street in the autumn. He told me that he was a member of the Back-bench Business Committee and that he might be able to obtain a debate for us on the floor of the Commons. He said with a smile that he had just one problem: he had to persuade some Tories and Liberals on the committee to support the debate. I did not envy his task. We were committed to collecting 100,000 signatures to secure a debate, but David was confident he could persuade them to hold one. David and I swapped emails and phone calls over the next few months and I travelled to Newcastle to meet with him and his agent, Paul Foy, who happened to be from Liverpool. They took copies of the documents I had prepared, to read and share with other sympathetic MPs. It was so refreshing to speak with people with whom I was not constantly on the defensive. David understood only too well what we were up against. As a former miner, he had been on strike in 1972, 1974, and 1984–5.

Tolpuddle Martyrs Festival

Another labour movement event that we decided to attend was the Tolpuddle Martyrs festival in Dorset, held the week after the Durham Miners' Gala. It is organised by the South West TUC and is supported by all the trade unions. It is a fitting commemoration of the six men who were convicted of swearing a secret oath to combine together and oppose the cutting of agricultural workers' wages. In 1834 they were sentenced to transportation to Australia. This was definitely the venue to talk about our campaign for justice for the pickets, even though it was a long way! Dorset in July is also usually very dry and sunny. We were fortunate that an old friend and supporter from

Bristol, Nigel Varley, went into a supermarket on his way down to Tolpuddle and bought a gazebo. We were old hands now and set up our stall of information sheets, books, mugs, T-shirts and CDs under the shade. We set about getting signatures, although with just three of us it was going to be tough. Then along came a familiar face, Jimmy Woods, who had travelled down from Liverpool with his wife. Jimmy had just retired as a full-time officer for UCATT and was a staunch supporter of our campaign. A Scouser through and through, he said, 'Give me a clipboard, Eileen. I'll get you signatures.' And so he did, like a whirlwind, accosting everyone who came within ten yards of our stall. No one was beyond Jimmy's reach. By the end of the two days, we were absolutely shattered but we had enjoyed the comradely spirit and atmosphere of Tolpuddle. We were to return each year with our stand until the pandemic put a temporary halt to the event.

Petition Presented to No. 10

During the second half of 2013 we had been out on the streets of Liverpool every Saturday with a stall, a banner and our petition sheets, thanks to the permit we were able to get through the mayor, Joe Anderson. He had been a student on one of my TUC courses in the early 1980s, when he was a shop steward for the National Union of Seamen. Often, I would walk up to the Green Room and bring Ricky down for an hour or so, which would attract a crowd. By the end of November, we decided we had collected enough. Plans were made to present the petition to the prime minister in Downing Street. A group of committee members, supporters and pickets, including Terry, John and Ricky, travelled down to London on 16 December and met up with leading trade unionists and MPs for a press conference at Portcullis House. Afterwards we walked across Whitehall, and a delegation, carrying some of the petitions, went past the armed police at the security gate and handed the petition into No. 10.

We Made It: The Debate in Parliament

The event at Downing Street attracted enormous publicity but did not get us our debate. It was David Anderson's hard work which was to finally triumph; he succeeded in persuading his fellow members of the Backbench Business Committee that this was an important issue that deserved to be debated. And so, on 23 January 2014, he was able to introduce a motion to the House of Commons:

> That this house is seriously concerned at the decision of the government to refuse to release papers related to the building dispute in 1972 and subsequent prosecutions and calls on them to reverse their position as a matter of urgency.

David organised an event the previous evening in the Churchill Room of the Commons to remind MPs to turn up for the debate the following day. He had also been in contact with the Labour leader, Ed Miliband, and got his agreement that the front bench would support the debate. Considering that the Labour government had abandoned the pickets in 1974, Miliband's support marked a huge and welcome political turnaround.

I drew upon my research to prepare a number of briefings for MPs who wanted to speak in the debate and sent them to David to distribute. Myself, Ricky and Karie Murphy, who worked for one of the Labour MPs that was supporting the campaign, were given seats on the ground floor of the chamber and could experience directly the atmosphere of the debate. The rest of the campaign committee and supporters were placed in the public gallery above us.

The debate was booked for three hours and was one of the most memorable times of my life. David Anderson gave a superb opening speech in which he analysed what happened to the building workers in 1972. Following his opening salvo there followed an unprecedented succession of speeches from Labour MPs talking in class terms about the forces in society that came down upon the pickets. They pointed to the collusion between the police, the employers and the Tory government. Among the

MP's there were powerful contributions from Ian Lavery, Ian Mearns, Dennis Skinner, Chris Williamson, Andy McDonald and Steve Rotheram (a former Liverpool bricklayer). They spoke about the deliberate abuse of executive power, culminating in the pickets' being prosecuted and jailed. In line with the thrust of the motion, they called upon the government to release all the outstanding documents relating to the Shrewsbury trials.

It fell to Simon Hughes, a justice minister, to respond for the coalition government. He repeated the line that the number of documents being withheld was tiny, but

> I hope colleagues understand that I am, at the moment, unable to change the position that the government have adopted over the years, but there are ways in which this matter can be reviewed again, I accept that. That is proper and appropriate. And therefore, the efforts of the hon. Member for Blaydon, and those of the petitioners and colleagues, are not in vain.[4]

Then came the vote: ayes 120, noes 3. We could hear everyone behind us in the public gallery cheering and clapping. When the debate ended it was clear that the Labour MPs had been energised. As they left the chamber, they started to sing the Red Flag! Despite Hughes's platitudes the government have still not released the papers. But David Anderson did us proud and we will never forget him.

The BBC and a Missing Case

While we were travelling back from the debate in Parliament to Euston Station, I was contacted by BBC Radio to ask if Ricky would do an interview. They sent a radio car to a side street near the station. We met up with the technician, who sat several of us in the vehicle with Ricky as he was being interviewed live on air. It was a great way to end the day. We then hurried into the station as we were running late. Just as we were about to board the train one of our supporters said, 'Eileen, here is your case. I'm fed up carrying it; what have you got in it? It weighs a ton.'

I looked at him and said, 'I have never seen that case before in my life.' I had my normal black leather briefcase with me. He replied, 'Stop joking, it is your case.' It was a large shiny aluminium case. I asked him where he got it from and he answered that it was next to me in the BBC van in which we had been sitting.

Harry piped up, 'Oh my god, you've taken the BBC's case!' Everyone panicked. I said, 'Quick, take it to Lost Property and I'll phone the BBC!' He said plaintively, 'I'll miss the train.' I snapped back that if he brought the case back to Liverpool there would be a nice big policeman waiting for him at Lime Street. With that, he turned and dashed up the platform. A couple of minutes later he entered our carriage, red-faced, puffing and blowing, just as the train pulled away. When I rang the BBC to apologise, the technician said, 'I know what you're worried about. You're all from Liverpool and something's been taken.' I could then hear a warm change in his tone, 'Well, I'm from Birkenhead. Don't give it another thought. I'm still by the station and I'll collect the bag from Lost Property. And the best of luck.'

We carried on campaigning. Our banner was seen in London, Birmingham and Manchester at all the national demonstrations against the austerity policies of the coalition government. We learned that an effective way to be seen at such a large event was to be as near to the front of the march as possible. Then, when it arrived at the rally, we would stand at the entrance of the park with our banner and leaflets so that the thousands who followed through would see us and stop to talk about the campaign.

We also received regular coverage in the daily *Morning Star*. Not only did it report on our press conferences and other events; they also published periodic articles that we wrote to highlight issues surrounding the pickets' case. I was helped in this by a member of the paper's management committee, Carolyn Jones (Cad). Her late father, Bill Jones, an active trade unionist throughout his life, had been involved with the strike in 1972 and was a prominent member of the North Wales Defence Committee afterwards. Cad kindly lent me her father's papers, which gave me further insights into the case. In the years that followed the debate in Parliament we would meet up regularly at trade union conferences and labour movement events with Cad, Bernadette Keaveney, Conrad Landin and other staff from the paper. Sadly, the other left press showed no interest in the case, and we did not receive a single telephone inquiry or email from any of them.

United We Stand: Townsend Productions

In 2013 I got a call from Sheila Coleman of the Hillsborough Justice Campaign. She wanted to know whether she could give my number to Neil Gore of Townsend Productions as he would like a chat about producing a play about the Shrewsbury pickets. I invited Neil to my house along with Terry, Harry and John. Neil was disarmingly open and honest as he explained his ideas. I gave him copies of the two books we had about the case, by Des Warren and Jim Arnison, and a number of our information sheets about the history of the strike and the trials.

Neil took it from there and, with his partner Louise Townsend, produced one of the best plays ever written about trade unionists. A brilliant idea was to use 1970s music, along with their own compositions, running throughout the play. Paul Fox played Des Warren and, although he had never met him, his portrayal was excellent. Neil wrote the play and portrayed Ricky Tomlinson. Each of them also played a variety of other characters during the performance, which was both comical and inspiring. It went on tour around the country, taking the tale of the Shrewsbury 24 to towns and villages that we could never reach. It included three packed houses in the Severn Theatre, Shrewsbury. We tried to have a member of the committee present at as many performances as possible to speak at the end about the campaign and to distribute information sheets. This play promoted our campaign immeasurably and in the following years we often saw comments on Twitter and Facebook from people who had seen it. We are indebted to Neil, Louise and Paul for their work and commitment.

Campaigning Together

We joined up with other justice campaigns as there were common threads linking us, primarily government secrecy. Our campaign was based in Liverpool, and we were inspired by the heroic Hillsborough campaigners. Their tireless work eventually succeeded in the establishment of an independent panel that was given a mountain of documents by every conceivable public body connected to the disaster, which had previously been withheld. One of the stalwarts of the Hillsborough Justice Campaign (HJC) was the late Gerry McIver, who ran the HJC shop opposite Anfield. He invited us to collect signatures for our petition on match days. There would always be tea and sandwiches for us. He introduced me to Chris Wignall and his dad Brian who had a small printworks next door. They are two amazing people, extremely skilled in their craft, designing and printing all our campaign Christmas cards and other material over the past ten years. They were generous with their time and always supportive of the campaign.

The Orgreave Truth and Justice campaign also became firm friends and supporters. They are demanding an inquiry to reveal the truth behind the Tory government's decision to plan a confrontation with miners at the Orgreave coking plant near Sheffield during the 1984–5 strike against pit closures. We proudly march with our banner on the annual Orgreave rally each June and have received unstinting backing from them. Kate Flannery, Chris Peace, Chris Hockney, John Dunn, Kevin Horne and Joe Rollin have become a great source of friendship and support. Kate's father, Martin, was a Sheffield Labour MP in the 1970s and would visit Des in prison and write regularly to him to keep his spirits up. Des kept all his letters.

Amnesty International: Prisoner of Conscience?

One of the mysteries that I was able to solve during my research concerned the decision of Amnesty International to adopt Des Warren as a prisoner of conscience on 25 July 1975, only to withdraw it in October 1975, while he was still in jail. He learned of their decision in a newspaper report while sitting in his cell in Lincoln prison, at the complete mercy of the state.

At the time, Amnesty claimed that there had been a mistake in the procedure used to adopt Des. The case worker dealing with his file in 1975 worked for 'Amnesty International UK' and not 'Amnesty International, International Secretariat'. They said that adopting a British prisoner of conscience could only be done by a non-British arm of the organisation. Many people at the time thought that this was an excuse, including Des himself.[5] I decided to investigate what happened and discovered that their reason for withdrawing the status was not supported by the evidence. Their own documents showed that they came under secret pressure from the Labour government to do so.

I assisted Des's son, Andy, to write to Amnesty on 13 February 2014 to ask why they had abandoned his father. We asked for a copy of his father's file and over the following months received a variety of excuses to fob us off. Andy asked me to continue pushing them on his behalf and so I wrote to Amnesty on 29 January 2015. Amnesty promised to send the papers to me and to meet us in Liverpool. I did not receive the papers and they cancelled the meeting. We were back to square one! I realised we were getting nowhere and that direct action was needed. I emailed them and said we would be in London on 11 March and would visit their office to pick up the documents from the file.

Harry, myself and Andy, travelled down to their office. Ricky came with us, although he had not been adopted as a prisoner of conscience as he had left prison in July 1975. The Amnesty officer we met had a list of the documents from Des's file. He said we could have a copy of the list but not the actual documents as they had not been cleared for release by their legal department. I informed him that we were not in a rush and were happy to wait there while he obtained clearance from the relevant legal team. He left us for ten minutes and when he returned agreed to our request. He then informed us that they would release some of the documents but the rest would have to be checked out further and sent to me at a later date.

Many of the documents he handed to me were poor photo-copies and some were redacted. When I asked him about this, he replied that the documents were old and some were copied from microfiche records. The redacted parts were the names of AI staff involved in the decisions forty years ago.

After sending further reminder emails to Amnesty, I eventually received the outstanding documents on 16 May. These were of the same poor quality. Names were redacted so I had to cross-reference dates and events to decipher the information, but it was worth it. I found conclusive evidence that the then Labour government had brought pressure to bear on Amnesty to withdraw prisoner-of-conscience status from Des Warren. From these documents I prepared the following timeline:

6 June 1975. Amnesty received an application for prisoner-of-conscience status from Des Warren's solicitor.

14 July 1975. Amnesty adopted Des as a prisoner of conscience. The letter to his solicitor was from Amnesty's International Secretariat. It stated, 'We have decided to "adopt" Dennis Warren. As you probably know, it is a rule of Amnesty International that members of the organisation do not work for cases in their own country. We are giving the case to a European Amnesty group who will appeal to the British Government for Dennis Warren's release; help support the family and publicise the case in their country.' It was signed by Angela Wright, Western European Research Department.

24 July 1975. Alex Lyon, MP and Home Office minister, wrote to Martin Ennals, general secretary of Amnesty International (and brother of David Ennals MP, minister of state in the Foreign Office and part of the Wilson government). Lyons wrote, 'I was a little surprised to read that Amnesty has adopted Des Warren as a prisoner of conscience. Could you give me your reasons for taking a view which seems to be at variance with a properly conducted trial where Warren was convicted of offences based on evidence of intimidation and violence?'

There were no copies of Martin Ennals's response in the Amnesty file. When pressed on this they carried out a search of the files but could not find it. They asked the Cabinet Office for a copy under the Freedom of Information Act but the Cabinet Office replied that they could not trace it.

After receiving the letter from Alex Lyon, Amnesty decided to refer Des Warren's case to its Borderline Committee for reconsideration. This committee consisted of three people, each from a different country, who considered cases where there was no outright agreement. In Des's case it had nothing to do with the original Amnesty caseworker being from the UK.

18 August 1975. After due consideration the Borderline Committee decided by two votes to one to retain Des as a prisoner of conscience.

20 August 1975. Alex Lyon wrote to Amnesty International again. This time it was a four-page letter and began, 'Thank you for your letter of 31st July inviting my comments on the case of Dennis Michael Warren.' The letter then set out in detail the case against the pickets that had been put by Drake in court. 'At the end of a long trial the jury decided in the light of the evidence – including that given by a number of the pickets who had accompanied Mr Warren as well as by men working on the building sites at which incidents had taken place – that Mr Warren was guilty of the three major offences.' Before signing the letter off he wrote, 'If you would like to examine the full trial transcript I can arrange for you to see it.'

21 August 1975. Amnesty sent a memo, with a copy of Alex Lyon's letter, to the Borderline Committee, copying in other Amnesty officers (names redacted). The memo stated, 'Enclosed is a copy of a letter we have just received from the Minister of State at the Home Office commenting on the above case "Dennis Warren". Given the careful and detailed nature of this letter I felt that it should be made available to you in your consideration of the suitability of Mr Warren for adoption by Amnesty International. If you have already committed your views to paper or, indeed, sent them you may wish to reconsider them in light of the enclosed letter.'

3 September 1975. One member of the Borderline Committee wrote, 'The letter from the Home Office does I think throw a different light on the Warren case ... In the light of the most recent evidence, I would be inclined to reverse my previous conclusion and say that while a slight doubt may remain and it is a very borderline case, on balance I think we would be wiser not to adopt this case, if only because it is very controversial and in case of doubt it would be wiser to be prudent.'

6 October 1975. A second member of the Borderline Committee wrote to say that, after considering the memo and Lyons's letter, they also agreed that Des Warren should not be adopted. The Borderline Committee vote was now two to one not to adopt Des as a prisoner of conscience.

None of this behind-the-scenes manoeuvring was disclosed to either Des Warren, his family or his solicitor. They were not aware that a Home Office minister had put pressure on Amnesty International to withdraw Des's status as a prisoner of conscience. This was to remain a secret for over forty years.

With this evidence from their own documents, I decided to confront Amnesty directly and ask them why they allowed this to happen, when they had such a well-earned reputation for highlighting repression of political prisoners. I requested a meeting with the secretary general of Amnesty, Salil Shetty, but was informed that he was out of the country. They agreed that I could meet with the acting director, David Griffiths, together with other heads of European departments. The meeting took place at their London office on 10 December 2015. Harry and Ricky accompanied me. Amnesty were represented by Griffiths and the director of the Europe and Central Asia Programme, John Dalhuisen; the deputy Europe director, Gauri van Gulik; and the EU campaigner/researcher, Kartik Raj.

They initially allowed just one hour for our meeting, but eventually agreed to two. It lasted almost three. Their delegation started the meeting by agreeing that Amnesty had an apology to make to Des Warren's family as they had failed to communicate to Des, his family or his solicitor that they had withdrawn prisoner-of-conscience status from him. Instead, they had simply informed the media and had written to the home secretary, Roy Jenkins, to notify him of their decision. I said that while these actions of exclusion were inexcusable and awful in themselves, the real issue was the political pressure put on Amnesty to reverse their decision.

I went through their documents systematically, pointing out how it showed clearly that Amnesty had bowed to pressure from the government and rescinded Des Warren's adoption as a prisoner of conscience. After a long discussion they conceded that the evidence was overwhelming and agreed that Amnesty's actions in 1975 were improper. They admitted that the decision to allow a government minister to interfere with their decision-making process was wrong and would not be repeated today. They accepted that their actions had left Des isolated during a further horrendous year in prison, where he suffered the cruellest of indignities, without any protection whatsoever. I asked for them to make a public statement setting out what happened, which they finally did on 9 May 2016.

A week after their apology appeared I attended UCATT's national conference at Scarborough. They recognised the enormity of this revelation and suspended standing orders to allow me to speak. As I recounted the meetings with Amnesty and the documents that I had obtained there were gasps around the conference hall. When I finished, many delegates were in tears. For my endeavours they gave me a standing ovation and reaffirmed their support for the Shrewsbury 24 Campaign's efforts to obtain justice for the pickets.

'My name is Dessie Warren'

Alun Parry is a remarkably talented singer–songwriter from Liverpool and produced a fundraising CD for the campaign, *Whose Conspiracy?*, which had songs from some of Britain's finest protest singers. Alun had also included a new song that he had written and recorded, 'My name is Dessie Warren'. He had clearly done his research as the lyrics of the song really captured

Des's socialist spirit and the stand he made against the authorities when he was imprisoned in 1973. Alun sings it beautifully, with its defiant refrain, 'The number it belongs to you, I'm only saying my name'. We had a thousand CDs made and we sold them all.

Alun called me a year or so later and told me that he had wonderful news. Another Liverpool singer-songwriter, the legendary Ian Prowse, had approached him and said that he would like to record the song. Alun generously said that Ian has got a much wider audience than him and the story about Des would spread far and wide. Ian contacted me and said he had recorded the song and wanted to shoot a promotional video. He asked me if I had any campaign papers and posters he could use as a backdrop on the film. I invited him to my home and showed him a variety of material that I had. He was delighted and said that Roger Appleton would be recording the film and would arrange the material for dramatic shots.

I said he was welcome to use them but I would need to take them to the film studio and bring them home with me. Ian laughed and said innocently, 'Eileen, don't you trust me?' But he understood that I did not want to take any chances in losing original material. So along I went with the papers to a freezing-cold warehouse near the Mersey where the video was recorded. Ian's version of the song is powerful and passionate, and he allowed us to put a copy of the video on the campaign's website. It has become a regular at his gigs and fans sing along to the chorus. We were so fortunate to have Alun and Ian giving us their time and their talents to support our campaign for justice.

Bolton Socialist Club: Ordinary Rebels

Supporters and friends at the Bolton Socialist Club, in the heart of the town centre, put on a number of fundraising events and meetings for us. One of the most memorable evenings was when local singer-songwriter Claire Mooney performed a rousing performance for us all, which lifted our spirits at a time when we needed it. Her rendition of her song 'Ordinary rebels' really hit

Frances O'Grady presents us with an award after delegates voted us the best stand at the 2018 TUC Congress in Manchester.

the spot. Although the club is a long way from Liverpool it was well worth the trip.

Bolton was on our doorstep compared with the other places campaign members visited throughout the period of the campaign. In particular, Harry and Terry would travel all over the country to speak at union branches, big and small, Labour Party meetings, trades councils, union conferences and rallies. It took them to Bournemouth, Brighton, Bristol, Birmingham, Sheffield, Newcastle, Cardiff, Shrewsbury, London and Glasgow to name just the bigger towns and cities.

Labour Party Manifesto

We made an important breakthrough in winning support from the Labour Party through Jim Kennedy, who became absolutely crucial to the campaign over the years. He was a member of the National Executive Committee and invited me to Portcullis House to meet with two MPs, Sadiq Khan and Andy Slaughter, to discuss our campaign. I went down by train and had only been with them for five minutes when Sadiq said politely, 'I have to go, I am late for a meeting, but I do support your campaign.'

I could not help myself and said back to him, 'I have been travelling from Liverpool since six o'clock this morning. All I am
asking is that you give me ten minutes of your time to hear
what I have to say.' Sadiq immediately apologised and sat back
down and we resumed our discussion. I informed them that we
were not asking the Labour Party to fight our corner. We were
asking them to support our call to the government to remove
the shackles of secrecy from all the documentation relating to
the Shrewsbury trials. They had no idea that they were being
held back from us. Sadiq and Jim were later to co-author the
pledge in the 2015 Labour manifesto to release all files relating
to the Shrewsbury trials. (It was maintained in the 2017 and
2019 manifestos.)

This was how we built the foundations of the campaign.
Hard work and a shared commitment to win justice for the
pickets. Along the way we received tremendous support from
unexpected quarters. It allowed us to create a national profile
that made us instantly recognisable at many demonstrations,
meetings and other events. We were on the map! We now had to
ensure that we had the fresh evidence to persuade the Criminal
Cases Review Commission to refer the pickets' convictions back
to the Court of Appeal.

15

The CCRC and the Road to the Court of Appeal

The work that I had undertaken on the master's degree proved to be well spent when we submitted the application to the Criminal Cases Review Commission. I was able to advise the pickets and campaign members of the way the CCRC was going to deal with it and, just as importantly, to warn everyone that there was going to be a delay. A long delay. I learned from the many articles and studies of the CCRC that a main complaint about it was the long periods that applicants had to wait, often with no communication, before they received a decision.

Ten of the convicted pickets had signed up with the campaign to submit an application, covering all three trials. We had wanted as many as possible but some had disappeared despite our best efforts to track them down. And there were some who did not want to be involved. We understood and accepted that we could not force anyone to make an application if they did not want to.

Our solicitors, Bindmans, had prepared a forty-six-page submission to accompany the applications that we delivered to the CCRC. We were asking it to refer the men's convictions to the Court of Appeal, as the only body with power to do that. We also called upon it, if necessary, to use its powers to obtain from government departments historic documents about the trials that were denied to us.

Our fundamental argument was that there had been an *abuse of process* in the way that the trials had been conducted, which had denied all the pickets a fair trial. From my knowledge of the commission, I anticipated two problems with the application. First, only four of the ten had ever appealed their convictions. Normally the CCRC would only accept cases from people who had exhausted the appeals process, and they could have told the other six to go away and do that first. The second problem was that some of them had pleaded guilty.

Bindmans submission had addressed both points and these were eventually accepted by the CCRC. If the trials had been tainted by an abuse of process, then those who pleaded guilty had done so under duress and in ignorance of facts about the way the trial had been conducted. And as the CCRC was going to deal with the issues raised by the four pickets who had appealed, it made sense to deal with the six others at the same time.

Eight reasons were put forward to support our claim that the pickets' convictions were unsafe, including that the prosecutions were the result of improper interference by the government; that the conduct of the trials was prejudicial, including the high security, the biased remarks of Judge Mais, and the improper communication between the jury bailiff and the jury; and that the continued withholding of government documents about the case prevented a fair hearing of any appeal. We asked the commission to deal with the applications as quickly as possible, pointing out that the trials were almost forty years ago and the men were getting on. It took over six months before we received a letter informing us that they were starting to examine the case and had allocated a case review manager.

Our solicitors' submission was well argued, but I wanted to strengthen the crucial fresh evidence that would be required to persuade the CCRC to refer our case back to the Court of Appeal. My research had to continue. I received an invaluable piece of advice from a former commissioner at a conference on miscarriages of justice. I was talking with him about all the issues that were raised by the pickets' case and wasn't sure what to submit and what to leave out. He said to me, 'Send them everything.' We should not police ourselves but instead present a wall of evidence to the CCRC. It was for them to batter it down if they thought it wasn't relevant.

In the next submission that Bindmans sent, eighteen months after the applications had gone in, we put forward further arguments. These were based mainly on new documents that I had found at Kew and Salford. First, Judge Mais had improperly told the jury to continue deliberating when they were sent to stay at a hotel overnight. Second, detailed evidence of the bias of the judge was set out, based upon the trial transcripts, particularly his summing-up. We also sent in a statement that Bindmans had obtained from David Altaras, one of the junior barristers at the trials. He set out his recollections of Judge Mais to support our claim that his bias against the pickets, particularly Des Warren, poisoned the jury against the men.

The most important part of this latest submission from Bindmans was the fresh evidence that I had unearthed that would eventually form one of the two strands of the appeal in 2021, *Red under the Bed*.

Red under the Bed: The Security Services

In 2012 I discovered details of a television programme, *Red under the Bed*, while researching government records about the case at Kew. The National Archives catalogue referred to a file described as 'Woodrow Wyatt's TV programme, "Red under the Bed"' but when I obtained the full reference it stated, 'Retained by Department under Section 3.4'. This was a reference to the Public Records Act 1958 that allows the government to retain any documents that it chooses, usually on the grounds of 'national security'.

On 1 August 2013 I made a request under the Freedom of Information Act for the file to be released to The National Archives for public viewing. The Cabinet Office agreed that it would be prepared for release to Kew but did not give a date. I made a weekly check of the catalogue until it eventually showed that the file had been transferred to The National Archives on 2 October 2013. I went back to Kew straight away and read it from cover to cover. I immediately realised the significance of the file and sent a copy by email to Bindmans to include in a further submission to the CCRC. I also sent copies to David Anderson MP, who was supporting us in trying to get our petition debated in Parliament.

I also began a search for a copy of the film. It had been made by Anglia Television for the ITV network. Anglia Television had been swallowed up by a succession of larger regional ITV companies in the 1990s but none of them had a copy; nor did the East Anglian Film Archive at the University of East Anglia. After several months I eventually tracked down a copy at the British Film Institute. They had it on two-inch film, which had to be transferred to a digital format for me to view it. I went to their London office with Harry on 25 September 2013 where 'Basement' Steve had set up a viewing room for us. He knew that we had travelled a long way and provided us with tea and biscuits. We watched the film and the studio discussion that had taken place afterwards.

The Cabinet Office file about the programme that I had discovered revealed the secret role that the government had played in producing the film. It was also clear that the film was prejudicial to the pickets in the way it depicted them in the programme and the association made between the building workers' strike, violence and communist subversion. There is no way that such a film would be allowed to be broadcast today during a trial dealing with the same subject matter.

Andy Burnham MP raised the issues surrounding *Red under the Bed* in a debate in Westminster Hall on 9 December 2015 that attracted significant media coverage.

Slow Progress with the CCRC

During the two years following the submission of the applications to the CCRC we held regular meetings with all the pickets either at Kevin Butcher's house near Mostyn, the Unite offices in Flint, the Council offices in Flint or in the St David's Hotel, Ewloe. It was a chance to update them on the application and

© Chris Gregory Photography

Pickets and committee at Ewloe, 2013. Back row: Bernard Williams, Kevin Butcher, Michael Pierce, Terry Renshaw and Ken O'Shea. Front row: Dawn and Mel McKinsie Jones (their father, John, was working away), Eileen Turnbull and Harry Chadwick.

the campaign. Most of them were delighted that we were gaining support from trade unions and Labour MPs. I admired them for their stoicism and kindness. They had waited a long time for justice and weren't expecting any quick fixes.

We had two meetings at the CCRC's offices in Birmingham, on 29 May 2013 and 26 February 2014, when we met the commissioners and case review managers dealing with the applications. During the lifetime of the case, we had a total of three different commissioners and four case review managers dealing with it. This change of personnel slowed down the progress with the case. Our meetings were unusual, as one of the criticisms of the organisation was that they rarely met with applicants. But I had insisted because of the age of the case and of the applicants involved. Our delegation included myself, Ricky, Harry and Terry, together with our lawyers, Rhona Friedman from Bindmans and Ben Newton from Doughty Street Chambers in London. Ben was to be with the campaign from the beginning, right through to the hearing in the Court of Appeal in 2021.

Three months after the second meeting at the CCRC, Bindmans sent them a third submission, on 2 June 2014. This contained the decisive evidence, though the CCRC did not think so. It was the memo that the West Mercia police had written for the prosecutor Desmond Fennell which revealed that they had destroyed original witness statements.

Although I believed that we had given the CCRC enough to allow it to refer the pickets case to the appeal court, we did not give up campaigning for the release of government files. In spring 2015, David Anderson gave an update in a Westminster Hall debate on the campaign's fight to get government papers released. Simon Hughes, minister of state for justice and civil liberties, made a statement in reply. Myself, Ricky and Harry then had a meeting with Hughes to continue the pressure. He confirmed that papers were still retained under the Section 23 exemption but promised a separate review of those relating to the trials. That year a general election ended the coalition government, when the Liberals were reduced to a rump in Parliament. It was not until the autumn that Oliver Letwin, the Cabinet office secretary, informed the House of Commons that he had held the review and no further documents would be released. He confirmed that the next review of all the historic documents withheld by the government would not be until 2021.

Andy Burnham

Despite the disappointment of Labour losing the election the campaign was energised when Jeremy Corbyn was elected Labour leader. He was a long-standing supporter, as was his new shadow chancellor, John McDonnell. The chairperson of the National Executive Committee was now Jim Kennedy, whom Harry, Terry and I had met up with at many conferences since our first meeting at UCATT's head office. When we took our campaign stand to the Labour Party conference in September 2015 Jim arranged for a pass for me so that I could sit on the second row in the conference hall to hear the speech of Jeremy's new shadow home secretary, Andy Burnham. I got odd looks from some of the old guard of MPs I was sat next to. I could see that they wondered who this upstart was as they didn't know me from Adam. As far as Jim was concerned our campaign needed all the help we could get and I had as much right to be there as they had. After all, we were all Labour Party members! A Liverpool MP, Steve Rotheram, who was Jeremy's parliamentary private secretary, sat next to me and gave me a knowing wink and a big smile. From the platform Andy gave his maiden conference speech as shadow home secretary. It was brilliant. He told the audience,

> Historic abuses must also be put under the spotlight – picking out the brutal attacks on striking mine workers in 1984, the Hillsborough disaster and the arrest of the twenty-four pickets at Shrewsbury after the national construction strike in 1972 … To understand how an anti-trade union culture developed in parts of the police, we need the full story about the false convictions and imprisonment of building workers in Shrewsbury.[1]

Andy quite rightly received a standing ovation from conference and then left the platform. With that, Steve grabbed my arm and ran with me behind the stage, catching Andy just as he descended the steps. Steve introduced me to him and I was invited to meet Andy in London. He repeated, 'I want to do all I can for your campaign and all justice campaigns.'

The Road to the Home Office: Knowledge and Information

Andy had pledged to support our demands for documents to be released and used his position to organise a Westminster Hall debate on the subject on 9 December 2015. Once again, I provided the Labour MPs with briefing papers and documents. I will never forget meeting Andy at a service station on the East Lancashire Road to hand over a file of papers that I had prepared for him to use during the debate. It was fortunate that he was an MP for Leigh, which was not too far from Liverpool. It was pouring with rain on that Saturday afternoon and we were both soaked through.

The debate was listed for an hour and a half. Among the MP's who spoke in support were Andy, Steve, Ian Lavery, Andy Slaughter and Diane Abbott, who were precise in their presentations and robust in their arguments. During the debate, a Home Office minister, Mike Penning MP, replied for the government. To my surprise he suggested that he meet with the campaign. We sat there listening to the debate and felt really proud of those MP's who stood their ground and argued for the veil of secrecy to be thrown off the Shrewsbury trials once and for all.

I was delighted with Penning's suggestion as I now had a pathway into the Home Office. Several days later, myself and another committee member, John Bohanna, travelled to London for the meeting, which Andy and Steve also attended. We faced Penning and half a dozen officials. Andy opened the meeting and then handed over to me. I outlined what documents were clearly missing from The National Archives at Kew. After listening to us, Penning said that he would arrange for me to meet with the 'head of Knowledge and Information', based in the Home Office. I never knew such a section existed. Two days later I was back in London accompanied by Kevin, from Andy Burnham's office.

The head of Knowledge and Information was a pleasant and extremely astute man. I handed him a list of documents and described to him what I was looking for and why we needed the missing information. He took it and told me that the papers might be spread out over a number of government departments as they tended to merge or be split up when governments changed. I sensed he wanted to help if he could, so I asked him a straight question: why would successive governments retain information about a building workers' strike over forty years ago? He replied, 'Last week, I had on my desk a number of documents from Ireland dated 1906. They included names of people who were "friendly" to Britain. My advice was that they remained retained by the department as the relatives of those people could still be living today in those areas. How would we attract friends again in any jurisdiction if it was known that, at some point in the future, we would release the information about them?' I said that our case was not about information-gathering on individuals, it was about government secrecy. Who in the government made the decisions to prosecute the Shrewsbury pickets, and why?

He told me he would circulate my list of documents to the various government departments that might hold them. I thanked him and we shook hands. He had been honest with us, even if he was not making any promises. I corresponded with him over the next few months as he endeavoured to seek out any files. He trawled every department twice, but only located a few documents that he could disclose to us.

CCRC's First Provisional Statement of Reasons: Rejection

After more than four years we finally received a 'provisional statement of reasons' from the CCRC: they were not going to refer the pickets' convictions to the Court of Appeal. The purpose of the provisional statement was to give us the opportunity to send in a response, including any further evidence, that might make it reconsider before it issued a final statement of reasons.

The CCRC dismissed the claim that there had been improper government interference in the case. It accepted the explanations that Rawlinson had given in 1975 when answering Roger Bolton's queries for the planned BBC *Panorama* programme. The CCRC also relied upon an interview it conducted with Maurice Drake, just a few weeks before he died on 6 April 2014. He had denied any political interference in the case and reiterated that the decision to proceed and to charge the pickets with conspiracy was his alone. The CCRC watched the copy of *Red under the Bed* that I had obtained for it but concluded that it did not prejudice the pickets' access to a fair trial. Many of our other grounds were also brushed away in the same way. In just six paragraphs it dismissed our claim that the police destruction of original witness statements was an abuse of process, denying the pickets a fair trial. It said that neither side could now say whether those original statements would have helped or hindered the defence. It was pure speculation today, which was insufficient to cause the Court of Appeal to overturn the convictions.

We were all very disappointed that the CCRC had reached that decision after four years' consideration of the application and fresh evidence. I had warned everyone at the beginning that my research into the CCRC had revealed that they were increasingly overcautious in referring cases to the Court of Appeal. This was due in part to criticism of them by appeal court judges for referring some cases that the court declared to be weak and speculative. In the ten years up to 2010, out of an annual average of 954 applications to the CCRC, only thirty-four were referred to the appeal courts, i.e. 3.6 per cent of all applications.

We held a meeting with the pickets at Ewloe on 16 June. Our lawyers, Rhona and Ben, travelled up from London. We were advised that the CCRC were wrong to dismiss our arguments about the prejudicial impact of the destruction of witness statements. It was agreed that Rhona would instruct Michael Mansfield to write an opinion on that point which could form part of our response. He was a leading criminal appeals QC and knew the law on this subject. This was going to cost the campaign, but we were willing to raise the money.

On 4 August Bindmans sent an eighty-three-page reply to the CCRC spelling out exactly where their analysis had gone wrong: 'It pains us to say that after four years of review the CCRC has … drawn erroneous conclusions based on a misapplication and misunderstanding of settled legal principles and case authorities.' The submission concluded, 'The unfair conduct of the trial process, the judicial bias, the misdirection of law, the jury irregularities, the unsafe identifications and the abuse of process by dint of the destruction of statements all combine to create a truly toxic combination.' It asked the CCRC to use its powers to obtain specified documents from public authorities and refer the men's cases to the appeal court.

We knew that we were in for another long wait but the over-whelming majority of pickets and campaign supporters remained confident. They knew that after all these years there were no quick fixes. Unfortunately, two of the pickets were losing faith in the possibility of winning, despite the huge support that we had built up in the trade union movement and the Labour Party. They were frustrated with the delays of the CCRC and the fact that we had been turned down. They were concerned that none of the pickets were getting any younger and were looking for an alternative avenue to bring about justice.

The first sign we saw of this came out of the blue at a fringe meeting at the Labour Party conference in autumn 2016, when two former supporters arrived with Ricky and a banner reading, 'The Shrewsbury 2 documentary team'. The 'two' were Ricky Tom-linson and Arthur Murray; all the other pickets and their families continued to support the campaign. We were very surprised and disappointed as our legal team were gearing up for another sub-mission to the CCRC. Ricky Tomlinson announced that they were going to make a documentary and were certain that the impact of a film and publicity stunts would bring about justice.

I was surprised to hear of one such stunt when I was research-ing the records of the T&GWU in the Modern Records Centre at the University of Warwick in March 2017. I had been granted access by a long-standing friend, Jim Mowatt, who is the direc-tor of education for Unite and is responsible for its archives. During the afternoon, my head buried in archive papers from the 1970s, my phone buzzed. It was a journalist from the *Daily Telegraph*. She wanted to know what evidence I had to support the claim that Richard Whiteley, the late presenter of *Count-down*, had been working for MI5. I did not know whether it was a wind-up. She quickly explained that the claim had been made that day by Ricky at a personal appearance he had made in Chester, opening a Wetherspoons pub. I explained that I had no evidence of this and she was best speaking to Ricky himself. On my way home I got a call from a journalist on the *Liverpool Echo* and I told him the same.

The issue made front-page news in print and online but it was reported negatively, as Ricky had been unable to substantiate the claims. I had a chat about it with him the next day and I explained that I had received several phone calls. I advised him that, in order to protect himself, he had to make sure that he had the evidence to back up whatever he said, as the media would undermine him otherwise.

Eureka! A Breakthrough at Last: The West Mercia Police Reports

The meetings that I had with government ministers and our constant campaigning for the release of documents did bear important fruit in early 2017. Bindmans contacted me to say that the CCRC had received a quantity of historical documents about the case from West Mercia Police. The head of Knowledge and Information at the Home Office had written to the police in the past to ask whether they had any and they had informed him that they had none. He later informed me that, by accident, they had discovered a quantity of documents that were buried among the archives of its police museum, which had been closed for several years.

I had to make a specific FOI request to gain access and was fortunate to receive the cooperation of the force's solicitor, who arranged for me to visit them in Telford on 13 March to inspect all the newly discovered documents. I went with Harry and we spent the day looking through the boxes of files. At last, after years of searching, I had found the West Mercia police report by Hodges and Glover that Chief Constable Willison had sent to the DPP on 18 December 1972, which had started the whole process. There were over a dozen files, containing witness statements and other evidence that the police had assembled for the trials. In addition, there was a second police report that I had not known about. It addressed complaints that had been made to the police by employers following the picketing in Shrewsbury and Telford on 6 September. An appendix contained a timeline of events and a transcript of the radio communications between police officers and the control room. These documents were to prove absolutely crucial to understanding how the police had acted that day. It took me a long time to study them and digest the information, but it was a massive step forwards in my understanding of how the case was manufactured against the pickets.

The CCRC's Second Provisional Statement of Reasons: Further Rejection

At the beginning of July 2017, we received the CCRC's second provisional statement. It rejected all the arguments that we had put forward a year earlier in response to the first statement. The most important part of its decision was its continued rejection of our arguments about the police destruction of witness statements:

> The CCRC reiterates that it is not possible to identify when any earlier statements that were not retained had been taken, and what their content may have been. There is no evidence of prejudice to the defence. Without knowing the number of and contents of any earlier statements and the process and reasons behind any destruction of them it is equally impossible, and speculative, to say that any earlier statements would have supported the defence case and/or undermined that of the prosecution.[2]

Several of us met with Bindmans and it was agreed that there was no point in sending a further detailed reply as the CCRC was not going to budge and we wanted its final decision as soon as possible. We met Jamie Potter, a quietly spoken but very shrewd public law solicitor at Bindmans who knew everything there was to know about judicial review. He was to become our close legal adviser for the rest of the case. We arranged for the legal team to meet with the pickets at Ewloe the following week. Unfortunately, there was disruption on the trains which prevented our lawyers getting up to north Wales, so the meeting went ahead without them.

I reported Bindmans advice, which was that we could take the CCRC to court through a judicial review. It wasn't enough to argue that we disagreed with its decision, though. We had to show that the CCRC had got the law wrong when analysing all the evidence and that its decision was irrational and perverse.

There were twelve of us at the meeting, including seven pickets. A lot of the discussion centred on whether we would ever get justice and two pickets were adamant that we had reached the end of the road. As far as Ricky was concerned only a documentary would expose the political nature of the trials and the government cover-up, leading to the quashing of their convictions. Most of the other pickets disagreed and wanted to see it through to the end. Terry Renshaw reminded him that he had already made one documentary in 2007, *Guilty My Arse*, which had not made any impact whatsoever. John McKinsie Jones, who had stood in the dock with Ricky Tomlinson for twelve weeks and was also imprisoned, tried to persuade him to stay with the case.

I understood how disappointed Ricky was and said that I would be happy to help him to make a documentary when the legal case had been completed, win or lose, as I was more familiar with it than anyone else, as he often acknowledged. I suggested that we all meet again, when the lawyers could attend and advise on any outstanding matters. This was agreed by everyone.

The CCRC's Final Statement of Reasons: Confirming Rejection

The CCRC issued its final statement of reasons on 30 October. This was it; they had turned us down and the ball was in our court. We met up again at Ewloe the following week and this time Jamie and Rhona were able to get there. They gave a full outline of the position we were now at and were able to answer the pickets' questions. Jamie expressed cautious optimism about the prospects of successfully challenging the CCRC through a judicial review. Ricky did not attend but Arthur told us that he had authority to speak on his behalf. He informed us that Ricky had advice from a QC that a judicial review had no chance of winning and that we were wasting the unions' money trying to challenge the CCRC. We should give up and instead make the documentary. Arthur said that he agreed with this. He informed us that Ricky had now withdrawn from the campaign and from the legal case. We asked him to share the QC's opinion with the rest of us, but it was never forthcoming.

We decided that the pickets present had to make the final decision themselves, so the rest of us left the room. When we returned, they were all keen to go ahead, except Arthur, who still agreed with Ricky. He said that he would let us know his final position but never contacted us again to join the legal action. We were all very disappointed but determined to go on. Kevin spoke for everyone when he said, 'This is about twenty-four people, not one or two.' We asked Jamie to prepare the paperwork to take proceedings against the CCRC. Eight of the original ten were still keen to have their convictions quashed. We needed money urgently to pay ongoing legal bills, so each member of the Committee agreed to lend the campaign £1,000 each. (This was repaid to each of us at the end of 2018.)

We were confident that we would win a judicial review but Bindmans advised us that if we lost, the combined costs of both sides could be as high as £150,000. I was confident that our supporters would not let us down. We had already started sounding them out and had received positive feedback from our affiliated unions, starting with a pledge from Unite. Many more unions were to follow. Mick Whelan, the general secretary of the train drivers' union, ASLEF, led the way in circulating our appeal to every branch, with a covering letter urging support. (Over the following year we ended up with more affiliations from that union, pro rata, than any other.) I made a number of visits to London at the start of 2018, often at short notice, to meet with general secretaries and executives, accompanied by Harry. We got support from the CWU, the FBU, the NUT, the PCS, the RMT and the TSSA.

There was a lot of hard work during the next few months and the campaign was to suffer a setback with the news that Ken O'Shea had passed away on Boxing Day, aged eighty-eight. Ken had been with us from the beginning and, despite being the oldest surviving picket, had attended as many meetings as possible. He was particularly pleased to have attended the UCATT conference in Llandudno in 2014 when all the pickets were invited to the front of the hall and given a standing ovation. We saw him for the final time a couple of weeks before he passed away. As I was saying my goodbyes, he squeezed my hand and said, 'You won't give up, will you?' 'Of course not, Ken,' I replied. 'We will keep going.'

Challenging the CCRC: The Pickets Fight Back

Bindmans sent the legal documents to the Administrative Court at the end of January 2018 and from that moment on we knew it was for real. Our submissions to the CCRC between 2012 and 2016 had covered up to ten different grounds but for the judicial review we concentrated on just two issues. These were the main ones where we thought that we could show that the CCRC had got it wrong: first, that the destruction of witness statements was an abuse of process that denied the pickets a fair trial; second, that the broadcasting of *Red under the Bed* halfway through the trial was prejudicial to the pickets.

Jamie had briefed us thoroughly on the procedure of a judicial review. Seemingly, applications go through a 'paper sift', where a judge considers whether it merits a full judicial review hearing. We received the news in the March that Judge Garnham had looked at our case and decided that it 'was hopeless'. Jamie said that it was not unusual for cases to be turned down at this stage, as the judge had not seen all the papers, just the application. We were forced to incur additional expense by making an application, which included a court fee, for a 'permission' hearing before a judge in open court to state why our case should go to a full trial.

The permission hearing took place on Friday 9 November in the Administrative Court in Birmingham. It was listed there because it was the home court for our opponents, the CCRC, but they did not send anyone to the hearing. When it began, I was pleasantly surprised to see that the judge was Mr Justice Jay. He was instantly recognisable as he had been on our televisions over several months as Robert Jay QC, the lead counsel at the Leveson inquiry, where he had led the questioning of Rupert Murdoch, David Cameron and others. Jamie had selected our barrister for the hearing carefully, Danny Friedman of Matrix Chambers. We had prepared a comprehensive bundle for the court that included a DVD of *Red under the Bed*. At the start of the hearing Jay announced that he had read everything and watched the film. He recalled that he had watched it when it was broadcast the first time around as a teenager.

During the next two hours we listened to Danny presenting the case and answering Jay's many questions. Then the judge decided he had heard enough. He was convinced that we did have an arguable case and, because of Garnham's negative comments, Jay decided to give a judgment which ran to four closely typed pages. We were now over the first hurdle. Better than that, Jay's judgment set out succinctly the main arguments showing why the CCRC had got it wrong. This was the first time the pickets' case had ever succeeded in court. We were overjoyed.

Now we just had to wait for the full hearing.

RMT, Machynlleth

Our campaigning and fundraising continued over the following months. It included an invitation from the Machynlleth branch of the RMT to a meeting on 29 April 2019. We put the date in our diaries and worked out how we would get there. Several of the pickets were keen to attend, as well as committee members. Then we got news from Bindmans that the Administrative Court had listed our full judicial review hearing for 30 April. At first we thought that the trip to Machynlleth would have to be postponed but we quickly changed our minds. After checking train timetables, we discovered that we could make it and decided that it would raise our spirits for what we had to face the next day in Birmingham. It was an excellent meeting, with lots of hot chips and bread provided. They were stunned when we told them that we were not returning home but were going on to Birmingham for the judicial review the next day. They were delighted to be the first to know and wished us well.

Judicial Review Hearing, Birmingham

The hearing was listed for the full day, with an 'early' start of 10:00 a.m. The case was heard by an appeal court judge, Lord Flaux, and a High Court Judge, Sue Carr. Jamie and Danny had travelled up from London the night before and were ready for the day ahead. This time the CCRC were there, in force. They were represented by Sam Karim QC and Ben Dylan Williams, plus a team of lawyers and officials from their nearby office. The case proceeded in a similar manner to the earlier permission hearing. Danny went through the case and answered points that were put to him by the two judges. It is not always easy to read the expressions and remarks of judges when the arguments are being debated, but there were one or two moments when I thought that they were with us.

It was during the most important discussion, about the way that the CCRC had analysed the issue of the destruction of witness statements, that Danny seemed to have the judges with him. He had been on his feet for nearly two hours when Sam Karim stood up and asked for an adjournment, 'so that I can take instructions from my client'. He knew which way the wind was blowing and was going to advise the CCRC to concede. After an hour or so of 'taking instructions' and to-ing and fro-ing, a form of words was agreed between us and their lawyers. They would withdraw their decision of October 2017 turning down the pickets' applications. They would also pay our lawyers' costs. We agreed to send in a new submission summarising the pickets' case on the two points – destruction of witness statements and the prejudice caused by *Red under the Bed*. This was the second time the pickets' case had succeeded in court and we were ecstatic.

After the hearing we asked Bindmans to write to Ricky and Arthur to inform them of the outcome and to contact the campaign to discuss it. They agreed to meet with the committee and I arranged a convenient location for them both. Sadly, the day before the scheduled meeting I received an email from each of them saying that they were not going to attend. They did not offer any alternative dates or suggest a further meeting.

Danny and Jamie quickly prepared a twenty-page submission to the CCRC within three weeks of the Birmingham hearing to maintain the momentum. But once again we witnessed how slow the CCRC was when dealing with cases. The problems it had from a lack of funding had only got worse. Significantly, the number of full-time commissioners was to drop from ten to zero. Their replacements were employed on a gig-economy-style contract. We were left waiting for months, despite getting Bindmans to send increasingly urgent requests for a decision.

By the beginning of March 2020, we had had enough. It had been nearly a year since the judicial review. I asked Bindmans to prepare a letter of protest and myself and three other members of the campaign travelled to Birmingham to hand it in. Again we met Justin Hawkins, the man who took the pickets' applications from us in 2012. I gave him two letters, one for the chief executive, Helen Pitcher, and the other for the case review manager. I asked Justin to hand them personally to the two people and we would wait there for their response. When he returned, he told us that the decision would be in the post that week and that we would never hear from the CCRC again. Two days later Bindmans received the letter that we had all been waiting for. The CCRC was going to refer the convictions of Des Warren, John McKinsie Jones, Ken O'Shea, Michael Pierce, Terry Renshaw, Kevin Butcher, Malcolm Clee and Bernard Williams to the Court of Appeal. We were absolutely delighted. Words cannot express our feelings as we always knew that this was the biggest hurdle.

The committee got the sensational news out to the pickets and their families. We explained that we had one final step to go, the appeal court. We arranged a celebratory meeting with everyone at Ewloe on Sunday 8 March. At the same time, we got the news out to all our affiliates and supporters. On the back of our success the CCRC announced on its website that any of the other convicted pickets, including Ricky and Arthur, could apply to them and they would also have their convictions referred to the Court of Appeal. Again, Bindmans wrote to the two men to explain the position and invited them to contact the campaign about the next steps. We did not hear from either of them, which saddened us. But we were delighted that the families of four deceased pickets – Alfred James, Graham Roberts, John Kenneth Seaburg and Samuel Roy Warburton – contacted the campaign and asked to join us. We now had twelve pickets' cases going forward to the appeal court.

In the Court of Appeal – the State Continues to Fight the Case

It had taken the CCRC eight years to finally refer the pickets' convictions and we were astonished when the Crown Prosecution Service (CPS) announced that it was going to defend the appeal. It meant that the government was going to fight us all the way. The Shrewsbury pickets would be up against the state again, in front of three appeal court judges. Danny prepared the grounds of appeal with Ben and they were supported by Jamie and a criminal law partner at Bindmans, Kate Goold.

At the beginning of 2021 we were informed that the appeal was to be heard over two days, 3–4 February, in the Royal Courts of Justice in the Strand, but were unsure whether we could or should appear in person. The government had brought in a new lockdown just before Christmas in response to the COVID pandemic. The hearing could take place remotely if all the parties wanted to. We thought about it long and hard and finally decided that some of us would go. John McKinsie Jones was determined to be there and drove down from north Wales with his wife, Rita. When we arrived outside the court the streets were empty except for a Press Association journalist and two press photographers, including Jess Hurd. The place was eerily empty, devoid of the normal queues you see when entering a court building at the start of the day. When I sat near John on that first day, suitably distanced and masked, he was very upset. He told me that the last time he had been there, in Court 4, he was in the dock. Harry and Terry stayed overnight on the Tuesday and Wednesday, which wasn't easy. Their hotel could not provide any food as all restaurants were required to shut. They had to use a takeaway for their breakfast and evening meal for two days.

Courtesy of Jess Hurd

Campaign members, pickets and solicitor outside the Royal Courts of Justice on the opening day of the appeal, 3 February 2021.

The first day of the appeal saw Danny on his feet for the entire day. The two pickets who had refused to join with us had used another legal team. They were also receiving Legal Aid. Their lawyers had no documents or other evidence to add as all the documents that the Court of Appeal had in front of it were ones that I had discovered. I even emailed a document to the judges, via Bindmans, on the second day when an issue arose about *Red under the Bed*. The CPS barrister did not put up a convincing show in the short time that he spoke and Danny dealt with his arguments in his summing-up at the end of the hearing. It just left us to wait for the decision.

Jamie Potter received an advance copy of the judgment, as was normal practice, but he was professionally bound not to divulge it until it was given out in open court. He said that he would ring me on Tuesday 23 March to give me the news. Harry came to our house as he wanted to be with us when we got the decision. Then, just before the appointed time, Jamie sent me a text to say that he would prefer to speak with me by Zoom. I feared the worst, as I thought that Jamie, being a decent person, wanted to face me when he broke the news, but I texted him back and agreed. We set up the laptop and dialled in at the allotted time. Jamie came on the screen immediately, grinned and said, 'We've won!' I jumped out of my seat and danced around the room. I could not contain myself. Harry joined me, the two of us jumping up and down. It was unbelievable; we had done it. The Court of Appeal had quashed the convictions of all the pickets in all three trials.

I rang Terry and told him the news. He fought back tears to tell me how pleased he was. 'After all these years, I'm now an innocent man.' He then rang Kevin, Michael and Ken's grand-daughter, Emma. After that he drove round to see Malcolm and Bernard. I called John McKinsie Jones. Apart from Des, he had felt the effects of his trial and sentence more than anyone else. It still chokes him to talk about it to this day. When he answered the phone, he was in a state of shock and kept repeating, 'Are you sure? Are you sure? Oh my god, are you sure?'

I spoke with the other members of our committee, Ann, Joe and John, who were speechless and absolutely delighted. Then I rang Elsa Warren, who had campaigned so tirelessly while Des was in prison and had suffered so much as a result of his absence from the family. 'Dessie should be here to see this, but he is here in spirit. I knew you would win. It's the best news I've ever had in my life. Thank you from the bottom of my heart.'

Once we had spoken with all the pickets we swung into action and sent out emails to everyone and posted the news on our website. The phone never stopped ringing. The first person to call was Frances O'Grady, who was so excited and pleased. She asked me to send the best wishes of the TUC to everyone involved and later sent a letter, which we put on our website along with letters from other unions. Messages of congratulation popped up on our Twitter and Facebook pages, like bubbles in a glass of champagne, but we didn't have time to celebrate – yet.

The COVID restrictions prevented us from having an immediate get-together but I decided to produce a celebration/thank-you card for all our supporters. Once again our printer, Chris and his dad, did not let me down. We spent another morning at his office, designing the card and the wording in between talking about the case. Then off home to the 'production line', which we had fine-tuned through several Christmases, sending out campaign greetings cards to our supporters. Harry signed each one and put them on a pile. I then signed it too and added a message before putting them into envelopes that I had stamped and put on address labels. Our local postbox was crammed full for several days but the local CWU members didn't mind.

Celebrations and Sadness

We wanted to organise a celebration for all the pickets and their families as soon as possible and made plans to hold an event at the end of June. It would be a great celebration but was to be tinged with sadness. In the months following the Court of Appeal decision two pickets died. First, Kevin Butcher in May. Several of us attended his funeral, including Terry, who made a dignified speech at the church. He tearfully recalled his final discussion with Kevin, who said to Terry with determination, 'We beat the bastards!' The priest's face was a picture. Then in August we lost Bernard Williams. At the service the vicar gave a wonderful speech about Bernard's participation in the strike and the fact that he never gave up seeking justice.

© Chris Gregory Photography

Victory celebration for the pickets, their families and the campaign, 26 September 2021.

We arranged the celebratory event for the end of June but the ongoing COVID restrictions in Wales forced us to postpone it. We finally got together on Sunday 26 September. The staff pulled out all the stops for us and had dressed the room for a special occasion. John McKinsie Jones, Michael Pierce and Terry Renshaw were there with their families, as were the families of the late Ken O'Shea, Roy Warburton, Kevin Butcher, Bernard Williams, Graham Roberts and John Seaburg. A video message from Elsa Warren was played. I was aware that many of the families might not know too much about the issues so we decided that we would show a short black-and-white film, *Free the Six*, which showed the reasons why the strike happened, including the awful working conditions on building sites. It had been made by Michael Rosen and Jeff Perks when they were students at a London film school in the early 1970s. Most of the people in the room were shocked that their relatives had worked in such dangerous conditions.

After our meal a representative of each family got up and spoke, which was very moving, as were the personal reminiscences from John, Terry and Michael. All the committee members spoke and the other indispensable supporters, including our website and IT expert, Richard; photographer, Chris; and driver, Neil. I was particularly pleased to introduce my two sons, Louis and Alex, who had accompanied us at many events and will always be remembered as our banner carriers. We also had supporters Chris and Sue from Manchester, Nigel from Bristol and Laurie Flynn from Edinburgh, who captured the mood when he praised the pickets and their families and said, 'You cannot take a photograph of dignity.'

Back to Shrewsbury

A week later, on 2 October, a group of us travelled to Shrewsbury as guests of our good friends at Shropshire & Telford TUC, who had put on a celebration. They invited a local Shropshire lad, Jeremy Corbyn MP, to speak. He was followed by Steve Gillan of the Prison Officers' Association who said, 'I was first

Marching through Shrewsbury, 2 October 2021, to a celebration organised for us by Shropshire & Telford TUC.

approached by Eileen Turnbull in 2012 and I didn't hesitate in getting involved in the campaign. This campaign for justice was essential for the Shrewsbury 24 and their families. Politically driven convictions have now been overturned and rightly so. I am proud to have been involved as the general secretary of the POA. This might have surprised some in the trade union movement given our role in society as Prison Officers but first and foremost I am a trade unionist and it was vital to get justice and speak up against the injustice. No self-respecting trade unionist should ever walk on the opposite side of the road to injustice, and I'm proud to say the POA didn't and you had mine and their full support. The success is tinged with sadness because people such as Dessie Warren didn't live to see the injustice overturned and the British political system that effectively carried out these political convictions should have been dealt with decades ago.'

We had a wonderful afternoon, meeting up with old friends and offering our thanks to them all for their steadfast support. We got a great shock when Ian Prowse walked in with his guitar slung over his shoulder. He was playing a gig in the town that evening and had dropped in to see us. It was the icing on the cake when he got on the stage and sang to us Alun Parry's 'My Name Is Dessie Warren'. It was a fitting end to the day.

Back to Parliament

The socialist MPs who had worked so hard for the pickets welcomed us to their meeting at the House of Commons on 24 November 2021 to hear about our success in the Court of Appeal. Many of them recalled the debate in Parliament in 2014 when so many of the Parliamentary Labour Party spoke up to highlight the injustices that the pickets had suffered over many years. We thanked them and emphasised that their support made a huge difference to us and all the other justice campaigns, and we were confident that they would continue to do so.

Conclusion

The most important word in the language of the working class is 'solidarity'.

Harry Bridges, leader of the International
Longshore and Warehouse Union

To overturn a miscarriage of justice affecting one person is an unusual occurrence and one that often gathers bold headlines. The quashing of the convictions of the Shrewsbury 24 pickets hardly got a mention in the media. It was not the subject of any debate on television news. None of the pickets were invited to discuss the issues surrounding the trials on BBC Radio 4's *Today* programme or BBC2's *Newsnight*. Yet the decision of the Court of Appeal covered three trials that stretched over six months, were presided over by two judges and had three separate juries, culminating in twenty-two men being convicted of serious public order offences during a strike.

This case is unprecedented, involving carefully orchestrated prosecutions against trade unionists, followed by long jail sentences. Six men went to prison and sixteen others received suspended prison sentences. Yet there is no statement of apology from the police and certainly no consideration of recompense for what these building workers had endured for over forty years. This was a miscarriage of justice on a seismic scale, but the government has been silent.

The three appeal court judges acknowledged that West Mercia police had destroyed original witness statements and, as a result, the building workers had been denied a fair trial. The prosecutions had been carefully orchestrated by the police, the DPP and the barristers, Drake and Fennell, to ensure that the successful picketing of building workers during the 1972 strike was criminalised.

Why the silence? The reporting of the successful appeal was scant by both the national and the left-wing press. They did not question why successive governments have refused all requests to release documents relating to the trials. The truth about the decisions that were taken at the highest level of government to bring these prosecutions remains a state secret, guarded by Section 23 of the Freedom of Information Act. The information that I have discovered throws some light on the way in which the state acted against the pickets, but I believe there is much more. The available documents show clear gaps in the exchanges of correspondence between government departments. And, of course, there are all the unrecorded discussions that took place between ministers, civil servants, police and employers whose paths crossed through a series of networks that bind these arms of the state together.

The government was determined to bring an end to effective picketing. The construction industry employers wanted to halt and reverse the rise of trade unionism and take back control of the sites. They were a driving force in pushing the police and the government to prosecute the pickets. The convictions and long prison sentences had a devastating impact upon building workers in the following years. Rank-and-file plans for bringing change to the industry disintegrated. During and after the strike there was an increase in trade union membership, but following the prosecution of the pickets numbers fell, continuing the trend that had been in place prior to the strike.

The Building Workers' Charter, in one of its final editions, summed up the position when discussing how to respond to the employers' 1978 wages offer:

> Charter is disappointed with the offer and at this stage can see no alternative to acceptance. Our reasons are based on experience since the 1972 strike. The strike itself was an example of

militancy and proved the fighting ability of building workers. Our drive and skilful dealings throughout the strike[,] coupled with determination to win, took the employers by surprise. The employers[,] determined never to let it happen again[,] took steps to weaken and undermine our movement. The trial at Shrewsbury was a major plank in their campaign which saw building workers jailed for trade union activity.

This attack, and the lack of leadership from the official trade union movement[,] left building workers in the lurch and feeling intimidated. It was in this climate that much of our site organisation was broken up, leading shop stewards sacked, and the blacklist rigorously operated. The growth of unemployment in the industry to 250,000 caused enormous difficulties for getting men into action. It must also be said that Charter, the rank and file, and the official unions, failed to consolidate the positive features of the 72 strike in a way that would have helped the movement continue its fighting spirit.[1]

In the same edition of the paper, Des Warren confirmed the local position: 'Following the 1972 strike, organisation in North Wales has steadily declined to such a degree, that now there is not one effectively organised site in the area.'

The construction employers – the McAlpines, the Bovis's, the John Laings – had won. They were not going to be troubled by an organised workforce in the future. Blacklisting of trade unionists in the building industry grew apace and spread to engineering and other workplaces. Casualisation and the lump increased and the number of apprenticeships declined significantly.

This account of the actions and prosecution of north Wales building workers is a chapter in the history of the British labour movement that should not be forgotten. Trade unionists need to remember the story of the Shrewsbury pickets to understand how the state can act against the attempts of working people to combine. We need to ensure that they never again imprison anyone for supporting strike action. The key to success is trade union solidarity and a willingness to take action to defend each other.

Afterword

How It Was for Some
of Those Involved

The Worst Time of My Life

John McKinsie Jones

Due to the magnificent efforts of the Shrewsbury 24 Campaign, we have won a great victory at the Court of Appeal. All the convictions of the pickets have been quashed. But the awful memories of what happened to me and my family all those years ago remain live in my mind. Being found guilty and imprisoned for something I did not do has haunted me throughout my life.

I was a young man of twenty-five with a wife and child of eighteen months. Rita was eight months' pregnant with our second child when, on 19 December 1973, I was found guilty at Shrewsbury Crown Court of conspiracy to intimidate, affray and unlawful assembly and sentenced to nine months' imprisonment. After I was sentenced, Judge Mais told the prison officers to take me down. I was in shock. I turned to look at the public gallery and saw my father looking at me. Then I felt a nudge from the officer to move, but my legs would not work. I can remember thinking, it is just six days before Christmas, will I ever get through it, could this be the end of me? This date and the horrific memories I associate with it have had a devastating impact on my life.

I find it remarkable that since this historic decision by the Court of Appeal to quash all convictions on 23 March 2021 the press and the politicians have all been completely silent. I have never received a letter from the Court of Appeal or the Crown Prosecution Service offering their apologies for the actions of the police, who deliberately destroyed witness statements, ensuring I did not receive a fair trial. A veil of secrecy continues to surround what happened to us in 1972–73. This book reveals for the first time what was going on behind the scenes which led to us being prosecuted and jailed. We know that this vital information, which was hidden for so many years, will restore our reputations as building workers whose only crime was to strike for better wages and conditions.

We Never Gave Up

Terry Renshaw

I, alongside my fellow pickets, was convicted of picketing offences at Shrewsbury Crown Court in 1974. I joined with the campaign in 2006 to overturn this historic miscarriage of justice. All of us have maintained from the outset that we were set up by the police. But it has taken forty-seven years to prove it.

The government has consistently refused to release documents relating to the Shrewsbury trials. We were forced to find fresh evidence which would show that the convictions were unsafe. This was an uphill struggle. It was made worse by the intransigence of the Criminal Cases Review Commission. Although Eileen Turnbull found irrefutable evidence showing that the police destroyed witness statements, they still rejected our applications. It was only when we successfully challenged them by way of a judicial review that they eventually, after seven years, referred our cases back to the Court of Appeal.

Midway through the pandemic, when the whole country was in lockdown, we attended the Court of Appeal hearing in London on the 3rd and 4th of February 2021. I cannot describe my feelings over those two days when listening to our QC, Danny Friedman, present our case in court. It was so good to hear the truth about what happened to us at Shrewsbury be put for the first time in a court of law. On 23 March I received the news from Eileen that we had won. I cried, and I admit to being emotional about it ever since. The tenacity and the driving force of the Shrewsbury 24 Campaign ensured victory for the pickets. We did it! We came back and we won.

Justice at Last

Elsa Warren

Dennis Warren was my husband and we had five children in 1973 at the time of the Shrewsbury trials. I would like to thank Eileen and all the Shrewsbury committee for all the work they had put in to bring about the victory that we have now after forty-seven years. It never left my mind at any time, and for the last few years Eileen has helped to keep that memory alive on frequent visits all the way from Liverpool, not always easy but I am very grateful for that.

At this point I would like to mention all of the rest of the pickets and the joy they must be feeling now that it is all over. It is finished and we have been vindicated. It has only taken forty-seven years, but what is that out of a lifetime? I am still here, and a few more of us are still here. I can remember the days when I was campaigning and standing outside 10 Downing Street with crowds around me, addressing them. I would go home and would feel, who was that? It was like somebody else. I had my up times, and I had my down times, but this is not the time to complain. However bad it was for us, it was never, ever as bad as it was for Dennis.

Dennis was brave, very brave. He not only fought for his own on building sites but also when he was in prison. He helped other prisoners who did not have the ability to help themselves and came to him for advice. He was an amazing man; no one can ever take that away from him. He was one of a kind; there will never ever be another Des Warren. I am absolutely amazed and pleased at the result and I am sorry that our friend and former picket Ken O'Shea is not here with us to celebrate this but I do believe that he is with us in spirit, along with Dennis. I wish to thank all of you who have helped overturn this miscarriage of justice and I send you my love and understanding and caring.

Immensely Proud

Harry Chadwick – Chairperson, Shrewsbury 24 Campaign

When Des Warren died in 2004 a number of us trade unionists in the North West got together and decided to campaign for justice for the Shrewsbury pickets. Des had always been the beacon for building workers. He was a trade unionist through and through. At the time we did not have a clue how to go about campaigning. It was a case of trial and error.

There were about ten people who initially formed our committee then, but it was a loose version of what it was to become in later years. We met once a month in the Casa, the dockers club in Liverpool, to talk about our strategy. It became clearer over time that we needed funds and we needed direction.

We asked Eileen Turnbull to join with us as treasurer as we were aware of her background in trade unionism. Without doubt her input changed the course of the campaign. She was always the optimist with an infectious sense of humour. Eileen proved to be a successful fundraiser, and later on a dedicated and forensic researcher, who steered us to victory in the Court of Appeal.

The six members of our committee – myself, Eileen, Terry Renshaw, John Bohanna, Ann Dobie and Joe Sim have worked tirelessly for over ten years. We have been through thick and thin, facing many problems, but we stuck together. I regard myself as fortunate in meeting and working alongside these people. There is not a doubt in my mind that the friendship, commitment and solidarity of our little group brought about justice for the Shrewsbury pickets, of which I am immensely proud.

Acknowledgements

Professor David Whyte brought enthusiasm and encouragement as he guided me through five years of study for the Master's and PhD, which laid the foundations for the first parts of this book. He has continued to be an inspirational source of knowledge and understanding of the issues covered by this book, and I wish him well in his new role as director of the Centre for Climate Crime and Climate Justice at Queen Mary, University of London. Thanks also to his colleague, Professor Gabe Mythen, professor of criminology at Liverpool, who always had wise words of advice. Lisa Hawksworth, the faculty librarian at the University of Liverpool, obtained copies of obscure but relevant books and journal articles for me from the libraries throughout the UK.

My thanks to all the staff at the National Archives, Kew, who never tired of my many queries about retained files. The staff at the Working-Class Movement Library, Salford, for going out of their way to make me feel welcome. Andrew, at Churchill Archives Cambridge, for alerting me to other relevant sources of files dealing with the 1970s. To the librarians and staff at the Bodleian, Oxford, the Modern Records Centre, Warwick, the Shropshire archives, the Hull History Centre, City of Westminster Archives Centre and the Marx Memorial Library and to Basement Steve at the BFI Stephen St site, London, for his assistance with *Red under the Bed*.

Thanks to Andy Warren for access to his father's archives and John McKinsie Jones for all his trial papers and personal archives; to Carolyn Jones for access to her father, Bill's archive papers.

Acknowledgements

I am indebted to West Mercia Police for providing me with the police reports concerning the investigation into picketing in Shrewsbury and Telford in 1972.

Thanks to Jim Mowatt, director of education at Unite, for allowing me to consult the records of the T&GWU at Warwick; and to Jim Kennedy, national political officer of UCATT (now National Officer for Unite), who gave me open access to UCATT's records at their head office in London.

We have respected and admired the pickets who never gave up and who had their convictions overturned by the Court of Appeal: Malcolm Clee, John McKinsie Jones, Michael Pierce, Terry Renshaw and the families of the late Des Warren, Ken O'Shea, Kevin Butcher, Bernard Williams, Alfred James, Graham Roberts, John Seaburg and Roy Warburton. A special thanks to Elsa Warren for her friendship, support and stoicism, and to Nick and Andy Warren.

There are so many trade unionists and socialists who have helped me and the campaign throughout these years, more than I can list. Apart from those mentioned in the book, I would particularly like to thank the following: Jacqui Richardson of the Casa, Liverpool; Ken Loach and Rebecca O'Brien at Sixteen Films; Mark Thomas, who has encouraged us every step of the way; Gary Leighton, a talented musician who has helped us fundraise for many years; Paul Fox, Neil Gore and Louise Townsend for bringing us the outstanding play *United We Stand*; Roger Phillips, legendary presenter on BBC Radio Merseyside, who always had time to have us on his programme to speak about the progress of the campaign; to our brilliant lawyers, Jamie Potter, Kate Goold and all the staff at Bindmans Solicitors for their unwavering belief in the pickets' case; to Thompsons solicitors, Birmingham, for their support during the two hearings in the Administrative Court; Bianca Todd for her solidarity and cheerful welcomes over the years; to everyone at Bolton Socialist Club for holding memorable fundraisers; to all the indefatigable campaigners of Merseyside Pensioners' Association and to Mike and Shirley Williams, Holywell.

I am so grateful to my fellow committee members of the Shrewsbury 24 Campaign, starting with the chairperson, Harry

Chadwick, for his unwavering support and comradeship, and to Terry Renshaw, Ann Dobie, Joe Sim and John Bohanna. We worked together as a team and never gave up. The many skills of Richard Grove, Chris Gregory and Chris and Brian Wignall were indispensable in ensuring that the campaign presented a serious profile to the labour movement. To Louis Healey and Alex Turnbull, who carried the campaign's banner with pride. To Ray Dodds and Neil Bowden for ensuring we all arrived safely.

Dennis Skinner, for all the help that he gave the pickets, 1972–76, when he was a newly elected MP for Bolsover. He visited Des Warren regularly and campaigned tirelessly for his release and justice for all Des's fellow pickets. When the Shrewsbury 24 Campaign was established in 2006 Dennis, along with other socialist Labour MPs, were unwavering in their support and put pressure on successive governments to release the documents that were being held back.

My thanks to Laurie Flynn for his support and guidance, which has been indispensable to me. To Tariq Ali at Verso Books, who readily agreed to publish this work and has been inspirational, providing me with many insights. Thanks also to the staff at Verso: Leo Hollis for his constant encouragement and kind words as I attempted to meet his demands and deadlines; Mark Martin, managing editor; and John Gaunt, copy editor, for putting my words in good order.

The following trade unionists gave vital support at crucial stages of the campaign.

Aslef: Mick Whelan (general secretary)

CWU: Dave Ward (GS); Billy Hayes, former GS; Carl Webb, NW regional secretary; Angela Teeling and Mark Walsh of the Mersey Amal,.

EIS: Larry Flanagan (GS).

FBU: Matt Wrack (GS).

GMB: Gary Smith (GS); Paul McCarthy, North West regional secretary.

Musicians' Union: Horace Trubridge (GS).

NAPO: Ian Lawrence (GS).

NEU: Mary Bousted and Kevin Courtney (joint GSs); Nigel Varley, Ann Lemon, Bristol.

PCS: Mark Serwotka (GS).

PFA: Gordon Taylor (GS).

POA: Steve Gillan (GS).

RMT: Mick Lynch (GS); Daren Ireland and John Tilley of the North West region; Stuart Holt, Central and North Mersey; Colin Rigby, Machynlleth; Jim Gray, Scottish regional council; Jim Mahon, Glasgow 1 and 2. A special thank you to the late Bob Crow, who went that extra mile.

TSSA: Manuel Cortes (GS).

TUC: Frances O'Grady (GS); Paul Nowak (AGS); Bill Adams, Yorkshire; Lee Barron, Midlands; Megan Dobney, former South East regional secretary; Jay McKenna, North West; Shavanah Taj, Wales.

UCATT/Unite: Billy Parry, Andy Fisher, George Guy, Jimmy Woods, Jamie Bramwell, Kenny Routledge, John Winstanley; Brian Clark, York; Jimmy Ellis, Wigan; Eddie Ward, St Budeaux; Peter Exon, South Sefton; George Fuller, Forest Gate.

Unison: Kevan Nelson, North West regional secretary; Glen Williams, Sefton; Bernadette Gallagher, Bolton; Ben Jackson and Neil McAllister, Manchester Mental Health; Paul Taylor, Tameside; Tracy Roberts, Wigan; Carol Coltman, Wigan retired members; Adrian Turner, Wolverhampton.

Unite: Sharon Graham (GS) and Tony Woodhouse (EC chair); Pat Rafferty, Scotland regional secretary; Ritchie James, North West RS (and his predecessor, Mick Whitley MP); Sarah Carpenter, South East RS; Steve Preddy, South West RS; Peter Hughes, Wales RS (and her predecessor, Jenny Formby, also as L.P. general secretary); Jim Mowatt, Unite director of education; Kate Purcell; John Lea, North West regional education officer; Karie Murphy and Amy Jackson; Steve Murphy and Sheila Coleman, Liverpool; Andy Howcroft, Bolton; Paul Conroy, Landrover Joint Shop Stewards Committee; Nick Kelleher, Wolverhampton; Jim Edgerton, Luton Retired Members; Dave Towers, NE/GEO/20; John Davies, NE/GEO/12; George White, BAe NW/64; Claire Williams, Prudential; Bryan Cottenden, Fylde Coast NW/520M; John Poland, Jaguar Halewood NW/562; Derrick Eastham, Preston 0754; David Bell, Scottish Borders Council; Frank Cammock, Short Belfast; Dwyer McKerr, Craigavon/USDAW: Paddy Lillis (GS).

The secretaries and PAs of several union general secretaries also deserve special mention: Jo Fontana, Unite; Liz Munro, PCS; Sharon Lester, FBU; Janina Dunn, CWU; Moya Jackson, USDAW; and Nicola Hubert, POA.

I am so grateful to my fellow committee members of the Shrewsbury 24 Campaign, starting with the chairperson, Harry Chadwick, for his unswerving support and comradeship, and to Terry Renshaw, Ann Dobie, Joe Sim and John Bohanna. We worked together as a team and never gave up. The many skills of Richard Grove, Chris Gregory and Chris and Brian Wignall were indispensable in ensuring that the campaign presented a serious profile to the labour movement. To Louis Healey and Alex Turnbull, who carried the campaign's banner with pride. To Ray Dodds and Neil Bowden for ensuring we all arrived safely.

Dennis Skinner, for all the help that he gave the pickets, 1972–76, when he was a newly elected MP for Bolsover. He visited Des Warren regularly and campaigned tirelessly for his release and justice for all Des's fellow pickets. When the Shrewsbury 24 Campaign was established in 2006 Dennis, along with other socialist Labour MPs, were unwavering in their support and put pressure on successive governments to release the documents that were being held back.

My thanks to Laurie Flynn for his support and guidance, which has been indispensable to me. To Tariq Ali at Verso Books, who readily agreed to publish this work and has been inspirational, providing me with many insights. Thanks also to the staff at Verso: Leo Hollis for his constant encouragement and kind words as I attempted to meet his demands and deadlines; Mark Martin, managing editor; and John Gaunt, copy editor, for putting my words in good order.

My two grandchildren, Karl and Katy Healey, remained an inspiration for me throughout the hard years of campaigning and writing this book. They grew from toddlers to teenagers during that time and were a constant source of humour and questioning.

Indebted as I am to all the above, I remain responsible for any errors of fact and for the interpretation of the events that I have set out in this book.

Notes

Introduction

1 Dominic Sandbrook, *State of Emergency. The Way We Were: Britain 1970–1974*, London, 2010; Alwyn Turner, *Crisis? What Crisis?*, London, 2013; Lawrence Black, Hugh Pemberton and Pat Thane (eds.) *Reassessing 1970s Britain*, Manchester, 2016. Most give only passing reference to the strike. Andy Beckett, *When the Lights Went Out: Britain in the Seventies*, London, 2009, while devoting a whole chapter to the miners' strikes of 1972 and 1974, does not contain a single word about the building workers' strike and the conspiracy trials. Ken Coates's introductory essay 'Converting the unions to socialism', in Michael Barratt Brown and Ken Coates, *Trade Union Register 3*, Nottingham, 1973, summarises a number of union struggles under Heath – the dockers strikes against containerisation, the Upper Clyde Shipbuilders work-in, various engineering factory sit-ins – but not the building workers' strike.

2 The Shrewsbury 24 Campaign republished Des Warren, *The Key to My Cell*, London, 1982, in 2007, and Jim Arnison, *The Shrewsbury Three*, London, 1974, in 2014.

3 West Mercia Police Complaints Report, paragraph 117.

4 Warren later sued the Home Office and received an out-of-court settlement.

5 This illness is discussed throughout his son's memoir: Nick Warren, *Thirty Years in a Turtleneck Sweater*, London, 2006.

6 Various terms have been used over the years to describe groupings of these pickets. 'Shrewsbury 24' refers to the total number charged and tried at Shrewsbury in the three trials in 1973–4. The term was used in 1973 when pickets were first arrested and charged. It is used by the campaign that was launched in 2006 to overturn their convictions. 'Shrewsbury 6' refers either to the

six pickets who were tried for conspiracy at the first trial, from October to December 1973, or subsequently to the six of the twenty-four pickets who were sent to prison. 'Shrewsbury 3' refers to the pickets imprisoned after the first trial: Des Warren, Eric Tomlinson and John McKinsie Jones. It is also the title of Jim Arnison's book. 'The Shrewsbury 2' was used by campaigners demanding the release of Warren and Tomlinson after McKinsie Jones was released.

7 The series J182, containing court papers of the Shrewsbury trials, were released on 1 January 2005. Other files, e.g. DPP2/5185 and DPP2/5159, were released later in that year, on 23 May 2005.

8 The office of the DPP was not a government department. It was supposed to be an arms-length body that took decisions on prosecutions without political interference, although it was answerable to the government's senior legal adviser, the attorney general. The DPP now heads the Crown Prosecution Service, which was formed in 1986 from an amalgamation of the DPP's office and local police prosecution departments. Joshua Rozenberg, *The Case for the Crown: The Inside Story of the Director of Public Prosecutions*, Wellingborough, 1987.

9 The term 'flying pickets' is used to describe the practice of pickets travelling by car and coach to other workplaces to persuade workers to support their strike either by stopping work themselves or by refusing to deliver supplies or collect goods. Since 1980 it has only been lawful to picket your own workplace (Employment Act 1980 s. 16, now re-enacted in s. 220 of the Trade Union and Labour Relations (Consolidation) Act 1992.)

1. A Strike Whose Time Had Come

1 John Gennard, *Financing Strikers*, London, 1970 pp. 166–7.
2 Royal Commission on Trade Unions and Employers' Associations (Cmnd. 3623, HMSO), London, 1968, though better known as the Donovan report after the name of its chairman.
3 *Hansard*, 'Royal Commission on Trade Unions and Employers' Associations (Report)', 16 July 1968, Volume 768, paragraph 1261, hansard.millbanksystems.com.
4 Ralph Darlington and Dave Lyddon, *Glorious Summer*, London, 2001, pp. 7–9.
5 *In Place of Strife* (Cmnd. 3888, HMSO), London, 1969.
6 *Heatons Transport (St Helens) Ltd* v. *Transport and General Workers Union* [1973] A.C. 15. The T&GWU was fined a total of £55,000 (approximately £800,000 in 2022 terms) arising from this dispute with this haulage firm. *Con-Mech (Engineers)*

Limited v. *Amalgamated Union of Engineering Workers* [1974] ICR 464. See Michael Barratt Brown and Ken Coates, *Trade Union Register 3*, Nottingham, 1973; Donald Macdonald, *The State and the Trade Unions*, London, 1976.

7   Darlington and Lyddon, *Glorious Summer*, pp. 31–73.

8   Ibid., p. 37.

9   Vic Allen, *The Militancy of British Miners*, Shipley, 1981; Arthur Scargill, 'The new unionism', *New Left Review*, 92 (July–August 1975) pp. 3–33.

10 For a full account see Scargill, 'The new unionism'; and Beckett, *When the Lights Went Out*, pp. 66–87.

11 Technology played its part. Fifty years earlier very few people had owned motor cars, certainly not coal miners. By the 1970s cars and coaches were increasingly available to take pickets long distances. 'The lesson of Saltley and the building strikes was that with the advent of motorways ... the days when picketing was normally a strictly local and peaceful affair ... appeared to have gone.' John Elliott, 'The restricted power of the picket', *Financial Times*, 7 February 1974.

12 The Official Solicitor is an officer of the court who is primarily responsible for acting for vulnerable individuals, including children and adults lacking mental capacity, but is also responsible for representing anyone committed to prison for contempt of court.

13 Jim Rand, a distinguished Liverpool bricklayer and trade union activist, winner of the silver trowel, often recounted to me the culture on building sites in the 1950s and 1960s. On a number of sites at which he had worked a chalk line had been drawn on the floor down the middle of the men's work hut to mark out which part could be used by labourers and which was reserved for the tradesmen.

14 Herbert Smith, *The 1973 Conspiracy Trials*, n.l., n.d., p. 42 (author's papers), from UCATT Liverpool's archives.

15 'Inter-union rivalry behind the building strikes', *Financial Times*, 29 August 1972. Elliot identified one of the drivers for the merger as the desire of the craft unions to avoid their members being poached by the general unions. He argued that UCATT's leadership were drawn into supporting strike action to prevent the more militant T&GWU from making itself attractive to building workers at their expense.

16 The Amalgamated Society of Woodcutting Machinists and the National Union of Furniture Trades Operatives.

17 Building Workers' Charter. Volume 2, No. 4, Appendix C of the West Mercia Police Report included an extract setting out the charter's demands.

18 Charlie McGuire, Linda Clarke and Christine Wall, 'Battles on the Barbican: the struggle for trade unionism in the British building industry, 1965–7', *History Workshop Journal*, 75, 1 (2013), pp. 33–57, for an excellent summary of the origins of the Building Workers' Charter.

19 'Negotiations in building were tough', *Viewpoint*, November 1972, p. 3.

20 Smith, The 1973 Conspiracy Trials, p. 11.

21 Patricia Hillebrandt, *Analysis of the British Construction Industry*, London, 1984. The NFBTE's archives are at the University of Warwick. It renamed itself in 1984 and was involved in an unsuccessful confederation of employers' organisations. Its present-day successor is the National Federation of Builders.

22 Leslie Wood, *A Union to Build: The Story of UCATT*, London, 1979, p. 129.

23 Today the FCEC is known as the Civil Engineering Contractors Association.

24 'He had grown up in considerable comfort. His father, Sir Samuel Joseph, a baronet, headed the family firm, Bovis, one of the biggest construction companies in the country, and also served a term as lord mayor of London.' Daniel Yergin and Joseph Stanislaw, *From Commanding Heights*, New York, 1998, p. 93.

25 HC Deb 22 January 1976, vol. 903, cc. 1631–60.

26 In 1966 Maudling became director of a property company headed by John Poulson and an adviser to the Peachey Property Company. Both companies collapsed when the chief executives were discovered to have been corrupt. Maudling's association with Poulson led directly to Maudling's resignation as home secretary on 18 July 1972, Lewis Baston, *Reggie: The Life of Reginald Maudling*, Stroud, 2004.

27 Jonathan Glancey, 'Life in the Fast Lane – Part Two', *Guardian*, 22 January 2007.

28 See 'Chichester-Clark, Robin (b. 1928)', at historyofparliament online.org.

29 See Owen's intervention in the debate on Eric Heffer's lump bill at *Hansard*, 'Labour-Only Sub-contracting Bill', Volume 856, 18 May 1973, hansard.parliament.uk.

30 These companies made direct donations to the Conservatives in 1971–2 totalling £13,915 (the equivalent of £201,538 in 2022). Another source of funds from industry to the Conservative Party was via British United Industrialists. It received £5,000 from Associated Portland Cement and £15,000 from Rugby Portland Cement (£20,000 is the equivalent of £289,671 in 2022). *Labour Research*, August 1975, pp. 162–4.

31 Ibid. In 2022 prices the amounts are £980,581 and £438,837 respectively.

32 *Labour Research*, August 1975, p. 163 (£630,614 in 2022 prices).

33 Ralph Morton, Construction UK: Introduction to an Industry, Oxford, 2002, pp. 73–4.

34 Speech by John Westacott, quoted in *NFBTE Newsletter*, 18 (22 September 1972), Warwick Modern Records Centre, MSS.187/3/1/10, emphasis added.

35 Department of Health & Social Security figures covering 1970–5 obtained from HSE, Bootle. *Occupational Safety Bulletin*, July 1972, reported that in 1971 there were 196 fatal and 34,272 non-fatal accidents in building and engineering construction. For a criticism of the accuracy of such figures see Sandra Dawson, *Safety at work: the limits of self-regulation*, Cambridge, 1988, pp. 27–30. What was often excluded was the many workers who were exposed to harmful dusts and chemicals by their employer. Such substances would cause premature and painful deaths in later years, such as from asbestos-related diseases, other lung diseases and cancers.

36 'Unsafe kiln kills three', *Viewpoint*, March 1972, p. 8 (Modern Records Centre, University of Warwick). £100 = £1,448 at 2022 prices.

37 Malcolm Deacon, Quentin Falk, Eileen Sheridan, Ian Soutar, *Wokingham Times*, 26 October 1972.

38 Factories Act 1961, s. 156.

39 Trial transcript, Working Class Movement Library (WCML), Salford, p. 1265.

40 'How the system works', *Socialist Worker*, 12 May 1973. See also 'Dumping the lump?', Vincent Hanna, *Sunday Times*, 19 April 1970.

41 Des Warren, evidence in the trial transcript, p. 1253. This is significant because the prosecution at Shrewsbury claimed that pickets chanted, 'Kill! Kill! Kill!', implying that the pickets were threatening violence against non-strikers.

42 John Platts-Mills, *Muck, Silk and Socialism: Recollections of a Left-Wing Queen's Counsel*, Wedmore, Somerset, 2002, p. 534.

43 On one part of McAlpine's Brookside site in Telford, which was picketed on 6 September 1972, there were fifteen sub-contractors including three bricklaying firms plus separate firms of scaffolders, electricians, plumbers, painters, roofers, plasterers and glaziers. Today the position is even worse due to the spread of employment agencies, many of which require workers to be independently registered with the tax authorities as self-employed.

44 The forms of employment in the construction industry have

changed significantly during the past fifty years. For recent studies of the greater use of agency workers, the self-employed and other contingent forms see Chris Forde, Robert MacKenzie and Andrew Robinson, 'Built on Shifting Sands: Changes in Employers' Use of Contingent Labour in the UK Construction Sector', *Journal of Industrial Relations*, 51: 5 (2009), pp. 653–67.

45 A fictional account of the working conditions of building workers, and techniques used by contractors to save money by using shoddy methods and materials, is Robert Tressell, *The Ragged Trousered Philanthropists*, London, 1965. Although written over 100 years ago it was based upon his experiences as a painter and signwriter. It was read by many building trade unionists in the twentieth century. Recent research into working conditions includes McGuire, Clarke and Wall, 'Battles on the Barbican'; Christine Wall, Charlie McGuire, Linda Clarke and Michaela Brockmann, *Building a Community: Construction Workers in Stevenage, 1950–1970*, London, 2011; Christine Wall, Linda Clarke, Charlie McGuire and Olivia Munoz-Rojas, *Building the M1 Motorway*, London, 2012; Christine Wall, Linda Clarke, Charlie McGuire and Olivia Munoz-Rojas, *Building the Barbican, 1962–1982: Taking the Industry out of the Dark Ages*, London, 2014.

46 In 1972, sites were covered by the Construction (Health and Welfare) Regulations 1966 and the Construction (Working Places) Regulations 1966. They were simply ignored by many employers as there was no official effective enforcement. The only way they would be policed was by trade union representatives.

47 Warren discusses this during his trial (trial transcript, pp. 1206–7); Arnison, *The Shrewsbury Three*, p. 65.

48 Mark Hollingsworth and Richard Norton-Taylor, *Blacklist: The Inside Story of Political Vetting*, London, 1988, pp. 147–55; Dave Smith and Phil Chamberlain, *Blacklisted: The Secret War between Big Business and Union Activists*, London, 2015. The prevalence of the blacklist in the building industry in the 1970s and 1980s led many militants to seek employment in the direct works departments of Labour-run local authorities. However, with the privatisation of council housing and the dismantling of their repairs departments, this option disappeared.

49 Again, just as Warren's comments about putting a match to a decrepit builders' hut at the Weir site in Shrewsbury was described at his trial as a threat of arson, so the need for him to take steps to avoid being blacklisted was condemned by the police as a sinister criminal act: 'Gwynedd Constabulary have put forward a suggested charge against him of obtaining the opportunity to earn remuneration by deception.' West Mercia Constabulary,

'Disorderly conduct by pickets at building sites in Shropshire on Wednesday 6th September 1972' (1972), p. 44 (author's papers).

50 *Morning Star*, 26 February 1972.

51 Wood, *A Union to Build*, p. 16.

52 See Warren's evidence at trial, Monday 3 December, trial transcript, p. 1216.

2. The Strike Begins

1 National Action Committee statement, 1 June 1972 (author's papers).

2 Quoted in Smith, *The 1973 Conspiracy Trials*, p. 9, emphasis added.

3 Ibid., p. 9.

4 Ibid., pp. 11–12.

5 *Morning Star*, 27 June 1972.

6 Harry Chadwick, personal communication.

7 *Workers' Press*, 7 September 1972, p. 10.

8 See photo in Wood, *A Union to Build*, p. 26.

9 Acceptance of the higher rates of pay by an employer on one site did not mean that the employer would pay it to their employees on every building site. Each one was a separate battle ground.

10 Speech notes relating to the unions' claim, 12 July 1972, p. 5 (author's papers).

11 UCATT special executive council minute, 19 July 1972, p. 1 (author's papers).

12 Ibid.

13 Minutes of the National Joint Council for the Building Industry (NJCBI) (operatives' side), meeting, 20 July 1972 (author's papers).

14 NJCBI operatives' side press release, 20 July 1972 (author's papers).

15 Minutes of the NAC with regional secretaries, 27 July 1972 (author's papers).

16 Report on the wage dispute to the NFBTE council, 17 August 1972, Warwick Modern Records Centre, MSS187/3/Mc/1/7.

17 Circular from George Smith to regional secretaries, 4 August 1972, UCATT Archives. See also the report on the wage dispute to the NFBTE council, 17 August 1972, Modern Records Centre, MSS187/3/Mc/1/7.

18 Darlington and Lyddon, *Glorious Summer*, pp. 192–3.

19 Smith, The 1973 Conspiracy Trials, p. 20.

20 Letter from G. F. Smith to all branch secretaries, August 1972 (author's papers).

21 *The Times*, 12 August 1972, quoted in Darlington and Lyddon, *Glorious Summer*, p. 193.

22 UCATT circular, GFS/ADM/RES/527/72, 'Construction industry dispute', August 1972 (author's papers).

23 Letter from G. F. Smith, UCATT general secretary, to all regional and branch secretaries, August 1972, UCATT archives.

24 Telex report from L. C. Kemp and G. P. Henderson to regional construction officials, 18 August 1972 (author's papers).

25 From letter, George Wright, regional secretary (designate), to officers concerned, 18 August 1972 (author's papers).

26 Minutes of meeting of the NAC with regional secretaries, 17 August 1972 (author's papers).

27 This was one of two mass-circulation evening papers in London in the 1970s; the other was the *Evening Standard*.

28 *Evening News* (London), 17 August 1972.

29 Minutes of meeting of the NAC with regional secretaries, 17 August 1972 (author's papers).

30 South Western Regional Action Committee Report to the National Action Committee, 24ᵗ August 1972, R. E. Heal, Regional Secretary (author's papers).

31 Arnison, *The Shrewsbury Three*, p. 24. Jim Arnison was a plumber and had been the union convenor of the building works department at Salford Direct Works. He resigned to become a full-time worker for the Communist Party and journalist on the *Morning Star*. He attended the Shrewsbury trials daily for the paper and wrote the first account of the jailing of pickets, *The Shrewsbury Three*.

32 Ibid., p. 24.

33 Report to council meeting, 17 August 1972, wage dispute, Warwick Modern Records Centre, MSS 187/3/MC/1/7 (author's papers).

34 *Newsletter* No. 4 of 18 August 1972, Warwick Modern Records Centre, MSS 187/3/MC/1/7.

35 Labour-only sub-contractors were lump workers. It was ironic that the employers made increasing use of lump labour to avoid the obligations that they would owe to employees, but when it came to a headcount for the purposes of a levy, the NFBTE pleaded that such workers should be included.

36 *Morning Star*, 6 September 1972.

37 UCATT Midlands regional secretary, letter to all members, 26 August 1972, capital letters in the original (author's papers).

38 Even a bitter opponent of trade unions, Major General Clutter-buck, recognised this: 'Building sites have no focus like the gate of a power station or a coke depot ... a building site has no perimeter and no gates, and the labour force changes weekly or

even daily.' Richard Clutterbuck, *Britain in Agony: The Growth of Political Violence*, London, 1980 p. 77.

3. The North Wales Pickets and the Fateful Day

1   Des Warren had been working at the Taylor Woodrow site up to November 1971 but was dismissed after campaigning against the use of lump labour and other issues. See Warren, *The Key to My Cell*, p. 13. He was blacklisted and had to use an alias, Michael Jones, to get work. This was known within UCATT. Albert Prest, 'Memoirs of Albert Prest, former UCATT regional organiser for the north west region', Modern Records Centre, MSS.78/UC/6/1, n.d., pp. 85–6. For Chester Telephone Exchange see report letter from E. V. Hughes, UCATT north west regional secretary, to George Smith, UCATT general secretary, 1 March 1973 (author's papers).

2   Statement, 20 September 1973, produced for Casson & Co. solicitors, acting for two T&GWU members in the first trial, Shrewsbury archives, WCML, Salford.

3   See the statement that the police prepared from information provided by Llywarch at an interview on 3 November 1972 (Exhibit 35, *R v. Carpenter and 5 Others*, TNA J182/48). Although Llywarch refused to sign it when he returned to the police station on 30 November, he said at his trial that 95 per cent of it was accurate. Trial transcript, pp. 941–1014. Tomlinson confirmed at the trial that he only joined the union in July 1972, after the Shotton pickets had visited the site, and 'when Llywarch organised it, when the members were picketing.' Trial transcript, pp. 1017–18.

4   Trial transcript, p. 1020.

5   Taken from the court indictments setting out the charges against the north Wales pickets at their trials at Mold and Shrewsbury Crown Courts a year later. None of the pickets were arrested or cautioned on the days that they went picketing in August and September. The first time that they were informed of any charges was six months later, in February 1973.

6   Although this was five weeks after the national strike had ended the police included an incident at the site to bring charges against Warren and a colleague, Glyn Davies.

7   Letter from Roberts to the T&GWU's two national officers for the building industry, Kemp and Henderson, 5 September 1973 (author's papers).

8   *Shropshire Star*, 21 August 1972.

9   West Mercia Constabulary, 'Disorderly conduct by pickets', para. 90.

10 Ibid., para. 93.

11 Confirmed in statements from two West Mercia PC's, Evans and Goodchild, and at trial by Inspector Needham.

12 According to Llywarch, 'Someone said Birmingham had been approached about it, but they had said it was too far for them to travel. I think the Shrewsbury area comes in with Oswestry, although it is not in the north west region of the union. Telford definitely does not – it is under the Birmingham branch.' Unsigned statement of John Elfyn Llywarch, p. 3 (author's papers). DCI Glover claims that the statement was based upon police interview notes taken on 3 November 1972.

13 Abrahams was a defence witness at the first Shrewsbury trial and his evidence describes the action committees in north Wales and the meeting on 31 August. Trial transcript, pp. 872–96.

14 Statement of Des Warren for Casson & Co. solicitors, (n.d.) p. 2 (author's papers).

15 According to Batterbee, 'During the meeting John LLYWARCH produced the newspaper report that 250 workers would be waiting for us and asked for support as far as Shrewsbury was concerned where some sites were still working.' Statement of J. W. Batterbee taken by Inspector Powell at Oswestry Police Station, 13 November 1972. Llywarch denied circulating the newspaper or encouraging a flying picket to Shropshire. He was trying to avoid incriminating himself but many other strikers at the Bull and Stirrup meeting confirmed that he was the source of the information – e.g. Warren. They saw nothing wrong in Llywarch or any other Oswestry strikers giving such a report or asking for support to picket out the Shrewsbury sites.

16 The article was included as Appendix D in the main West Mercia Constabulary report. The article said, 'Sub-contractors working for many of the big building firms, including Frank Galliers, Fletchers, Ashleys and Watking [*sic*],Starbuck and Jones have agreed to join the anti picket force. Their "army" was formed on Friday and sub-contractor Mr John Price at the Severn Meadows estate said he hoped to raise enough men to ward off the pickets and persuade them to leave.'

17 Trial transcript, p. 877.

18 Statement of Dennis Michael Warren for Casson & Co. solicitors (n.d.), p. 3.

19 Police radio log, Radio Communications Console No. 2, 16:57, in West Mercia Constabulary, appendix file, n.d. Details of the Chester coach were not given by the police as it had returned home and did not proceed to Telford in the afternoon.

20 Statement of John Kenneth Seaburg, Exhibit 8 in the third Shrewsbury trial, *R* v. *Renshaw and Others* (author's papers).

21 Trial transcript, p. 882. They were both members of the Communist Party.

22 Warren, *The Key to My Cell*, p. 18.

23 Statement of Dennis Michael Warren for Casson & Co. solicitors (n.d.), p. 4.

24 Detective Constable Philip Davies made a statement that he witnessed Warren addressing a group of 200 pickets and local workmen on 6 September: 'The picket spokesman was asking for support for the strike and asked for local workers to picket sites in the Telford area. He said, "It will only take about a dozen of you to police this area."'

25 The West Mercia Constabulary was the police authority covering Shropshire, and two other counties, Worcestershire and Herefordshire. It was a predominantly rural area and the police had little experience in policing industrial disputes. In the months following the picketing in Shropshire the police produced two reports. These were not made public until the successful appeals of the Shrewsbury pickets in 2021. The circumstances in which I obtained them are dealt with in Chapter 15. The first report was entitled 'Disorderly conduct by pickets'. It was submitted to the Director of Public Prosecutions with a large quantity of statements and other documents. The second was simply called 'Report file', and was prepared for internal purposes to address complaints that the police had received from local builders. It had a separate appendix file of documents. These documents contain valuable information about the conduct of the police on the day and their attitude towards the north Wales building workers.

26 Statement of Desmond Michael Warren for Casson & Co. solicitors (n.d.), p. 4 (author's papers).

27 The first incident was at Brynford on 18 August. The police prepared a statement from a joiner, Raymond Jones, who claimed to witness his employer, Stanley Rawson, having a camera snatched and smashed. (Contractors throughout Britain were known to be taking photographs of pickets to use for blacklisting.) 'I then saw Mr. Rawson pick up a shotgun and he appeared to be loading it. As Mr Rawson had the gun cocked open they rushed him again and pushed him from the hallway into the back room ... The pickets were milling around telling us that we should be in a union and should not be working.' PC Ellis arrived at the site and questioned Rawson, who made a statement: 'I asked RAWSON if he did point the gun at them. He replied "Yes, I did, I just wanted to scare them off." The pickets then handed to me a shotgun which Mr. RAWSON identified as his gun.' Statement of Police Constable Michael Ellis, 5 April 1973 (author's papers).

28 The contractor was never prosecuted and at the first Shrewsbury

trial Judge Mais declared that he was legally entitled to have it in his possession provided he had a licence! Llywarch gave a statement to the police while pickets boarded their coaches for the next site but the facts of the incident were turned on their head. When Sergeant Bourne sent a message from the control room to police at Telford at 1:35 p.m. he gave the impression that the pickets had a weapon with them: 'Coaches should be with you within the hour. Pickets may use violence. A shotgun was stolen from a car in Shrewsbury not known if any ammunition – and it is suspected that one of the pickets is responsible.' Extract from Wellington telephone book, West Mercia Constabulary, appendix file.

29 West Mercia Constabulary, 'Report file', para. 26.

30 Ibid., para. 95. A better indication of the concern with which West Mercia police took the pickets than Hodges's hindsight was the decision to send just a solitary police motorcyclist to follow the pickets' coaches from Shrewsbury to Telford.

31 Statement of Dennis Michael Warren for Casson & Co. solicitors, p. 5.

32 Police statement of Tecwyn Price, 4 October 1972 (author's papers).

33 West Mercia Constabulary, 'Report file', para. 35.

34 Warren believed that the pressure to investigate and prosecute the north Wales pickets came from Sir Alfred McAlpine & Son Ltd. Warren, *The Key to My Cell*, pp. 25–6. The McAlpine family were very influential nationally and in north Wales. The son-in-law of Sir Alfred McAlpine and a company director, Peter Henry Bell, became the high sherriff of Denbighshire in 1973. A short history of the family companies was set out in litigation between them, *Sir Robert McAlpine Limited* v. *Alfred McAlpine Plc* [2004] EWHC 630 (Ch) para. 2.

35 Statement made to D.C. 974 Jones at St Asaph Police station 14 November 1972 (author's papers). See also the police 'record of interview' with John Bithell (author's papers).

36 Index of Counts, Defendants and Witnesses, second indictment, count 42. TNA J182/15.

37 Statement of Dennis Michael Warren for Casson & Co. solicitors, p. 7.

38 West Mercia Constabulary, 'Report file', para. 114.

39 Statement of Chief Superintendent Christopher Meredith, 2 March 1973.

40 Statement of Superintendent George Landers, 2 April 1973.

41 West Mercia Constabulary, 'Report file', para. 117.

42 Ibid., para. 17.

43 Ibid., para. 49.

44 Ibid., para. 48.
45 Ibid., para. 52.
46 Statement of Dennis Michael Warren for Casson & Co. solicitors, p. 7.
47 Warren, *The Key to My Cell*, p. 46.
48 Ibid., p. 18.
49 West Mercia Constabulary, appendix file, Radio Communications Console No. 3, 1347.
50 Ibid., Console No. 5, 1431.
51 Ibid., Console No. 5, 1454.
52 The pickets had all travelled from north Wales or Shropshire, not from Liverpool. The comment would fit in with a prejudice and fear in West Mercia of anyone from this trade union-organised city.
53 West Mercia Constabulary, appendix file, Radio Communications Console No. 6, 1539.
54 Ibid., Console No. 5, 1700.
55 Memorandum, T. McTurk to DC Macgregor re. Glasgow Action Committee Report, 6 September 1972 (author's papers).
56 Letter, 15 September 1972, UCATT archives.
57 At this stage there was no indication of a government-imposed wage freeze. On 14 September the government held a meeting at Chequers of the tripartite National Economic Development Council (NEDC). It included six TUC and six CBI representatives, alongside government ministers. The meeting was chaired by the prime minister. The TUC stated that its target was twenty pounds basic pay for a forty-hour week. The talks eventually collapsed on 2 November and the government imposed statutory wage controls on 6 November. Trades Union Congress, *The Chequers and Downing Street Talks, July to November 1972: Report by the TUC*, London, 1972.
58 Letter, L. C. Kemp to officers concerned in building dispute (author's copy).
59 Copy minutes from UCATT (author's papers).
60 Letter, D. W. Craig, secretary Aberdeen Action Committee to Mr G. F. Smith, secretary National Action Committee, 18 September 1972 (author's papers).
61 Warren, *The Key to My Cell*, p. 16.
62 Prest, 'Memoirs', pp. 108–9.
63 Ibid., p. 93.
64 Darlington and Lyddon, *Glorious Summer*, p. 1.
65 Arnison, The Shrewsbury Three, p. 40.
66 Interviewed in *Arise Ye Workers* (London: Cinema Action, 1972), at nineteen minutes fifty seconds.

4. The Employers Mobilise

1   Letter to the Confederation of British Industries (CBI), Ref. 2035, City of Westminster Archives, London, emphasis added.
2   NFBTE emergency letter no. 6, 14 September 1972, Warwick Modern Records Centre, MSS.187/3/PIC/1/11.
3   *NFBTE Newsletter*, no. 18, Warwick Modern Records Centre, MSS.187/3/1/10.
4   *The Times*, 21 August 1972.
5   *NFBTE Newsletter*, no. 17, Warwick Modern Records Centre, MSS.187/3/1/10.
6   Ref. 2035, City of Westminster Archives, London.
7   Letter from M. A. P. Harnett, NFBTE press officer, 20 September 1972, Warwick MSS/187/3/PIC/1/14.
8   Letter, 22 August 1972, UCATT archives.
9   NJCBI press release, 17 August 1972 (author's papers).
10 John Elliott, 'Report tells of building strike "mobster tactics"', *Financial Times*, 30 October 1972. The *NFBTE Newsletter* no. 20, 13 October 1972, reported, 'we have compiled a dossier on the thuggery and intimidation on building sites this summer which will shortly be sent to the Home Secretary.' The exact date that the dossier was sent to the Home Office is unknown because there is no correspondence about it in Home Office files at Kew or in any publicly accessible records of the NFBTE.
11 Copies available in the file TNA LAB10/3510, and in the file MSS.187/3/PIC/1/1-13, Modern Records Centre, University of Warwick.
12 The case of Growcott is discussed in more detail in Chapter 10.
13 *Sunday Times*, 29 October 1972.
14 *Financial Times*, 30 October 1972, cutting in TNA LAB10/3510.
15 'Curbing the industrial bullies', *Financial Times*, 31 October 1972.
16 Justinian, 'Uncertainty about limits of peaceful picketing', *Financial Times*, 25 September 1972, copy in TNA LAB10/3510.
17 Note of a report in the *Financial Times*, 30 September 1972, in TNA LAB10/3510.
18 Cutting from the *Guardian*, 30 September 1972, in TNA LAB10/3510.
19 'Picket clash and a boss's fear – Court story', *Yorkshire Evening Post*, 14 December 1972.
20 Minutes, TNA LAB 10/3510. The EPC was the Employment Policy Committee.
21 TNA LAB10/3510.
22 TNA HO325/103.
23 'Pickets may face mobile police units', *Guardian*, 12 October

1972; 'Hope for code of picketing practice to stop troublemakers', *The Times*, 14 October 1972. Their speeches had been discussed in advance at a Cabinet committee on 9 October 1972, attended by Heath. He summed up the discussion by repeating that no change in the law was necessary. 'Picketing and secondary industrial action', 10 October 1972, TNA FV62/110.

24 Quoted in *The Times*, 8 November 1972, cutting in TNA LAB10/3510. The full debate is at HC Deb 7 November 1972, vol. 845, cc. 801–4.

5. The Conservative Party Reacts

1 TNA LAB 10/3510.
2 TNA LAB10/3510.
3 Letter, 12 July 1972, TNA LAB10/3510.
4 Note in the Churchill Archives Centre, Churchill College, Cambridge, HLSM/2/30/18.
5 Churchill Archives Centre, HLSM/2/30/18.
6 Letter to Macmillan, 5 October 1972, TNA LAB 43/718, and Churchill Archives Centre, HLSM 2/30/17.
7 In 1972 there were just three television channels available in Great Britain: BBC1, BBC2 and ITV. The vast majority of the population watched one of them every evening, giving evening programmes such as BBC's *9 O'clock News* or ITV's *News at Ten* an audience each of over 10 million. This compares with the hundreds of channels that can be viewed today.
8 Seven years later the Conservative leader of the opposition, Margaret Thatcher, commended Rawlinson's speech during a House of Commons debate on the industrial situation: 'the law on the nature of picketing has not changed for a very long time. The best exposition that I know on this ... is an exposition given by the Conservative Attorney-General, then Sir Peter Rawlinson in a speech in September 1972 ... The only right is that of peaceful persuasion. There is no right to stop a vehicle. There is no right to threaten loss of a union card ... But now we find that the place is being practically run by strikers' committees and that they are using such language as "allowing" access to food, "allowing" certain lorries to go through.' Prime Minister James Callaghan replied, 'Picketing, even today when the balance of strength has changed, is intended to stop the blackleg from doing the work of the man on strike.' HC Deb 16 January 1979, vol. 960, cc. 1524–1641.
9 Newspaper cuttings of these reports are in TNA LAB10/3510 and DPP2/5159.

10 *Daily Telegraph*, 22 September 1972.

11 The speech contained large sections of an earlier, less publicised speech that Rawlinson gave to a constituency club, the 1964 Club, on 19 March 1972. An extract was attached to an internal Home Office document dealing with contingency planning during the upcoming miners' strike, 'Picketing: contingency planning 31 January 1974', in TNA HO287/2194/1, PREM15/2117, DEFE70/367 and T357/490.

12 *Financial Times*, 6 October 1972, cuttings in TNA LAB 10/3510 and LAB 43/632.

13 The speeches of Carr and Shawcross were cited in the letter from Robert McAlpine and Sons Ltd to the Metropolitan Police commissioner, 26 February 1973 (author's papers).

14 *Financial Times*, 6 October 1972. The phrase 'unlawful conspiracy' and his own and Rawlinson's suggestion that sheer numbers alone could be intimidatory would be taken up by the prosecution to formulate a novel charge, 'conspiracy to intimidate', that was laid against six of the Shrewsbury pickets in February 1973.

15 Cutting from article by Colm Brogan, Monday 9 October 1972, in TNA LAB10/3510.

16 *Daily Telegraph*, 12 October 1972, cutting in TNA LAB10/3510.

17 Ian Aitken, 'Pickets may face mobile police units', *Guardian*, 12 October 1972, cutting in TNA LAB 10/3510. These tactics were to be implemented in the miners' strike of 1984–5.

18 TNA HO 325/103.

19 Note of 5 October 1972, Churchill Archives Centre, GBR/0014/WLFF3/3/9.

20 Richard Barber, *Picketing: The Law of Violence*, London, 1972. The Bow Group is a think tank linked to the Conservative Party.

21 Churchill Archives Centre, GBR/0014/WLFF3/3/9, emphasis added.

22 A conspiracy charge was tried, unsuccessfully, against a group of London and Liverpool dockers. The prosecution was led by the Labour Attorney General, Hartley Shawcross. Hilary Heilbron, *Rose Heilbron: The Story of Britain's First Woman Queen's Counsel and Judge*, Oxford, 2012.

23 This was one of the lessons that the government learned from the success of flying pickets. If trade unionists organised groups of 250 to 500 pickets to visit a workplace, the police had to be able to assemble a force of a similar size to deal with them. This approach was used most effectively during the coal miners' strike against pit closures in 1984–5. Bob Fine and Robert Millar (eds.), *Policing the Miners' Strike*, London, 1985.

24 *The Times*, 9 November 1972, cutting in TNA 10/3510. No

records of Carr's meetings with police constables have been found at The National Archives.

25 Note of meeting, TNA FV 62/110. For related documents see TNA HO325/103.

26 *Financial Times*, 2 November 1972.

27 HC Deb 1 November 1972, vol. 845, cc. 173–315: 261. The falseness of the reports in the *News of the World* is shown in Chapter 6.

28 HC Deb 8 December 1972, vol. 847, c. 1891. The 'book' he referred to was the NFBTE dossier, National Federation of Building Trade Employers, 'Violence and intimidation: a dossier of examples of personal violence, injury, arson and damage during the building strike 1972', Modern Records Centre, University of Warwick, MSS.187/3/PIC/1/1-13.

29 Brown was an unusual Conservative MP. He was a trade union member and led the 'Conservative Trade Union Movement'.

30 Forty pounds is approximately £580 in 2022 values.

31 HC Deb 18 December 1972, vol. 848, c. 984.

32 Confidential note from H. P. Brown to Mr Woolmer, 21 September 1972, TNA LAB 43/718.

33 Memo, T. R. Hornsby, 9 January 1973, TNA T357/490.

34 The Trades Disputes Act 1927 was introduced by the Conservative government a year after the General Strike. It outlawed mass picketing and secondary strikes. It was repealed by the Labour government in 1946.

6. The Propaganda War against Mass Picketing

1 Dod's Parliamentary Companion, Epsom, 1971, p. 515.

2 The article on picketing from the September 1972 edition of *East–West Digest* is in TNA LAB10/3510.

3 Letter, 15 September 1972, TNA DPP2/5159.

4 Letter to Mr Prior and Lord Carrington, 5 October 1972, Churchill Archives Centre, WLFF 3/2/4.

5 Letter, 19 September 1972, TNA DPP/2/5159.

6 *East–West Digest*, September 1972, p. 645, TNA LAB10/3510.

7 Letter, 4 October 1972, TNA DPP 2/5159.

8 The abbreviation 'ass.a.b.h.' refers to assault occasioning actual bodily harm. Section 47, Offences against the Person Act 1861.

9 19 October letter, TNA DPP2/5159.

10 Photographs in TNA DPP2/5159.

11 *East–West Digest*, September 1972, p. 645. The report was based upon a statement from 'Yorkshire building trades employers, issued in mid-August'.

12 Report of 13 October 1972, TNA DPP2/5159.
13 Letter Wilfred Proudfoot to Robert Carr, 16 October 1972. TNA DPP2/5159.
14 See correspondence between the DPP, the Attorney General and police forces in TNA DPP2/5159.
15 *East–West Digest*, September 1972, p. 646.
16 Report in TNA DPP2/5159.
17 The *News of the World* was the UK's biggest-selling Sunday newspaper. In the 1970s it sold more than 5 million copies each week.
18 Letter from John Glover, Attorney General's Department, to the DPP, 25 October 1972, TNA DPP2/5159.
19 Cutting from *News of the World*, 29 October 1972, TNA LAB10/3510.
20 Cutting from *News of the World*, 22 October 1972, TNA DPP2/5159.
21 Letter, 17 November 1972, and report, TNA DPP2/5159.
22 Statement to police, 13 November 1972, in Northampton police report, TNA DPP2/5159.
23 *Red under the Bed*, at explore.bfi. Wyatt was a former Labour MP who moved politically to the Conservative right and promoted anti-communist causes in a column, 'The voice of reason', in the *News of the World* (see Terence Lancaster, 'Obituary: Lord Wyatt of Weeford', *Independent*, 9 Dec. 1997).
24 *News of the World*, 22 October 1972, p. 3.
25 Ibid.
26 The Oswestry Action Committee was told that Birmingham strikers could not even travel to Telford, in their own region, because they were too busy picketing other sites in the West Midlands. See Llywarch's unsigned statement, p. 3. A rank-and-file bulletin, *Site Action*, produced by Charter supporters in Wolverhampton after the strike, also rebutted the false claims of Regan. *Site Action*, 1 Nov. 1972, p. 5 (author's papers).
27 Report, 20 November 1972, TNA DPP2/5159.
28 Letter from assistant chief constable to the DPP, 20 November 1972, p. 3, TNA DPP2/5159.
29 *Morning Star*, 22 September 1972, cutting in TNA LAB10/3510.
30 Ten pounds in 1972 would be worth £145 in 2022.
31 The file dealing with the *Red under the Bed*, programme is at TNA PREM15/2011.
32 Hugh Wilford, 'The Information Research Department: Britain's secret Cold War weapon revealed', *Review of International Studies*, 24 (1998), pp. 353–69; Paul Lashmar and James Oliver, *Britain's Secret Propaganda War*, Stroud, 1998. The IRD was closed down in 1977.

33 Industrial Research and Information Services Limited. IRIS was a covert grouping funded by the government and private businesses to promote pro-capitalist ideas and individuals within the trade unions. See Seumas Milne, *The Enemy Within: The Secret War against the Miners*, London, 2004, pp. 386–7.

34 Barker ended his note by advising that a copy of it be shown to Sir John Rennie, the director of the Secret Intelligence Service (MI6) from 1968 to 1973 and previously director of IRD.

35 Trial exhibit item B, Bundle 7, TNA J182/23. It had no direct evidential value of Warren's guilt; it was simply an unauthored newspaper article that was published on 10 September. But the prosecution did not need it to prove a particular allegation. Instead, a page-long article containing Warren's photograph below a headline, 'The wrecker', was useful to them to reinforce a point; it could have a visually potent effect. A copy of the article was kept in his prison file. Warren, *The Key to My Cell*, p. 107.

36 Warren, *The Key to My Cell*, p. 18.

37 *News of the World*, 22 October 1972.

38 Carter, Lewis, Abrahams and Tattam were named by Conservative MPs during debates about industrial relations: HC Deb 18 December 1972, vol. 848, c. 927; and HC Deb 8 December 1972, vol. 847, c. 1891.

39 Clutterbuck, *Britain in Agony*, p. 83. The *Morning Star* carried a report on 21 September 1972 (copy in TNA LAB10/3510) that four masked men broke into his house and attacked him, causing a broken arm, a broken toe, badly crushed ribs and a smashed-up face.

41 Letter, Christopher Roberts to Geoffrey Holland, Department of Employment, 18 August 1972, in TNA LAB 43/718. Bernie Steer was also one of the 'Pentonville 5' who was imprisoned for contempt of court in July 1972.

42 West Mercia Constabulary, 'Disorderly conduct by pickets', p. 24. Despite the reference in the police report, no article on picketing and the building workers' strike has been identified in the *Observer* between June and December 1972.

7. West Mercia and Gwynedd Police Investigate

1 West Mercia Constabulary, 'Report file', p. 2.

2 Maurice Graham Ltd was the main contractor on the Mount construction site. Sir Alfred McAlpine & Son Ltd was the main contractor of the Brookside site at Telford. The company has been referred to as McAlpine, although there were linked companies that included the surname in their titles.

3   West Mercia Constabulary, 'Report file', pp. 2–3.
4   Untitled report of Watkin Starbuck & Jones Ltd, West Mercia Constabulary, appendix file, Appendix C.
5   Letter, John Biffen to Robert Carr, 18 September 1972, in West Mercia Constabulary, appendix file.
6   Letter, West Mercia Constabulary, appendix file. The 1972 Annual Report of the West Mercia Constabulary recorded that Smith submitted a complaint to the chief constable in September 1972 about a 'lack of police action in Shropshire when an organised group of travelling strikers caused damage on a number of building sites'. Annual Report 1972, 14, TNA HO 287/1946. The report noted that Assistant Chief Constable Rennie was leading the investigation into this complaint.
7   West Mercia Constabulary, appendix file, Appendix B.
8   Ibid., Appendix D: telex from R. J. McAlpine, Esq., Telford, to Sir Robert McAlpine & Son Ltd head office, Hooton, 7 September 1972.
9   West Mercia Constabulary, 'Report file', p. 4.
10 Only two police officers were appointed to the Halifax investigation, a detective sergeant and a detective chief inspector. Statements were taken from just ten people, including three full-time UCATT union officials who had attended the site with the pickets. The three officials were not interviewed until 15 January 1973, though the Home Office had asked for a report into Mr Fee's complaint on 30 October 1972. They were not interviewed individually, but as a group. One of the officials, Arthur Harrison, echoing the praise that Warren had received from Inspector Meredith on departing Telford, pointed out, 'well, we haven't had any complaints about this. In fact, our relations with the police were very good. They even commended us for our behaviour on the sites in that area.' Statement of DS John Boyle, p. 2, in TNA DPP2/5159.
11 Report of West Mercia Constabulary by Mr R. G. Fenwick, 31 December 1974, p. 39, TNA HO287/1948. Rennie became chief constable on 1 January 1975.
12 Alex Rennie, *Farmhand to Chief Constable*, Bicester, 2009, p. 92.
13 Ibid., pp. 78, 90, 99–116.
14 Home Office organisation chart, June 1972. Obtained as an FOI request, 26 May 2017.
15 West Mercia Constabulary, appendix file, Appendix 7.
16 10 October 1972. The two letters are in the West Mercia Constabulary, appendix file, but neither of Rennie's reports to the Home Office have been traced.
17 Article headed 'Ex-officer: Ricky was no political prisoner', *Shropshire Star*, 8 July 2009.

18   Rennie, *Farmhand to Chief Constable*, p.227.
19   West Mercia Constabulary, 'Report file', pp. 2–3.
20   Ibid., p. 5.
21   West Mercia Constabulary, 'Disorderly conduct by pickets', p. 3.
22   Report of Superintendent C. Glover for the chief constable of West Mercia, 29 March 1974, following the end of the third Shrewsbury trial. TNA DPP2/5159. See also West Mercia Constabulary, 'Report file', p. 16, though no record of the Chester conference has been traced.
23   *Liverpool Daily Post*, 30 November 1972. The *Daily Post*, although Liverpool-based, also published a separate edition, which was the main daily newspaper in north Wales.
24   Report of Superintendent C. Glover for the chief constable of West Mercia, 29 March 1974.
25   West Mercia Constabulary, 'Disorderly conduct by pickets', p. 26, emphasis added.
26   Ibid., p. 27.
27   See summing-up of Judge Chetwynd-Talbot at the end of the first Mold trial of *Hughes and Others*, pp. 65–88 (author's papers).
28   Warren, *The Key to My Cell*, pp. 34–6.
29   See Chapter 10 for the way Llywarch's unsigned statement was used at the first Shrewsbury trial.
30   Witness statements (author's papers).
31   Summing-up of Judge Chetwynd Talbot, pp. 71–80 (author's papers).
32   Memo from Superintendent Glover to the West Mercia Chief Constable, 14 March 1975, TNA DPP2/5159. Bithell and Skinner were not charged subsequently.
33   Pro forma for Des Warren; see letter, ACC Hodges to J. Walker at DPP, 25 March 1975, TNA DPP2/5159.
34   Letter, Walker, Smith & Way to J. McKinsie Jones, 30 January 1973, Shrewsbury archives, WCML, Salford. The police report identified that John Heath gave telephone advice to several pickets prior to interview, West Mercia Constabulary, 'Disorderly conduct by pickets', p. 30.
35   Letter, chief constable to DPP, 18 December 1972, TNA DPP2/5159.
36   No exchange of correspondence about these investigations between the DPP and the West Mercia and Gwynedd police forces before 18 December 1972 has been found in government files at The National Archives This contrasts with the reports sent to the DPP by police forces in Rotherham, Lincolnshire, West Yorkshire, Birmingham and Northampton. The covering letters from each police force make reference to the DPP's request for the report.

37 The two reports were not with Willison's letter in the DPP file at The National Archives or with any other document that referred to the police reports, e.g. the form from the DPP to the Attorney General asking for the nomination of counsel said that the two police reports were attached (TNA DPP2/5159), but no copies were discovered in the law officers' files at TNA either.

38 West Mercia Constabulary, 'Disorderly conduct by pickets' (author's papers).

39 A Gwynedd report has not been identified but documents have been discovered from Gwynedd police which set out offences allegedly committed by pickets in north Wales. It was the basis for the prosecutions of pickets at Mold Crown Court in June and July 1973.

40 West Mercia Constabulary, 'Disorderly conduct by pickets', para. 117.

41 Ibid., para. 97.

42 Ibid., para. 118.

43 West Mercia Constabulary, 'Report file', para. 71. It may seem surprising that a police force in largely rural north Wales was identified as having such an efficient Special Branch but this area included one of the main transit points between Britain and Ireland, the port of Holyhead. This was kept under constant surveillance in the 1970s for movements of IRA members and weapons.

44 West Mercia Constabulary, 'Disorderly conduct by pickets', p. 45.

45 West Mercia Constabulary, 'Report file', pp. 14–15. The Economic League was a secretive body set up by employers just after the First World War to gather intelligence on trade union and political activists. It established a blacklist that member firms could use to deny employment to someone. When it closed in 1993, personnel and the blacklist transferred to the Consulting Association, which was funded largely by construction companies. See Smith and Chamberlain, *Blacklisted*.

46 West Mercia Constabulary, 'Report file', p. 19. IS were the International Socialists, publishers of *Socialist Worker*. They are now known as the Socialist Workers Party (SWP).

47 West Mercia Constabulary, 'Disorderly conduct by pickets', p. 44. It would have added insult to injury if a trade unionist who was blacklisted by employers was then prosecuted by the police for using a false name to gain employment and earn a wage. Smith and Chamberlain, *Blacklisted*, have shown how the police actually assisted the employers in compiling the blacklist by sharing intelligence with the Consulting Association.

48 West Mercia Constabulary, 'Report file', p. 15.

49 Prest, *Memoir*, pp. 96–7. Hodges recommended that the police cultivate contacts with employers and employers' federations, and with trade unions and their spokesmen. 'Many of these are prominent in public life as magistrates and the like and it may be that this contact can be maintained at senior officer level.' West Mercia Constabulary, 'Report file', para. 85. He reported that he had already started by forming a relationship with the directors of the NFBTE at Birmingham and Bristol. Ibid., para. 135(a) 3.

50 West Mercia Constabulary, 'Disorderly conduct by pickets', para. 134.

51 The report quotes a speech given in the House of Commons to the '1964 Club' on 10 March 1972. No record of this speech has been found and the reference could reveal an error by the police. The 1964 Club was a discussion forum established by Conservatives in Epsom and Ewell, for which Rawlinson was the current MP. It held talks in the Surrey area rather than at the House of Commons. The section of the speech quoted in the report is almost identical to the reported speech Rawlinson gave to his constituency on 21 September 1972.

52 West Mercia Constabulary, 'Disorderly conduct by pickets', para. 139.

8. The Prosecution 'Construct' a Case

1 West Mercia Constabulary, 'Report file', p. 4.

2 TNA DPP2/5159. Although a number of the early papers were headed *R. v. Barton and Others*, Barton was not included in any proceedings. It was believed that Barton was a pseudonym for a picket who could not get work in his real name due to blacklisting.

3 This was a Monday and a normal working day. Only in the following year, 1974, did 1 January become a public holiday in England and Wales.

4 Pro forma, TNA DPP2/5159.

5 Fennell was a Conservative Party member and sought selection as a parliamentary candidate in 1972. See Sir Desmond Fennell's obituary, *Daily Telegraph*, 5 July 2011.

6 At 4 Paper Buildings, now known as Hailsham Chambers. Drake succeeded Quintin Hogg QC as head of chambers. *Daily Telegraph*, 9 April 2014. Both were Freemasons and Drake was president of the Masonic Court of Appeal for twenty years. In 1964 Max Mosley became a pupil barrister under Drake.

7 TNA LAB10/3510.

8　The closed investigations concerned events at Neap Wharf, London Stock Exchange, various Birmingham sites and so on discussed in the previous chapter. The West Yorkshire police were still investigating the picketing at the site of J & J Fee Ltd in Halifax in August 1972. The chief constable wrote to the DPP four days *after* Rawlinson's letter to Carr to report that their inquiries had now been exhausted. TNA DPP2/5159.

9　The only reference on the letter is 9/5/479.

10　TNA DPP2/5159.

11　TNA T357/490. Carr was appointed home secretary on 17 July 1972.

12　Chronological table of important events, author unknown, TNA DPP2/5159.

13　Home secretary's engagement diaries 1973, TNA HO317/24. The Dorchester Hotel in London's Park Lane was owned by the McAlpine family.

14　*The Times*, 3 February 1973.

15　*Shropshire Star*, 3 February 1973.

16　Gwynedd police memo, DCI Salisbury to DCS Clarke, 15 February 1973, TNA DPP2/5159.

17　TNA DPP2/5159. The words 'Contrary to Common Law' were written in hand at the end, making clear the law under which the six pickets were being charged. See Chapter 10 for a fuller discussion about the nature of this offence.

18　The other contractors included North West Holst, Flathers, Monks, London Marine, William Press and Simon Calves. The Holst workers were selected to strike from 26 June but after a week the others voted to join them.

19　This policy was unpopular with many workers because the wage rates of local authority building departments were tied to those agreed by the NJCBI. It was argued that if they had an interest in the outcome of the dispute, they should take part in it too.

20　West Mercia Constabulary, 'Disorderly conduct by pickets', p. 36.

21　Handwritten note of a discussion with Fennell after the trials, following a query on the subject from BBC *Panorama*, 27 March 1975, TNA DPP2/5159.

22　West Mercia Constabulary, 'Disorderly conduct by pickets', para. 126.

23　West Mercia Constabulary conclusion report, 29 March 1974, TNA DPP2/5159.

24　Warren, *The Key to My Cell*, pp. 27–8. The Krays were twin brothers who organised a violent criminal gang in London in the 1950s and 1960s. They were tried for two murders and convicted in 1969 at a highly publicised Old Bailey trial. They were sentenced to life imprisonment.

25 Ricky Tomlinson, *Ricky*, London, 2003, pp. 114–15.
26 Unlawful picketing at Shrewsbury: opinion of Maurice Drake QC, 21 February 1973, TNA DPP2/5159.
27 Ibid.
28 The police had suggested that every picket present in Shrewsbury and Telford could be charged with affray. West Mercia Constabulary, 'Disorderly conduct by pickets', para. 139.
29 Opinion, 21 February 1973, TNA DPP2/5159.
30 Letter, Sir Robert McAlpine and Sons Ltd to the 'Commissioner of Police of the Metropolis', 26 February 1973 (author's papers).
31 The committee developed out of the North Wales Action Committee that had existed during the strike and continued to meet after it ended to organise solidarity among building workers for future disputes that arose in the construction industry.
32 Conclusion Report by Superintendent Glover, 29 March 1974, TNA DPP2/5159. One of the pickets' counsel later claimed, 'An enormous delay suggested something untoward. Everything was suspicious. Now we know from Maurice Drake's opinion that he wasn't asked to prepare an indictment[;] he was asked "what can we get these chaps for?". He was a very able chap but I criticize his bona fides in this.' CCRC interview with Keith McHale, 17 March 2014 (author's papers).
33 Gwynedd police memo, DCI Salisbury to DCS Clarke, 15 February 1973, TNA DPP2/5159.
34 Memo, C. Hall to Mr Walker, 24 April 1973, TNA DPP2/5159.
35 Warren, *The Key to My Cell*, p. 29.
36 Letter, G. Smith, operatives secretary, to L. C. Kemp (T&GWU), J. Lewis (G&MWU) and A. Tomkins (FTATU), 8 March 1973 (author's papers).
37 Letter, John L. Williams to G. F. Smith, 12 March 1973, p. 4 (author's papers).
38 George Smith, 'U.C.A.T.T. and the building strike prosecutions', n.d. (author's papers).
39 Ibid., pp. 46–8.

9. The Mold trials and the Lessons Learned by the Prosecution

1 Letter, Hodges to Mr Hall at the DPP's office, 22 May 1973, TNA DPP2/5159.
2 Under Section 9 of the 1875 Act a person charged with intimidation under section 7 had the right to elect whether they wanted to be tried in the Crown court before a jury. If they chose not to, the case would be heard summarily, in the magistrates' court.

The right of a defendant to elect a jury trial for certain offences punishable by imprisonment was a new development in 1875 and applied to just a handful of criminal statutes.

3   Warren, *The Key to My Cell*, p. 34.

4   CCRC interview with Sir Maurice Drake, 24 February 2014, question 8, p. 2 (author's papers).

5   He was represented by Mr Roberts of Mason & Moore Dutton solicitors, Chester.

6   West Mercia Constabulary conclusion report of Superintendent Glover, 29 March 1974, para. 14, TNA DPP2/5159.

7   Letter, Jackson to the T&GWU district secretary, Shotton, 9 April 1973, Shrewsbury archives, WCML, Salford.

8   Costs forms Ref. 11927/72, TNA DPP2/5159.

9   'Defence protest at number of policemen at court', *The Times* 27 June 1973.

10 The picketing had not been planned in advance. A strike meeting in Ellesmere Port on 11 September was due to be followed by a demonstration in the town, but bad weather caused the march to be cancelled. Two coaches of striking building workers that had travelled from north Wales decided to go to the reservoir site instead.

11 Arnison, *The Shrewsbury Three*, p. 47.

12 *R v. Derrick Hughes and Others*, summing-up, 10–12 July 1973, TNA J302/40.

13 Headlined 'The wrecker', *Sunday People*, 10 September 1972; see Chapter 6 above.

14 At 2022 prices, respectively £203 and £676. Chetwynd-Talbot ruled that there was no evidence against Hughes and Pierce on count 3, damaging the rig, that would allow a jury to give a verdict, and therefore the question was not put. Kelly still faced the same charge and the jury found him not guilty.

15 Equivalent to £2,637 in 2022.

16 Davies's trial was not relisted until Drake, Fennell and Wadsworth had finished prosecuting all the pickets at Shrewsbury.

17 Drake had considered prosecuting Warren for an offence on 26 October at the same site, Greenfield Sewerage Works, Flintshire, but he decided later not to proceed. Nevertheless, at Warren's trial Drake referred to those events as evidence of Warren's behaviour. See report from DCI Salisbury of Gwynedd Constabulary to DC Superintendent Clarke, Building Workers' Dispute, TNA DPP2/5159.

18 Handwritten note headed 'A/D Country 31.7.1973', TNA DPP2/5159.

19 'Re. Building Workers Dispute 31 July 1973', TNA DPP2/5159.

20 Hayes's report is referred to in the document 'Matters discussed

with Mr. Drake 17th September 1973', TNA DPP2/5159. His report has not been identified.

21 The DPP ordered a copy of the transcript of the four Mold trials (letter, John M. Walker to Lee & Nightingale, 20 August 1973, TNA DPP2/5159).

22 TNA J301/29. Keith McHale QC and Anthony Rumbelow for Kelly, Roberts and G. Williams; David Turner-Samuels QC and J. L. Reide for O'Shea and E. L. Williams; Frank Hiorns QC and Norma Negus for Pierce and Seaburg. The solicitor for Derrick Hughes instructed T. M. Dillon QC and Alex Carlile.

23 Ruling on intimidation by Judge Chetwynd-Talbot, TNA DPP2/5159.

24 *R v. Taylor* [1973] AC 964.

25 TNA J182/9.

26 Court record of the Petty Sessional Division of Wenlock, TNA J182/16.

27 It should be noted that Wales is not a separate legal jurisdiction. The United Kingdom has three separate jurisdictions for criminal cases: England and Wales, Northern Ireland, and Scotland.

28 Letter, 18 December 1972, TNA DPP2/5159.

29 Reported in a letter from the chief whip, Francis Pym, to Robert Carr, 29 November 1972, TNA HO 325/103.

30 Letter, deputy circuit administrator, Midland and Oxford Circuit, to the DPP, 19 July 1973, TNA DPP2/5159.

31 Norma Negus (for Casson & Co's eleven pickets), E. Edwards (Walker, Smith & Way, twelve) and K. Barnett (Gwilym Hughes & Partners, one).

32 A front-page article in the weekly *Shrewsbury Chronicle*, 28 September 1973, gave details of the upcoming case. It referred to six pickets facing forty-two charges, and to 250 witnesses to be called during a trial that was expected to last for nearly five months, and highlighted the estimated cost. This painted a picture of a major criminal trial.

33 TNA J182/26.

34 Report in 'Memo of Supt. Glover to West Mercia Chief Constable 14 March 1975', TNA DPP2/5159.

35 Note in TNA DPP2/5159.

36 'Conclusion report re. trial of "Flying Pickets"', Superintendent C. Glover, 29 March 1974, TNA DPP2/5159.

37 *Who's Who*, London, 1973. Mais, like Drake, was a Freemason. See also Platts-Mills's description in *R v. Jones, Tomlinson and Warren*, notes of proceedings, before Lord Justice James, 11 January 1974, p. 11, para. E, Shrewsbury archives, WCML, Salford.

38 CCRC interview with David Altaras, 19 May 2014, p. 5. Contained

in CCRC's bundle of documents submitted to Court of Appeal, 4 March 2020.

39 Statement of David Altaras for the CCRC prepared by Bindmans, 14 November 2013, (author's papers).

40 CCRC interview with Sir Maurice Drake, 24 February 2014, question 15, p. 3 (author's papers). 'Widgery LCJ' was Lord Chief Justice Widgery, the most senior judge in England and Wales, who had responsibility for overseeing criminal trials.

41 See Peter Hain, *Political Trials in Britain*, London, 1985, pp. 137–44.

42 This right, of peremptory challenge, was abolished by the Criminal Justice Act 1988, s. 118(1)

43 Arnison, *The Shrewsbury Three*, p. 46; Platts-Mills, *Muck, Silk and Socialism*, pp. 532–3.

44 CCRC interview with Sir Maurice Drake, 24 February 2014, question 8, p. 2 (author's papers). See also his answer to question 25, p. 5.

45 Hailsham was a hereditary peer when Drake joined the chambers but was able to renounce the title in 1963 and revert to Quinton Hogg QC. He became Lord Hailsham again in 1970 when he was appointed Lord Chancellor in Heath's government and made a life peer.

46 Section 31(2) states, 'The arrangements to be made by the Lord Chancellor under this Part of this Act shall include the preparation of lists (called panels) of persons summoned as jurors, and the information to be included in panels, the court sittings for which they are prepared, their division into parts or sets (whether according to the day of first attendance or otherwise), their enlargement or amendment, and all other matters relating to the contents and form of the panels shall be such as the Lord Chancellor may from time to time direct.'

47 CCRC interview with Sir Maurice Drake, 24 February 2014, question 9, p. 3 (author's papers).

48 *New Law Journal*, 11 October 1973, pp. 918–19. See also the report in the *Daily Telegraph*, 5 October 1973.

49 One of those cases with political overtones was the 'Mangrove 9', a group of Afro-Caribbean men and women who, in August 1971, were charged with incitement to riot. Some defended themselves and demanded a jury composed exclusively of black people. This was refused but they challenged sixty-three potential jurors between them to get a jury closer to being their peers than the initial twelve who were called. They were all acquitted of incitement and five of them were acquitted of all charges. See Robin Bunce and Paul Field, 'Mangrove nine: the court challenge against police racism in Notting Hill', *Guardian*, 29 November 2010.

50 HC Deb 12 November 1973, vol. 864, c. 25.

51 HC Deb 3 December 1973, vol. 865, c. 909.

52 A request was made to the House of Commons library and the Cabinet Office but neither of them could locate a copy. On many occasions when the direction was requested a copy of an earlier direction was mistakenly produced.

53 Other directions are included in these reports, e.g. a 'Practice Direction (Jurors)' made by Lord Widgery CJ on 12 January 1973 dealing with excusal from jury service, [1973] 1 W.L.R. 134.

54 *Archbold Criminal Pleading, Evidence and Practice in Criminal Cases*, supplement to the thirty-eighth edition (1973), Section 4-274, p. 459. It simply states, 'In 1973 the Lord Chancellor issued a directive stating that information contained in jury panels should no longer include the particulars of prospective jurors' occupations.' *Archbold* is the leading textbook on procedure in the criminal courts in England and Wales and has been updated regularly since it was first published in 1822.

55 TNA DPP2/5159.

56 TNA DPP2/5159.

57 Warren, *The Key to My Cell*, p. 38.

58 Arnison, The Shrewsbury Three, p. 51.

59 'Matters discussed with Mr. Drake', 17 September 1973, TNA DPP2/5159.

60 'West Mercia Police operational order', TNA J182/26.

61 Platts-Mills, *Muck, Silk and Socialism*, p. 538.

10. The First Trial at Shrewsbury Crown Court

1 Emlyn Hooson QC, Liberal MP for Montgomeryshire, had been briefed by Walker, Smith & Way to represent John Llywarch but two weeks before the trial Hooson withdrew and recommended a fellow parliamentarian, the Labour MP, Sir Arthur Irvine. The latter took the brief but after two weeks was sacked by Llywarch, who continued to be represented by his junior barrister, Mr M. O. Garrett, and another, James Pyke.

2 West Mercia Constabulary conclusion report, 29 March 1974, para. 16, TNA DPP2/5159.

3 Letter, Casson & Co. to DPP, 4 September 1972, TNA DPP2/5159.

4 The pickets' solicitors did not receive the signed first indictment from the court until 14 September. Letter, Shrewsbury court clerk to Casson & Co., Shrewsbury archives, WCML, Salford.

5 Section 3 of the Act dealt with conspiracy and it actually benefited trade unionists because it declared that an agreement between two or more workers to act 'in contemplation or furtherance of a trade dispute' could not be tried as a criminal conspiracy. If the Act was simply repealed the law would revert to the pre-1875 position, when trade unionists were charged with criminal conspiracy for organising strikes and other action.

6 This was an example of overcharging by the prosecution as a tactical device. Multiple charges can also pressurise a defendant to plead guilty to some of the offences. See John Baldwin and Michael McConville, *Negotiated Justice: Pressures on Defendants to Plead Guilty*, London, 1977.

7 Taken from West Mercia police report, paras. 94–7.

8 Ibid., p. 29.

9 Ibid., p. 36, emphasis added.

10 Trial transcript, p. 10, para. C, Shrewsbury archives, WCML, Salford.

11 John Platts-Mills, *Muck, Silk and Socialism: Recollections of a Left-wing Queen's Counsel*, Wedmore, Somerset, 2001, p. 537.

12 See the evidence of Alan Abrahams, chairman of the regional action committee and member of UCATT's north-west regional council, trial transcript, p. 880.

13 Platts-Mills, *Muck, Silk and Socialism*, p. 536. Meredith's evidence on this point is at pp. 642–3 and Warren's at p. 1221 of the trial transcript. Shrewsbury archives, WCML, Salford.

14 Platts-Mills 2001, p. 534. See Hall's report letter to Walker at the DPP, 15 November 1973, which noted that Platts-Mills had put these points 'and has received some dusty answers from our witnesses.' TNA DPP2/5159.

15 Trial transcript, p. 1197.

16 Letter, 6 November 1973, TNA DPP2/5159.

17 Platts-Mills 2001, p. 537.

18 Minutes of a meeting between J. P. Wadsworth (second junior Crown counsel), CCRC case review manager Adam Barnes and Commissioner David James Smith, 18 March 2014, p. 9 (author's papers).

19 Tomlinson, *Ricky*, p. 120.

20 Warren discusses the trial in *The Key to My Cell*, pp. 38–68; Platts-Mills in *Muck, Silk and Socialism*, pp. 532–40.

21 The trial did not proceed on Friday 5 October as a juror was ill. It resumed the following Monday, when Drake completed his opening.

22 *The Times*, 5 October 1973.

23 Drake's opening address, trial transcript, p. 9.

24 Ibid., pp. 57–63 (WCML and author's papers).

25 An objection was later made but it was too late – see supplemental grounds of appeal for Tomlinson drafted by David Altaras, TNA DPP2 5185/2.

26 Irvine had only been instructed to represent Llywarch two weeks before the trial began.

27 Trial transcript, vol AE 10, p. 973.

28 Llywarch's unsigned statement, p. 8.

29 Arnison, The Shrewsbury Three, p. 61.

30 Glover's statement, p. 57.

31 Copy of Llywarch's police statement with handwritten comment at the end by Glover. Item G in a bundle of trial documents headed 'Exhibits' in the author's possession.

32 Llywarch's evidence is in the trial transcript, vol. AE 10, pp. 941–1014, Shrewsbury archives, WCML, Salford.

33 Summing-up of Judge Mais, p. 157 WCML, Salford.

34 Llywarch's unsigned statement, p. 5. On the final page Glover wrote, 'Statement prepared from notes made on Friday, 3rd November 1972 by D/C/I C. Glover'.

35 Trial transcript, p. 972.

36 Hain, *Political Trials in Britain*, pp. 117–18.

37 Platts-Mills 2001, p. 535. Tom Rhys-Roberts was leading counsel for John McKinsie Jones.

38 Trial transcript, p. 893.

39 Trial transcript pp.895–6.

40 During an interview on BBC Radio 2 on 25 March 2021, Tomlinson claimed that the late John Carpenter was a police informant. The claim has never been substantiated.

41 Letter, West Mercia police to DPP, 18 December 1972, TNA DPP2/5159.

42 Matters discussed with Mr Drake, 17 September 1973, TNA DPP2/5159.

43 Rewriting of witness statements was a central theme of the Hillsborough case. Phil Scraton, *Hillsborough – The Truth*, London, 2016, p. 448, noted that the IPCC had reported that 240 police officers' statements appeared to have been altered.

44 The *Shropshire Star* received information to their office on 6 September 1972 alerting them to go to the Brookside site. They sent a reporter and a photographer. The West Mercia police report, p. 24, states that the photographs taken 'were shown to all the witnesses with a view to identifying persons involved in the disorderly picketing … The task would have been virtually impossible without press photographs.' None of the photographs showed scenes of violence.

45 Warren, *The Key to My Cell*, p. 44. James's evidence is at p. 587 of the trial transcript.

46 Evidence of Henry Vivien James, trial transcript, pp. 588–9.

47 Conclusion report of Superintendent Glover, 29 March 1974, TNA DPP2/5159.

48 See the cross-examination of Jones (trial transcript, p. 368E); Harry James (trial transcript, pp. 328–30); Hordley (trial transcript, p. 408) and Gradwell (trial transcript pp.21D-22B).

49 Cross-examination of Henry James, trial transcript, p. 569.

50 Trial transcript, p. 225. The word 'not' is a mistake and the sentence should be read without it, a point agreed by all parties at the Court of Appeal hearing on 3 February 2021.

51 Trial transcript, pp. 257–8.

52 Trial transcript, pp. 456–7.

53 The *Daily Mail* article, 11 September 1972, was headlined 'Terror ordeal of a man who defied a strike' and said, 'The attack has left Mr Growcott temporarily blinded in one eye and only partly sighted in the other.'

54 Clutterbuck, *Britain in Agony*, also peddled these inaccurate claims. 'Though there were no really serious casualties (one man lost the sight of one eye) there were many minor injuries … A photograph by a news cameraman of this meeting shows the bricklayer who had already received injuries which were to result in the loss of the sight of an eye standing at the back of the crowd.' p. 88

55 Extract shown on the BBC's *One Life: Guilty, My Arse*, 2007: 'There is one member of a union who is now partially blind based on the fact that he was kicked off the scaffold.' Growcott was not a union member.

56 West Mercia police bundle of evidence, 'Statements 11 Police', statement of Chief Superintendent Meredith, p. 5, Growcott's statement, p. 2 (author's papers).

57 Trial transcript, p. 619.

58 Statement in Shrewsbury archives, WCML, Salford.

59 *Shropshire Star*, 8 September 1972. The West Mercia police report believed that the attitude of the pickets at Brookside was due in part to the fact that it was a McAlpine site. It was 'held in special regard by many of the pickets.' Llywarch and Tomlinson were employees on a McAlpine site in Wrexham but at Brookside 'subcontracting "lumpers" were the norm, whereas self-employed men are an exception in heavy construction work.' West Mercia Constabulary, 'Disorderly conduct by pickets', p. 29.

60 Trial transcript, p. 618.

61 Ibid., p. 623.

62 A picket who suffered far more serious injuries than any reported case involving a non-striker was Mike Shilvock, chairman of the Birmingham Builders' Action Committee. 'Brum builders'

leader is "beaten up"', *Morning Star*, 21 September 1972, TNA LAB10/3510. No one was ever caught for this assault.

63 Police record of interview with John Bithell (author's papers).

64 'Reds in industry', *Shropshire Star*, 13 November 1973. The television guide of the *Daily Mail*, 13 November 1973, showed that the programme was being broadcast in all ITV regions of the UK except Westward (covering south-west England from Plymouth) and Channel (covering the Channel Islands).

65 The film, including the thirty-minute studio discussion, is available to view at the British Film Institute, London.

66 Defence application, Shrewsbury archives, WCML, Salford. The application was accompanied by a witness statement in the name of one of the six, Carpenter. It gave more detail of scenes from the programme that were considered to be prejudicial.

67 Minutes of a meeting between J. P. Wadsworth (second junior Crown counsel), CCRC case review manager Adam Barnes and Commissioner David James Smith, 18 March 2014, p.8 (author's papers).

68 March 1974 report, para. 25(d), TNA DPP2/5159.

69 Witness statement of John Carpenter, para. 2(xx), Shrewsbury archives, WCML, Salford. His statement exhibited the television page of the *Shropshire Star* for Tuesday 13 November 1973 and claimed, 'On page 7 the programme is referred to as a Star spot and described in a special article.'

70 TNA PREM15/2011. Ordinarily the file should have been released to The National Archives thirty years later. When it was identified in their online catalogue in 2013 it said 'Retained by Dept.' and was not released until an FOI Act request was made by the author.

71 Memo, 'Red Under the Bed', T. C. Barker to Mr Reddaway, 21 November 1973, TNA PREM 16/2111. Sir Conrad Heron KCB, OBE was a permanent secretary at the Department of Employment from 1973 to 1976.

72 Handwritten notes on compliments slip headed '10 Downing Street Whitehall', 17 January 1974, TNA PREM15/2011.

73 IBA archives, Bournemouth University. Buxton's proposal may have been scuppered by a government attempt to defeat the upcoming miners' strike: it imposed a three-day working week on industry and directed the television companies – the BBC and ITV – to stop broadcasts each evening at 10:30 p.m. from 17 December.

74 Mais's summing-up, pp. 155–68 (author's papers).

75 'Note received from Jury 4.20pm 18/12/73 Howell. Clerk of the Court', handwritten note, TNA DPP2/5159. The jury were split eight to four for a conviction.

76 *Financial Times*, 19 December 1973.
77 Trial transcript, 18 September 1973, p. 218, emphasis added.
78 *R v. Thakaran* [1995] 2 Cr. App. R. 368 at 374. Although this
    case post-dated the Shrewsbury trials the principle was long-
    standing. 'On the facts which we have related, it is ... quite clear
    that there is abundant room for speculation that the jurors, or
    some of them in this case, did continue their deliberations in
    the hotel. It is quite impossible for the Court to conclude that if
    there were further deliberations, all 12 of the jurors were there
    together. As James L.J. said in *Goodson (1974) 60 Cr.App.R.
    266*: "... where there is room for speculation there is ... room for
    possible injustice."'
79 Statement of Elsa Warren to CCRC, 14 May 2015. See also letter
    from Elsa Warren to UCATT, 24 March 1974, UCATT archives.
    'The two jury men walked out before the sentence was passed
    and had to be called back before the judge finished his sentenc-
    ing. I was there at the court – when sentence was passed and
    spoke with these men – who were disgusted with the men being
    found guilty of these trumped up charges.'
80 Platts-Mills, *Muck, Silk and Socialism*, p. 539.
81 Warren, *The Key to My Cell*, pp. 62–8, 65.
82 Trial transcript, 13–19 December 1973, p. 246.
83 *Socialist Worker*, 5 January 1974.
84 Norman Atkinson MP raised the issue in a letter to Labour col-
    leagues, 9 April 1974, listing five questions to be put to a meeting
    with the Attorney General, including, '(e) Why did the Foreman
    of the jury protest after sentence?' TNA DPP2/5185; see also
    Barry Cox, *Civil Liberties in Britain*, Harmondsworth, Middle-
    sex, 1975, p. 48.
85 Platts-Mills, *Muck, Silk and Socialism*, p. 539.
86 Note headed 'John Gasson 405/7641 Ex. 3417', TNA DPP2/5159.
87 Transcript attached to letter from Mais's clerk to Sir John Wil-
    lison, 19 December 1973, TNA J182/9.

11. The Prosecution on a Roll

1 Letter, T. J. Taylor of the DPP to Casson & Co., 3 January 1974,
   TNA DPP2/5159.
2 See the first indictment for the wording of both offences.
3 Glover acknowledged that Drake changed the wording of the
   two counts when he saw the grounds of appeal lodged by lawyers
   for warren et al. West Mercia Constabulary conclusion report, 29
   March 1974, TNA DPP2/5185.
4 The transcript runs to fifty pages.

5 Drake's opening speech for the prosecution, 15 January 1974, p. 49 (author's papers).

6 Ibid., p. 37.

7 Handwritten note from jury, 29 January 1974 (10:58), *R* v. *Clee and Others*, TNA DPP2/5185.

8 Superintendent Glover noted that 'an extra count was added in each case in respect of Renshaw'. West Mercia Constabulary conclusion report, para. 30, TNA DPP2/5159.

9 Letter, A. K. Pal, surgeon, to the clerk to the court, 19 February 1974, TNA J182/26.

10 *Broome* v. *Director of Public Prosecutions* [1973] UKHL 5, also known as *Hunt* v. *Broome* [1973] Q.B. 691 in the court below. Broome was a UCATT official and had persuaded a lorry driver to stop at the picket line so that he could talk to the driver about the building workers' strike. After several minutes a police officer told him to move away. Broome refused and was arrested for obstruction.

11 *Sunday Telegraph*, 23 December 1973.

12 Ibid.

13 *Daily Mirror*, 20 December 1973, p. 7.

14 Letter from R.C. to the prime minister, headed 'Picketing', 18 January 1974, TNA PREM/15/2117.

15 Minutes of Cabinet committee meeting, 4 February 1974, TNA CAB130/716.

16 Ibid., emphasis added.

17 Letter of thanks from Assistant Chief Constable F. R. Hodges, West Mercia police, to the Crown Court Office at Shrewsbury, 29 March 1974, at the conclusion of the three trials, TNA J182/26.

18 UCATT executive statement, 28 January 1974. UCATT's position was also set out in a five-page document by the general secretary, George Smith, 'The Shrewsbury convictions', 16 June 1974 (copy in UCATT archives).

19 George Smith, *UCATT and the Shrewsbury Trials*, London, 1974.

20 Throughout 1973 there were no articles in UCATT's monthly journal, *Viewpoint*, of the arrests, magistrates' court hearings or trials at Mold and Shrewsbury. The first mention was December 1973, when it included an appeal for a hardship fund. Modern Records Centre, Warwick, MSS.078/UC/4/1.

21 Letter, Roy Jenkins to Lionel Murray, 15 November 1974, TNA LAB10/3743.

22 Originals with author's papers.

23 Letter, Tom Litterick MP to Des Warren, 8 August 1976 (author's papers).

12. The Court of Appeal

1 Warren was sent to Bedford prison on 4 January 1974, followed by Liverpool on 17 January and then Stafford on 22 January, where he remained until 17 May 1974, apart for two weeks in London prisons during his appeal. In January Jones was transferred to Ranby prison, where he remained for the rest of his sentence, apart from the appeal. Tomlinson was sent from Shrewsbury straight to Stafford in the new year.

2 *R v. Jones, Tomlinson and Warren*, notes of proceedings before Lord Justice James, 11 January 1974, p. 11, para. E, Shrewsbury archives, WCML, Salford.

3 Several separate grounds of appeal were prepared by the various barristers representing the pickets. After they were lodged with the court in January the defence teams collated them into eight agreed points. Copies are at the Shrewsbury archives, WCML, Salford.

4 *R v. Jones and Others*, CACD, 21 February 1974, Appeal Nos. 54, 111, 112, 171–3/R/74 unreported.

5 *R v. Jones and Others* [1974] IRLR 119, para. 14.

6 *R v. Jones and Others* [1974] IRLR 117, para. 15. Note James's use of the phrase 'interests of justice'. Nowhere is this phrase defined. It is whatever the courts decide it to mean. To state that the Crown's case could not be adequately presented simply by prosecuting the pickets on the many counts of intimidation was designed to subvert Parliament's 1875 Act.

7 This point was made by Stan Thorne, Labour MP for Preston South, when moving a ten-minute rule bill on 25 February 1975: 'It is an insult to the authority of Parliament that any outside body, even the judges, should be able to pass heavier sentences for attempting to commit a crime if that crime was alleged to have been part of a conspiracy, when Parliament has fixed a maximum penalty for the crime itself.' HC Deb 25 February 1975, vol. 887, cc. 300–10. Some critics argued that Warren could have gone to prison for longer if he was tried on all the other charges that he faced, but this assumed he would have been convicted of them and would have received consecutive prison sentences for them all, both highly unlikely.

8 Grounds of appeal settled by Keith McHale QC, Shrewsbury archives, WCML, Salford.

9 *R v. Jones and Others*, CACD, 22 March 1974, unreported (author's papers).

10 *R v. Jones and Others* [1974] IRLR 117, para. 44.

11 Memo from C. D. Hall, 8 April 1974, to the A/D, country ref. 11927 72, TNA DPP2/5159.

12 Court of Appeal, form of judge's order ref. 834/R/74, Shrewsbury archives, WCML, Salford.

13 Not all the evidence from the first trial was transcribed.

14 A record of the various bail applications is given in *R v. Tomlinson and Warren* [1974] IRLR 349, paras. 36–45. Warren believed that bail was only granted in June to release the pressure on the government from the labour movement, which had built up during the winter and spring.

15 McKinsie Jones had been released from Ranby prison, Retford, at 7:00 a.m. on 18 June, having served two-thirds of his nine-month sentence. Michael Pierce, Brian Williams and Arthur Murray were released from Drake Hall open prison, Eccleshall, at 7:00 a.m. on 12 June.

16 Quoted by Lord Justice James, *R v. Tomlinson and Warren* [1974] IRLR 348, para. 13.

17 *R v. Tomlinson and Warren* [1974] IRLR 346, para. 34.

18 *R v. Jones and Others* [1974] IRLR 121, para. 40.

19 *R v. Tomlinson and Warren* [1974] IRLR 350, para. 49.

20 *New Law Journal*, 9 January 1975, pp. 25–6.

21 'The Shrewsbury pickets' (16 January 1975), paper by Ivan Lawrence MP, Churchill Archives Centre, HLSM 2/8/5.

22 Letter, Roger Bolton to the DPP, 14 March 1975, TNA DPP2/5159.

23 Handwritten note headed 'Mr J. Walker' and signed MJJ, 17 March 1975, TNA DPP2/5159.

24 Letter, Tony Hetherington to Michael Jardine, 25 March 1975, TNA DPP2/5159.

25 Letter, Rawlinson to Skelhorn, with enclosure, 21 March 1975, TNA DPP2/5159.

26 Hetherington suggested to Jardine that 'it might be prudent to have a word with Counsel' in case either Drake or Fennell said anything to the BBC that might contradict their line. Letter, 25 March 1975, TNA DPP2/5159.

27 Letter, Rawlinson to Bolton, 8 April 1975, TNA DPP2/5159.

28 Letter, Bolton to Scragg, 2 April 1975, Shrewsbury archives, WCML, Salford.

29 Letter, Bolton to Jardine, 17 April 1975, TNA DPP2/5159.

30 One of the draft grounds did include it: 'The judge erred in imposing a sentence for conspiracy to intimidate that exceeded the statutory maximum of three months' imprisonment for committing the substantive offence under section 7.' Shrewsbury archives, WCML, Salford.

31 '"New Law Journal" article – 3rd July – by Lustgarten', TNA LAB10/3743.

32 Law Commission, *Report on Conspiracy and Criminal Law*

Reform (No. 76, HMSO), London, 1976. Copy in TNA BCI/78.

33 Draft report on conspiracy, p. 42, para. 71, TNA BC3/228. *Hansard*, lord chancellor's speech, Lord Cairns, 26 July 1875, api.parliament.uk (paras. 37–8 in particular). Labour's Employment Secretary, Michael Foot, raised these points in a paper for the Cabinet, 'The Law on Picketing', 23 September 1975, TNA CAB129/185/1.

34 Draft report, p. 42, para. 73.

35 Law Commission, *Report on Conspiracy and Criminal Law Reform*, p. 42, para. 1.111.

36 'Intimidation: the Shrewsbury pickets decision questioned', *New Law Journal*, 3 July 1975, pp. 636–7.

37 See letter from E. M. Chadwell of the Home Office to J. Bacon at the Department of Employment, 14 July 1975, LAB10/3743.

38 He wrote to Labour colleagues on 9 April 1974, listing five questions to be put to a meeting with the Attorney General, Sam Silkin. TNA DPP2/5185. See Gasson's letter to Walker, DPP's Office, 25 April 1974, asking for his comments to assist Silkin. TNA DPP2/5185. Atkinson asked the home secretary, Roy Jenkins, whether notes that passed between previous Attorneys General, Home Secretaries and Directors of Public Prosecutions about the case had been destroyed. HC Deb 6 February 1975, vol. 885, cc. 1549–50. Jenkins refused to inquire into it.

39 'Re: The Conspiracy and Protection of Property Act 1875', 25 Feb 1976, TNA DPP2/5185/2.

40 Document headed 'Deputy director' by K. Dowling, 26 February 1976, TNA DPP2/5185/2.

41 Letter, 27 February 1976, TNA DPP2/5185/2, emphasis added. The Court of Appeal does not decide what is appealed if a party – prosecution or defence – does not want to raise it.

42 The affray conviction had been quashed, leaving just unlawful assembly. K. Dowling had argued in his comments on Pearson's paper, 'I hardly think that the sentences of three years and two years [on Warren and Tomlinson respectively] could be upheld solely on the basis of unlawful assembly.'

43 Opinion prepared by Laurence Lustgarten, Associate Research Fellow, Oxford University, 4 April 2013 (author's papers).

44 When appeals were lodged in January 1974 one ground was that a sentence 'of the same period for unlawful assembly and affray, if the sentence for conspiracy was unlawful, was outside the permissible range on the basis of the degree of criminality for such offences and the previous convictions, or lack thereof, of each defendant.' Copy of grounds of appeal in author's papers.

45 I was kindly given a copy of the Economic League's blacklist by George Guy, UCATT North West Regional Secretary. I discovered that I was on it too!

46 19 July 1975, p. 16.

47 Tomlinson, *Ricky*, Chapter 13.

48 Warren, *The Key to My Cell*, pp. 81–82.

49 Among Warren's papers was a pamphlet issued to all prisoners, *Parole: Your Questions Answered*, Home Office, autumn 1972. All prisoners are reviewed for parole automatically unless they state that they do not want to be. Both Warren and Tomlinson wanted parole, but on their terms, not the Prison Service's.

50 Warren, *The Key to My Cell*, p. 127. He pointed out that it was exceptional for a prisoner to receive a letter from another prisoner in a different jail.

51 Tomlinson wrote that he visited Warren in the late 1980s when the latter was housebound from the worsening effects of Parkinson's disease. The initiative for his visit did not come from Warren. They did not become friends, although Tomlinson did attend Warren's funeral in 2004.

52 Warren, *The Key to My Cell*, pp. 108–9.

53 Tomlinson, *Ricky*, p. 86; *Liverpool Daily Post*, 9 May 1969.

54 Ibid., pp. 134–85.

55 Ibid., pp. 142–8.

56 See Chapter 14 for more details.

57 Warren's papers, which I have, reveal that he was a prolific writer, sending many letters to MPs and others asking them to campaign for a public inquiry. He also had a lengthy correspondence with Bert Ramelson and other CP leaders requesting action to get him released, just as the Pentonville 5 had.

58 Warren, *The Key to My Cell*, p.191.Tomlinson incorrectly states that Warren was 'thrown out of prison at midnight so that there would be no TV cameras or journalists', *Ricky*, p. 188.

59 Warren, *The Key to My Cell*, p. 74.

13. The Shrewsbury 24 Campaign

1 Author's notes.

2 Letter, Jack Straw to Peter Kilfoyle, 8 April 2009 (author's papers).

3 Ian Cobain, *The History Thieves: Secrets, Lies and the Shaping of a Modern Nation*, London, 2017.

14. The Campaign Gets Going

1 UK Parliament Early Day Motions, 'Shrewsbury 24', edm.parliament.uk, 12 June 2012.
2 See petition, 'Full disclosure of all Government documents relating to the 1972 building workers strike and the conspiracy trials at Shrewsbury', petition.parliament.uk, closed 27 June 2013.
3 Letter, Chris Grayling to David Hanson, 20 November 2012 (author's papers).
4 *Hansard* 2013–4 session, Volume 574, Column 517, hansard.parliament.uk.
5 Warren, *The Key to My Cell*, covers this in Chapter 29.

15. The CCRC and the Road to the Court of Appeal

1 Shrewsbury 24 Campaign website, 'Labour Party Conference 2015', shrewsbury24campaign.org.uk, 23 October 2015.
2 CCRC Provisional Statement of Reasons in the applications of Tomlinson, Warren, Jones and O'Shea, 29 June 2017, para.281 (author's papers).

Conclusion

1 *Building Workers Charter*, 3, 14 (Summer 1978). The front-page article was headlined, 'Settle now, prepare for battle!'.

Index